FREDERICK DOUGLASS

Frederick Douglass,

FREDERICK DOUGLASS

by

BOOKER T. WASHINGTON

Author of "Up from Slavery," "Working
with the Hands," etc.

HASKELL HOUSE PUBLISHERS Ltd.

Publishers of Scarce Scholarly Books

NEW YORK, N. Y. 10012

1968

First Published 1907

HASKELL HOUSE PUBLISHERS Ltd.
Publishers of Scarce Scholarly Books
280 LAFAYETTE STREET
NEW YORK. N. Y. 10012

Library of Congress Catalog Card Number: 68-25001

Haskell House Catalogue Item # 253

Printed in the United States of America

PREFACE

THE chance or destiny which brought to this land
of ours, and placed in the midst of the most progressive and the most enlightened race that Christian civilization has produced, some three or four
millions of primitive black people from Africa
and their descendants, has created one of the most
interesting and difficult social problems which any
modern people has had to face.   The effort to solve
this problem has put to a crucial test the fundamental principles of our political life and the
most widely accepted tenets of our Christian faith.
Frederick Douglass's career falls almost wholly
within the first period of the struggle in which this
problem has involved the people of this country, —
the period of revolution and liberation.   That
period is now closed.   We are at present in the
period of construction and readjustment.   Many of
the animosities engendered by the conflicts and
controversies of half a century ago still survive to
confuse the councils of those who are seeking to
live in the present and the future, rather than in
the past.   But changes are rapidly coming about
that will remove, or at least greatly modify, these
lingering animosities.   This book will have failed
of its purpose just so far as anything here said shall
serve to revive or keep alive the bitterness of those

controversies of which it gives the history ; it will
have attained its purpose just so far as it aids its
readers to comprehend the motives of, and the men
who entered with such passionate earnestness into,
the struggle of which it gives in part a picture—
particularly the one man, the story of whose life is
here narrated.

In the succeeding chapters, an effort has been
made to present an account of the life of Frederick
Douglass as a slave and as a public man during the
most eventful years of the anti-slavery movement,
the Civil War, the period of reconstruction, and
the after years of comparative freedom from sectional agitation over the "Negro problem."

To bring this study within the plan and purposes
of the American Crisis Series of Biographies, such
subjects as "The Genesis of the Anti-Slavery Agitation," "The Fugitive Slave Law," "The Underground Railway," "The American Colonization
Society," "The Conflict in Kansas for Free Soil,"
"The John Brown Raid," "The Civil War," "The
Enlistment of Colored Troops," and "Reconstruction," have been given more space than they have
received in earlier biographies.

While it is true that Frederick Douglass would
have been a notable character in any period, it is
also true that in the life of hardly any other man
was there comprehended so great a variety of incidents of what is perhaps the most memorable
epoch in our history. The mere personal side of
Douglass's life, though romantic and interesting, is
here treated only in outline.

S. Laing Williams, of Chicago, Ill., and his wife, Fannie Barrier Williams, have been of incalculable service in the preparation of this volume. Mr. Williams enjoyed a long and intimate acquaintance with Mr. Douglass, and I have been privileged to draw heavily upon his fund of information. He and Mrs. Williams have reviewed this manuscript since its preparation and have given it their cordial approval.

In addition to these sources of information, I wish to make grateful acknowledgment of my indebtedness to Major Charles R. Douglass for the use of many printed addresses, and for interesting data showing his father's work in the Underground Railway.

I must also acknowledge my sense of gratitude for the opportunity afforded in this work of getting close to the heart and life of this great leader of my race. No Negro can read and study the life of Frederick Douglass without deriving from it courage to look up and forward.

CONTENTS

CHRONOLOGY

1817—February. Born on a plantation at Tuckahoe, near the town of Easton, Talbot County, on the eastern shore of Maryland; the exact date not known. His mother, Harriet Bailey, was the slave of Captain Aaron Anthony, the manager of the estate of Colonel Edward Lloyd.

1825—Sent to Baltimore to live with Hugh Auld, a relative of his master.

1833—Returns to Maryland and becomes the slave of Thomas Auld, at St. Michaels, Talbot County; while here he has an encounter with the Negro slave breaker, Covey.

1836—First attempt to run away results in his being sent back to Baltimore where he is apprenticed by Thomas Auld to William Gardiner of Fells Point, to learn the trade of ship-calker.

1838—September 3d. Makes his escape from Baltimore, reaching New York the next day. September 15th, according to the marriage certificate, possibly a day earlier, he marries a free colored woman, Anna Murray, who on receiving the news of his escape follows him to New York. They are directed to New Bedford, Mass., by Anti-Slavery friends where Douglass begins his life as a freeman. He changes his name from Frederick Augustus Washington Bailey, to Frederick Douglass.

1841—August 11th. Makes his first speech before an Anti-Slavery convention and becomes a lecturer in the Anti-Slavery cause.

1842—Participates in the campaign for equal rights in Rhode Island during the " Dorr Rebellion."

1843—Takes part in the campaign of " A Hundred Anti-Slavery Conventions "; his hand broken in a fight with a mob at Pendleton, Indiana.

1845—Writes, in order to prove that he is what he proclaims himself, a fugitive slave, *Narrative of Frederick Douglass*, giving the names of his owners. This book was published by the Anti-Slavery Society. August 16th, sails for Liverpool, England, lest the publication of his biography should lead to his capture and reënslavement. He is received with enthusiasm in England and his freedom is purchased by two members of the Society of Friends.

1846—August 7th. Addresses the " World's Temperance Convention " at Covent Garden Theatre, London. December 5th, the papers are signed which grant him his freedom.

1847—April 20th. Reaches America again. December 3d, the first issue of the *North Star*, subsequently *Frederick Douglass's Paper*, is published, he having first removed to Rochester, N. Y. Following its establishment came his rupture with Garrison and the Abolitionist wing of the Anti-Slavery party.

1848—September. Delivers an address before a colored convention at Cleveland, O., on farming and industrial education.

1851—Announces his sympathies with the voting Abolitionists.

1852—Supports the Free Soil party and is elected a delegate from Rochester to the Free Soil Convention at Pittsburg, Pa.

1853—Visits Harriet Beecher Stowe at Andover, Mass., with reference to the forming of an industrial school for colored youth.

1855—*My Bondage and My Freedom* published in New York and Auburn.

1856—Supports Frémont, the candidate of the Republican party, for President.

1858—*Douglass's Monthly* is established. Its publication is continued until 1864.

1859—August 20th. Visits John Brown at Chambersburg, Pa. This was his last interview with the old Anti-Slavery hero before the attack on Harper's Ferry, three weeks later. At this interview John Brown made a final effort to induce him to join in the dangerous enterprise.

1859—November 12th. Sails from Quebec on his second visit to England. This trip is undertaken because he is in danger of being implicated in the plot to cause an uprising of the slaves for which John Brown had already been executed.

1860—Returns to the United States, called home by the death of his daughter, Anna.

1860—December 3d. Attempts to speak in Tremont Temple, Boston, but the meeting is broken up.

1863—Publishes in *Douglass's Monthly* his address to colored men urging them to enlist in the Federal Army. He is instrumental in forming the Fifty-fourth and Fifty-fifth Massachusetts Regiments of colored soldiers. Subsequently he visits President Lincoln to secure fair treatment of the colored soldiers and is promised, by Secretary Stanton, a commission as Assistant Adjutant to General Thomas, which, however, he does not receive.

1866—February 7th. Interviews President Johnson to urge upon him the wisdom of granting the suffrage to the freedmen. Issues shortly afterward an address in reply to President Johnson's argument against granting the suffrage to Negroes. In September, is elected a delegate to the "National Loyalists' Convention" in Philadelphia.

1869—Becomes editor of the *New National Era* which he continued to edit until 1872, at a pecuniary loss of about $10,000.

1871—Visits San Domingo as Secretary to the Commission, consisting of B. F. Wade, Dr. S. G. Howe and Andrew D. White, to determine the attitude of that country toward annexation to the United States. He is appointed a member of the upper house of the territorial legislature of Washington, D. C., but shortly resigns his position in favor of his son, Lewis. May 30th, he delivers the Decoration Day address at Arlington National Cemetery. Becomes president of the "Freedmen's Savings and Trust Company."

1872—April. Presides at the National Convention of colored citizens held in New Orleans. Chosen elector-at-large from the State of New York on the Presidential ticket which elected General Grant to a second term and is afterward designated to carry the vote of the electoral college of New York to Washington.

1876—April 14th. Delivers an address at the unveiling of the Lincoln Monument in Lincoln Park, Washington, D. C.

1877—Appointed Marshal of the District of Columbia, which office he held until 1881.

1878—May. Visits St. Michaels and is reconciled to his old master, Thomas Auld.

1879—September 12th. Reads a paper before the American Social Science Association in which he opposes the Negro exodus to Kansas.

1881—May. Appointed Recorder of Deeds in the District of Columbia. June 12th, visits the Lloyd plantation.

1882—January. *Life and Times of Frederick Douglass* published. August 4th, his first wife dies: she was the mother of five children.

1884—January 24th. Marries Miss Helen Pitts, of New York.

1889—Appointed Minister and Consul General to Hayti.

1893—Commissioner for the Haytian Republic at the World's Fair at Chicago. Makes an address on Negro Day at the Fair.

1895—February 20th. Dies at his home at Cedar Hill, Washington. Buried with honors from the Metropolitan Church (African Methodist Episcopal); public services being held subsequently in Rochester. His body finally interred beside those of his wife and daughter, in Mount Hope Cemetery, Rochester, N. Y.

FREDERICK DOUGLASS

CHAPTER I

FREDERICK DOUGLASS, THE SLAVE

THE life of Frederick Douglass is the history of American slavery epitomized in a single human experience. He saw it all, lived it all, and overcame it all. What he saw and lived and suffered was not too much to pay, however, for a great career. "It is something," as he himself said, "to couple one's name with great occasions, and it was a great thing to me to be permitted to bear some humble part in this, the greatest that had come thus far to the American people."

Tradition says he was of noble lineage, but of this there is no written record. Frederick Douglass was born in the little town of Tuckahoe in Talbot County on the eastern shore of Maryland, supposedly in the month of February, 1817. The exact date of his birth was made the subject of diligent search by him in the days of his manhood and freedom, but nothing more definite than the month and year could be established. He gleaned so much as this, he says, "from certain events, the date of which I have since learned."

In the early life of this child of slave birth, there were several incidents that seemed to mark him for a high destiny. The very pretentiousness of the name he bore, Frederick Augustus Washington Bailey, was a possible indication of something unusual and promising in his appearance and demeanor. Though it is not known who was his father, it is fortunate that, out of the many uncertainties of his lowly origin, a reasonably clear outline of the personality of his mother has come to light and has been preserved. We cannot know her name or pedigree. The slave-child saw little of his slave-mother, but he made a great deal of this little. His references to her were frequent in his writings and public addresses, and they all indicate the pride and love of a heart true to its primal instincts.

While he was a child, his mother was employed on a plantation, a distance of twelve miles from Tuckahoe. Her only opportunity of seeing her son was by walking the distance after her day's work, to return to the field of her labors by dawn of the next day. To use his own language: "These little glimpses of my mother obtained under such circumstances and against such odds, meagre as they were, are indelibly stamped upon my memory. She was tall and finely proportioned; of dark and glossy complexion, with regular features; and among slaves she was remarkably sedate and dignified. She was the only slave in Tuckahoe who could read." That she was a woman of marked superiority, and that her child inherited from her much that raised him above the other slaves among whom he lived, can be easily believed. When he had grown to manhood and while reading Prichard's *Natural History of Man*, he found in the features of "King Rameses the Great" a strong resemblance to his mother. There were four other children, one boy named Perry and three girls. So far as is known, the brother and sisters showed none of the marks of superiority that distinguished Frederick Augustus Washington Bailey.

Whatever training Frederick had up to eight years of age, he received from his Grandmother Bailey. It was in her cabin that he was born, and it was by her that he was cared for and nourished. He was very fond of this grandmother and has paid an affectionate tribute to her memory. She was a woman of strong character and of unusual intelligence. There were many things that she could do uncommonly well, such as gardening, and her good luck in fishing was proverbial. She was also famed as a fortune-teller and as such was sought far and wide by all classes of people. Because of her intelligence and natural gifts, she was allowed many privileges and a great deal of liberty ; in her old age she was amply provided for by her master, and saved from hard toil. Judging from his frequent and fond references to his grandmother, young Douglass had better care and more attention than the ordinary slave-child ; he probably had plenty to eat, and was taught good manners. Whatever it was possible for an impressionable mind to gain from contact with a strong and vigorous nature, the lad received from this unusual woman.

Until he was seven years of age, young Fred felt few of the privations of slavery. In these childhood days, he probably was as happy and carefree as the white children in the "big house." At liberty to come and go and play in the open sunshine, his early life was typical of the happier side of Negro life in slavery. What he missed of a mother's affection and a father's care, was partly made up to him by the indulgent kindness of his good grandmother.

The owner of Fred and of his mother, grandmother, sisters, and brother, was Captain Aaron Anthony. He was the proprietor of several plantations and about thirty slaves near Tuckahoe. But Captain Anthony was something more, and this fact became important in the subsequent history of young Frederick Bailey; he had the distinction of being the manager of the vast estate of Colonel Edward Lloyd, who belonged to one of the foremost families of Maryland, and who owned between twenty and thirty plantations with over one thousand slaves. His home was on a plantation situated about thirty-five miles southeast of Baltimore and on the banks of the Wye River, the mansion and its surroundings being typical of the splendor and power of the wealthy slave-holder. When young Douglass first gazed upon all these signs of wealth, he says: "I became impressed with the baronial splendors of the Lloyd mansion and the princely mode of living; the vast army of enslaved men, women, and children ; the completeness of the government that made it almost impossible for any of these slaves to escape ; the subordination of my own master ; the great number of mechanics that were skilled in all the trades, and the tutors from New England that were hired to teach the Lloyd children."

Near the mansion stood the plain but commodious home of Fred's master, Captain Anthony. The Anthony family consisted of Mrs. Lucretia Anthony, the wife ; Richard and Fred Anthony, sons ; and an only daughter, Lucretia, who became the wife of Captain Thomas Auld.

When Fred was between seven and eight years of age, his grandmother was directed by her master to take her grandson to the Lloyd plantation. After the boy arrived at his new home, he was put in charge of a slave-woman for whom the only name we know is "Aunt Katy." This change brought him the first real hardship of his life. As an early consequence of it, he lost the care and guidance of his grandmother, his freedom to play, good food, and that affection which means so much to a child. When he came under the care of Aunt Katy, he began to feel for the first time the sting of unkindness. He has given a very disagreeable picture of this foster-mother. She was a woman of a hateful disposition, and treated the little stranger from Tuckahoe with extreme harshness. Her special mode of punishment was to deprive him of food. Indeed he was forced to go hungry most of the time, and if he complained, was beaten without mercy.

He has described his misery on one particular night. After being sent supperless to bed, his suffering very soon became more than he could bear, and when everybody else in the cabin was asleep, he quietly took some corn and began to parch it before the open fireplace. While thus trying to appease his hunger by stealth, and feeling dejected and homesick, "who but my own dear mother should come in?" The friendless, hungry, and sorrowing little boy found himself suddenly caught up in her strong and protecting arms. "I shall never forget," he says, "the indescribable expression of her countenance when I told her that Aunt Katy had said that she would starve the life out of me. There was a deep and tender glance at me, and a fiery look of indignation for Aunt Katy at the same moment, and when she took the parched corn from me and gave me, instead, a large ginger-cake, she read Aunt Katy a lecture which was never forgotten. That night, I learned, as never before, that I was not only a child but somebody's child. I was grander on my mother's knee than a king upon his throne. But my triumph was short. I dropped off to sleep and waked in the morning to find my mother gone, and myself again at the mercy of the virago in my master's kitchen."

There is no record of another meeting between mother and son. She probably died shortly afterward, because if she had been within walking distance, he certainly would have seen her again. Her memory in his child's mind was always that of a real and near personality. When he became older, and conscious of his superiority to his fellows, he was wont to say: "I am proud to attribute my love of letters, such as I may have, not to my presumed Anglo-Saxon father, but to my sable, unprotected, and uncultivated mother." Thus, after his mother died, his vivid imagination kept before him her image, as she appeared to him that last time he saw her, through all his struggles for a fuller and freer life for himself and his race.

With the loss of his mother and grandmother, he came more and more to realize the peculiar relation in which he and those about him stood to Colonel Lloyd and Captain Anthony. His active mind soon grasped the meaning of "master" and "slave." While still a lad, longing for a mother's care, he began to feel himself within the grasp of the curious thing that he afterward learned to know as "slavery." As he grew older in years and understanding, he came also to see what manner of man his master was. He described Captain Anthony as a "sad man." At times he was very gentle, and almost benevolent. But young Douglass was never able to forget that this same kindly slave-holder had refused to protect his cousin from a cruel beating by her overseer. The spectacle he had witnessed, when this beautiful young slave was whipped, had made a lasting and painful impression upon him. Vaguely he began to recognize the outlines of the institution which at once permitted and, to a certain degree, made necessary these cruelties. It was at this point that he began to speculate on the origin and nature of slavery. Meanwhile he became, in the course of his life on the plantation, the witness of other scenes, quite as harrowing, and the memory mingled with his reflections, and embittered them.

During this time an event occurred which gave a new direction and a new impetus to the thoughts and purposes slowly taking form within him. This event was the successful escape of his Aunt Jennie and another slave. It caused a great commotion on the plantation. Nothing could happen in a Southern community that excited so many and such varied emotions as the escape of a slave from bondage :— terror and revenge; hope and fear, mingled with the images of the pursued and the pursuers, with speculation in regard to the capture of the fugitive, and with prayers for his success in the minds of the slaves.

Young Douglass had begun to feel the burden of slavery and already had a dim consciousness of its fundamental injustice, but up to this point, he had known no other world than this immense plantation, and no other people than these masters, overseers, and slaves. His horizon was further enlarged and his imagination quickened by talking with certain Negroes on the Lloyd plantation, who could recall the event of their being brought from far-off Africa in slave-ships. Speaking of his own state of feeling at this time, he says: "I was already a fugitive from slavery in spirit and purpose."

From now on his quick and comprehending mind saw and suffered things that formerly never affected him. The hard and sometimes cruel discipline, toil from sunrise to sunset, scant food, the stifling of ambitions,—all these began now to be perceived and felt, and the impression they left sank into the soul of this rebellious boy. He saw a slave killed by an overseer, on no other charge than that of being "impudent." "Crimes" of this nature were committed, as far as he could see, with impunity, and the memory of them haunted him by day and by night.

Thus far Douglass had not felt the overseer's whip. He was too small for anything except to run errands and to do light chores. Of course, he had been cuffed about by Aunt Katy ; he says he seldom got enough to eat and he suffered continually from cold, since his entire wardrobe consisted of a tow sack. He was fortunate, however, in having two friends, who often saved him from the pangs of hunger, and who now and then gave him a word of kindness. One was young Daniel Lloyd, of the "great house," and the other, Miss Lucretia, his master's daughter. This lady seems to have had a real fondness for the boy, and would often give him something good to eat and at times caress him in such a way as to recall to his mind the few blessed moments he had known with his mother. Young Lloyd also often protected him from the impositions of other boys.

To show how far the lad had advanced in his thinking, it is well to quote his own words on this point: "I used to contrast my condition with that of the blackbirds, in whose world and sweet songs, I fancied them so happy. Their apparent joy only deepened the shadows of my sorrow. There are thoughtful days in the lives of children, at least there were in mine, when they grapple with all the primary subjects of knowledge, and reach in a moment conclusions which no subsequent experience can shake. I was just as well convinced of the unjust, unnatural, and murderous character of slavery when nine years old, as I am now (1881). Without any appeal to books, to laws, or to authorities of any kind, I came to regard God as our Father, and condemned slavery as a crime.''

When Fred became nine years old, the most important event in his life occurred. His master determined to send him to Baltimore to live with Hugh Auld, a brother of Thomas Auld. Baltimore at this time was little more than a name to young Douglass. When he reached the residence of Mr. and Mrs. Auld and felt the difference between the plantation cabin and this city home, it was to him, for a time, like living in Paradise. Mrs. Auld is described as a lady of great kindness of heart, and of a gentle disposition. She at once took a tender interest in the little servant from the plantation. He was much petted and well fed, permitted to wear boy's clothes and shoes, and for the first time in his life, had a good soft bed to sleep in. His only duty was to take care of and play with Tommy Auld, which he found both an easy and an agreeable task.

Young Douglass yet knew nothing about reading. A book was as much of a mystery to him as the stars at night. When he heard his mistress read aloud from the Bible, his curiosity was aroused.

He felt so secure in her kindness that he had the boldness to ask her to teach him. Following her natural impulse to do kindness to others and without, for a moment, thinking of the danger, she at once consented. He quickly learned the alphabet and in a short time could spell words of three syllables. But alas, for his young ambition! When Mr. Auld discovered what his wife had done, he was both surprised and pained. He at once stopped the perilous practice, but it was too late. The precocious young slave had acquired a taste for book-learning. He quickly understood that these mysterious characters called letters were the keys to a vast empire from which he was separated by an enforced ignorance. In discussing the matter with his wife, Mr. Auld said : "If you teach him to read, he will want to know how to write, and with this accomplished, he will be running away with himself." Mr. Douglass, referring to this conversation in later years, said : "This was decidedly the first anti-slavery speech to which I had ever listened. From that moment, I understood the direct pathway from slavery to freedom."

During the subsequent six years that he lived in Baltimore in the home of Mr. Auld, he was more closely watched than he had been before this incident, and his liberty to go and come was considerably curtailed. He declares that he was not allowed to be alone, when this could be helped, lest he would attempt to teach himself. But these were unwise precautions since they but whetted his appetite for learning and incited him to many secret schemes to elude the vigilance of his master and mistress. Everything now contributed to his enlightenment and prepared him for that freedom for which he thirsted. His occasional contact with free colored people, his visit to the wharves where he could watch the vessels going and coming, and his chance acquaintance with white boys on the street, all became a part of his education and were made to serve his plans. He got hold of a blue-back speller and carried it with him all the time. He would ask his little white friends in the street how to spell certain words and the meaning of them. In this way he soon learned to read. The first and most important book owned by him was called the *Columbian Orator*. He bought it with money secretly earned by blacking boots on the streets. It contained selected passages from such great orators as Lord Chatham, William Pitt, Fox, and Sheridan. These speeches were steeped in the sentiments of liberty, and were full of references to the "rights of man." They gave to young Douglass a larger idea of liberty than was included in his mere dream of freedom for himself, and in addition they increased his vocabulary of words and phrases. The reading of this book unfitted him longer for restraint. He became all ears and all eyes. Everything he saw and read suggested to him a larger world, lying just beyond his reach. The meaning of the term "Abolition" came to him by a chance look at a Baltimore newspaper.

Slavery and Abolition! The distance between these two points of existence seemed to have lessened greatly, after he had comprehended their meaning. "When I heard the word 'Abolition,' I felt the matter to be my personal concern. There was hope in this word." As he afterward went about the city on his ordinary errands, or when at the wharf, even performing tasks that were not set for him to do, he was like another being. That word "Abolition" seemed to sing itself into his very soul, and when he permitted his thoughts to dwell on the possibilities that it opened to him, he was buoyed up with joyous expectations. He tried to find out something from everybody. He learned to write by copying letters on fences and walls and challenging his white playmates to find his mistakes; and at night when no one suspected him of being awake, he copied from an old copy-book of his young friend Tommy. Before he had formulated any plans for freedom for himself, he learned the important trick of writing "free passes" for runaway slaves.

Notwithstanding his progress in gaining knowledge, his considerate master and kind mistress, his loving companion in Tommy, his good home, food and clothes, he was not happy or contented. None of these things could stifle his yearning to be free. He has aptly described his own feelings at this time in speaking of Mrs. Auld : "Poor lady, she did not understand my trouble, and I could not tell her. Nature made us friends, but slavery made us enemies. She aimed to keep me ignorant, but I resolved to know, although knowledge only increased my misery. My feelings were not the result of any marked cruelty in the treatment I received. It was slavery, not its

mere incidents, I hated. Their feeding and clothing
me well, could not atone for taking my liberty from
me. The smiles of my master could not remove the
deep sorrow that dwelt in my young bosom. We
were both victims of the same overshadowing evil,—
she as mistress, I as slave. I will not censure her
too harshly.''

But if his hopes and aspirations were excited by
the vast and vague horizon which the thought of
emancipation opened to him, he was, on the other
hand, driven to something like despair when he
considered how distant and inaccessible was this
''land of freedom'' of which he dreamed. The
nearer and clearer appeared to him the possibility
of this larger life, the more torturing became the
restraints that kept him from seeking it. It was
when thus pursuing in thought this phantom of a
greater world although at the same time in despair
of ever attaining it, that he found peace for a while
in the consolation of religion. His imagination had
been aroused by the preaching of a white minister,
a Methodist, named Hanson. Feeling himself
wretched and alone, he was in a state of mind, as so
many others have been before and since, to find comfort in the thought of a kindly and overshadowing
Power, a Protector to whom he might turn, in his
great distress, without reserve and without misgiv-
ing. He surrendered himself completely to this new
faith in God. In his search for more light, he met
a lasting friend and guide in the person of a colored
preacher to whom he fondly refers as '' Uncle Lawson.'' This good and pious old man lived very near

the home of Mr. Auld. Young Douglass said of
him : "He was my spiritual father. I loved him
intensely, and was at his house every chance I could
get."

Douglass's master and mistress knew that he had
become religious, and though they were at that time
but lukewarm in their support of the church, they
respected the piety in the young slave and seem to
have encouraged it. But unfortunately the boy's
interest in religion had increased his desire to read,
in order to become thoroughly acquainted with the
Bible. "I have gathered," says Mr. Douglass,
"scattered pages of the Bible from the filthy street-
gutters, and washed and dried them, that in moments
of leisure I might get a word or two of wisdom from
them."

Uncle Lawson could read a little and Douglass,
who went frequently with him to prayer meeting,
spent much of his spare time on Sunday helping him
decipher its pages. When his master learned what
he was doing, he threatened to whip him if he went
to Lawson's again, but he stole away whenever he
could and got his needed instruction in the simple
lessons of faith.

Uncle Lawson was probably the first colored person that young Douglass had met who appreciated
his longings and powers. He was also the first person who awakened in him a dim consciousness that
he was destined for a public career. Speaking of
this, Douglass once said : "His words made a deep
impression upon me, and I verily felt that some
such work was before me, though I could not see

how I could ever engage in its performance." The
old preacher could go no further than to give utterance to the familiar exhortations : "Trust in the
Lord, the Lord can make you free" ; "Ask in
faith and He will give you what you ask." The
boy's great respect for the honesty and piety of
Uncle Lawson lent these words a deep significance,
and he never forgot the lessons that he learned from
this simple-minded man. How important was this
teaching is evidenced by Mr. Douglass's own testimony : "Thus assisted and thus cheered on under
the inspiration of the preacher, I worked and prayed
with a light heart, believing that my life was under
the guidance of a wisdom higher than my own. I
always prayed that God would in His great good
mercy and His own good time, deliver me from my
bondage." After Douglass learned how to write
with tolerable ease, he began to copy from the Bible
and the Methodist hymn-books at night, when he
was supposed to be asleep. He always regarded
this religious experience as the most important part
of his education ; it had the effect, not only of enlarging his mind, but also of restraining his impatience,
and softening a disposition that was growing hard
and bitter with brooding over the disadvantages
suffered by himself and his race. He greatly needed
something that would help him to look beyond his
bondage and encourage him to hope for ultimate
freedom.

While he was undergoing this, to him, novel religious experience, and while he was gradually being
adjusted to the situation in which he found himself,

there came one of those dreaded changes in the
fortunes of slave-masters that made the status of the
slave painfully uncertain. His real master, Captain
Anthony, died, and this event, complicated with
some family quarrel, resulted in Douglass being recalled from Baltimore to the plantation. This was
a depressing incident in his slave-life. It is true
that Mr. and Mrs. Auld were not at this time as
gentle with him as when he first came to the city.
He was under stricter discipline, was constantly
watched, and his liberties were circumscribed in
many ways that were both inconvenient and irritating. But in spite of all this he was comparatively free
from the usual severities of slavery. He had many
interests and many happy relationships that he was
able to cultivate outside of the Auld household.
He had become something of a leader among the
young colored men of the city. He had taught
many of them their letters. Among the white boys
of his acquaintance he also had a large circle of
friends, who loved him and were loyal to him.
Most important of all was his affection for his religious teacher, Uncle Lawson. Through these attachments in the more complex life of the city, and
the opportunities for mental and spiritual growth
which they offered, he was able to throw off to a
great degree the gloom and doubt of his earlier
youth. He had begun to feel that he was actually
preparing himself for that larger life of leadership
in freedom, that had been hinted to him by Uncle
Lawson. But all these happy relations were rudely
severed when he was recalled to the plantation.

"It did seem," he said, "that every time the young tendrils of my affection became attached, they were rigidly broken off by some unnatural, outside power, and I was looking away to Heaven for the rest denied to me on earth."

CHAPTER II

BACK TO PLANTATION LIFE

WHEN young Douglass left Baltimore to go back to the plantation, he was about sixteen years of age; —strong, healthy, and fully capable of the hard work of a field hand. But this was not the most difficult task he now had to face. Conditions that he met there were to test his character as it had never been tested before, and the trials he endured during this period profoundly influenced all his future life. For the first time in many years, he was to feel the "pitiless pinchings of hunger." He says: "So wretchedly starved were we that we were compelled to live at the expense of our neighbors, or steal from our own larder. This was a hard thing to do, but after much reflection, I reasoned myself into the belief that there was no other way to do—and after all there could be no harm in it, considering that my labor and person were the property of Master Thomas, and that I was deprived of the necessaries of life. It was simply appropriating what was my own, since the health and strength derived from such food were exerted in his service. To be sure, this was stealing according to the law and gospel I had heard from the pulpit, but I had begun to attach less importance to what dropped from that quarter, on certain points."

Having found a principle upon which he could justify, against the precepts of morality, the practice of stealing from his own master, in order to get enough to eat, it was not difficult to go farther and discover a warrant based on grounds quite as logical, for the habit of stealing from others beside his master, when the same necessity seemed to justify it.

"I am not only a slave of Master Thomas," he argued, "but I am also a slave of society at large. Society at large has bound itself in form and fact to assist Master Thomas in robbing me of my liberty and the just reward of my labor; therefore whatever rights I have against Master Thomas, I have equally against those confederated with him." It is thus that Mr. Douglass, writing years afterward, construed the argument with which the boy solved the doubts and questions arising in his mind when he found himself following the custom, prevalent among the slaves, of persistent petty stealing.

Whatever one may think of this theory as a justification for the practice, it is interesting as showing in Douglass, even as a boy, the tendency to get clear ideas in regard to his own conduct and the conduct of those about him, and to make his actions conform to some fundamental rule. A boy who was disposed to think thus clearly and to apply the test of elementary principles to the lives and actions of those about him, was already a dangerous slave. And so the summer of 1833 found Douglass more determined than ever to run away.

Meanwhile he tells us that there were several incidents which served still further to shape in his

mind the view of his master and the class his master represented. About this time there was a religious revival in the neighborhood of St.
Michaels, where Douglass lived. Master Thomas became
converted and was afterward a devoted member and
class-leader in the Methodist church. Young Douglass attended the camp-meeting, and, from his position behind the preacher's stand, where a space had
been marked off for colored people, watched the
process of conversion in his master with great interest and close attention.

Another episode tended to add to the perplexity
in the young slave's mind and still further undermine his faith in the moral superiority of the mas-
ter-class, and in the religion which based its justification of slavery on the fact of that superiority.
To add further to his confusion, he had read somewhere, in the Methodist discipline, that "the slave-
holder shall not be eligible to an official station in
the church." When he saw Mr. Auld making
open confession of his sins, and afterward given
official position in the church, he felt sure that a
great change must necessarily come over his disposition and character. But his master's face,
Douglass said, became more stern with increasing
piety, and the discipline he enforced upon his slaves
was even more rigid. This was a severe test of the
religious convictions of the young slave-boy. He
knew that religion had made him better, kinder,
and more appreciative of all that was true and
beautiful. It had also given him comfort during
the period of his servitude. He had looked for-

ward, with sincere faith in the power of religion, to some marked change in Master Thomas. The resulting experience left him disappointed and confused.

At the request of an earnest and sincerely pious white man, named Wilson, Douglass had joined in an attempt to conduct a Sunday-school for young colored people. During the second meeting of this innocent company, it was violently broken up by a mob, chief among whom was his master, Thomas Auld. The men were armed with sticks and other missiles and drove away both pupils and teachers, warning them never to meet again. The only explanation given for this violent interruption of what seemed a harmless and worthy occupation, was the rough remark of one member of the party, that Douglass wanted to be another Nat Turner. The fear inspired by his unfortunate slave insurrection was responsible for much of the hardship which Negroes in the South, free and slave, were at this period compelled to endure. The memory of it hardened the heart of many a master against his slaves and made him cruel and suspicious where he would naturally have been kind and confident.

But Thomas Auld seems not to have had even this excuse for some of his acts which still further embittered the young slave, already grown critical and suspicious of all that his master did. It was not long after his conversion, Douglass says, that he began to beat the boy's crippled and unfortunate cousin, Henny, with unusual barbarity, finally setting her adrift to care for herself. All

these incidents crowded quickly upon the young
slave's mind at a time when he had already begun
to test and measure the actions of his master and
those about him by the principles of universal
right and justice, which his study of the *Columbian
Orator* had furnished him, and which his reflections
and comparisons were steadily making more clear
and definite. The effect was to render him bold
and rebellious to such an extent that he soon became a fit subject to be " broken in " by some overseer, who knew how to handle "impudent" slaves.

A man named Edward Covey, living at Bayside,
at no great distance from the camp-ground where
Thomas Auld was converted, had a wide reputation
for "breaking in unruly niggers." Covey was a
"poor white" and a farm renter. To this man
Douglass was hired out for a year. In the month of
January, 1834, he started for his new master, with his
little bundle of clothes. From what we have already
seen of this sensitive, thoughtful young slave of sev-
enteen years, it is not difficult to understand his state
of mind. Up to this time he had had a comparatively easy life. He had seldom suffered hardships
such as fell to the lot of many slaves whom he knew.
To quote his own words : "I was now about to
sound profounder depths in slave-life. Starvation
made me glad to leave Thomas Auld's, and the
cruel lash made me dread to go to Covey's." Escape, however, was impossible. The picture of
"the slave-driver," painted in the lurid colors that
Mr. Douglass's indignant memories furnished him,
shows the dark side of slavery in the South. Dur-

ing the first six weeks he was with Covey, he was whipped, either with sticks or cowhides, every week. With his body one continuous ache from his frequent floggings, he was kept at work in field or woods from the dawn of day until the darkness of night. He says : "Mr. Covey succeeded in breaking me in body, soul, and spirit. The over-work and the cruel chastisements, of which I was the victim, combined with the ever growing and soul-devouring thought, 'I am a slave—a slave for life, a slave with no rational ground to hope for freedom,' had done their worst."

He confesses that at one time he was strongly tempted to take his own life and that of Covey. Finally, his sufferings of body and soul became so great that further endurance seemed impossible. While in this condition, he determined upon the daring step of returning to his master, Thomas Auld, in order to lay before him the story of abuse. He felt sure that, if for no other reason than the protection of property from serious impairment, his master would interfere in his behalf. He even expected sympathy and assurances of future protection. In all this he was grievously disappointed. Auld not only refused sympathy and protection, but would not even listen to his complaints, and immediately sent him back to his dreaded master to face the added penalty of running away. The poor lone boy was plunged into the depths of despair. A feeling that he had been deserted by both God and man took possession of him.

Covey was lying in wait for him, knowing full

well that he must return as defenseless as he went
away. As soon as Douglass came near the place
where the white man was hiding, the latter made a
leap at Fred for the purpose of tying him for a
flogging. But Douglass escaped and took to the
woods where he concealed himself for a day and a
night. His condition was desperate. He felt that
he could not endure another whipping, and yet
there seemed to him no alternative. His first impulse was to pray, but he remembered that Covey
also prayed. Convinced, at length, that there was
no appeal but to his own courage, he resolved to
go back and face whatever must come to him. It
so happened that it was a Sunday morning and,
much to his surprise, he met Covey who was on his
way to church, and who, when he saw the runaway,
greeted him with a pleasant smile. "His religion," says Douglass, "prevented him from breaking the Sabbath, but not from breaking my bones
on any other day in the week."

On Monday morning, Douglass was up early,
half hoping that he would be permitted to resume
his work without punishment. Covey was astir be-
times, too, and had laid aside his Sunday mildness
of manner. His first business was to carry out his
fixed purpose of whipping the young runaway. In
the meantime Fred had likewise fully decided
upon a course of action. He was ready to submit
to any kind of work, however hard or unreasonable,
but determined to defend himself against an attempt
at another flogging. In the cold passion that took
possession of him, the slave-boy became utterly

reckless of consequences, reasoning to himself that
the limit of suffering at the hands of this relentless
slave-breaker had already been reached. He was
resolved to fight and did fight. He began his morning work in peace, obeying promptly every order
from his master, and while he was in the act of going up to the stable-loft for the purpose of pitching
down some hay, he was caught and thrown by
Covey, in an attempt to get a slip knot about his
legs. Douglass flew at Covey's throat recklessly,
hurled his antagonist to the ground, and held him
firmly. Blood followed the nails of the infuriated
young slave. He scarcely knew how to account for
his fighting strength, and his dare-devil spirit so
dumbfounded the master, that he gaspingly said :
" Are you going to resist me, you young scoundrel ? "
" Yes, sir," was the quick reply.

Finding himself baffled, Covey called for assistance. His Cousin Hughes came to aid him, but as
he was attempting to put a noose over the unruly
slave's foot, Douglass promptly gave him a blow in
the stomach which at once put him out of the combat and he fled. After Hughes had been disabled,
Covey called on first one and then another of his
slaves, but each refused to assist him. Finding
himself fairly outdone by his angry antagonist,
Covey quit with the discreet remark : " Now, you
young scoundrel, you go to work ; I would not have
whipped you half so hard, if you had not resisted."

Douglass had thus won his first victory and was
never again threatened or flogged by his master.
The effect of this encounter, as far as he himself

was concerned, was to increase his self-respect, and
to give him more courage for the future. He said
that, "when a slave cannot be flogged, he is more
than half-free." To the other slaves he became a
hero, and Covey was not anxious to advertise his
complete failure to break in this "unruly nigger."
It speaks well for the natural dignity and good sense
of young Douglass that he neither boasted of his
triumph, nor did anything rash as a consequence
of it, as might have been expected from a boy of his
age and spirit.

On Christmas Day, 1834, young Douglass's time
with Covey was out. He then learned that he had
been hired to a William Freeland, who owned a
large plantation near St. Michaels, and by January
1st, was with his new master. Mr. Freeland was a
great improvement upon Covey. He was less direct
in his professions, but more humane in his manner
toward his slaves. He was what was called a "kind
master." He did not overwork or underfeed his
slaves and he was sparing of the lash. All this was
Paradise to young Douglass, when compared with
the strenuous life he had led with Covey. The effect
of so much kindness was evidenced in the character
of the Freeland slaves. Mr. Douglass describes
them as a superior class of men and women, and he
loved, esteemed, and confided in them, as with real
friends, generous and true.

With these new and better conditions and with
these superior companions in bondage, Douglass
felt a renewal of that old impulse to do something
for his fellow slaves. He naturally first turned

to the thought of teaching them to read and write. He found time and spirit again to look at his library,—the blue-back speller and the *Columbian Orator*. He first started a Sunday-school under the trees, at a safe distance from the "big house," gathering together some thirty young people. They were making fine progress, when, one Sunday, his former experience was repeated, and they were rushed upon and scattered. The school was again started, however, and this time Douglass seems successfully to have evaded the vigilance of his master. In addition to the Sunday-school, he devoted three evenings a week to his fellow slaves.

His leadership among all the Negroes was recognized and respected by them. This brought with it his first consciousness of that peculiar power over men, which in after-life made him so conspicuous a figure among the heroes of the Abolition struggle. The whole year at Freeland's was spent in self-development and in the mental and spiritual improvement of his companions in bonds.

At the end of this time he learned that his services had been hired for another twelve months to Mr. Freeland. This seemed to promise good for him in the future. The Bible, the spelling book, and the *Columbian Orator* were read and re-read and, at each new reading, he felt an enlargement of mind and an increasing thirst for liberty. The kindness of Mr. Freeland and the pleasant companionship of the Harris brothers and other slaves, served only to increase his discontent. He liked his master and would gladly have remained with him

as a free man, but he could never overcome his
increasing impatience of the restraints of slavery,
and, with this ambition for liberty, his troubles
began. He made a solemn vow to himself that the
year should not close without witnessing some
earnest effort on his part to escape. This vow
also included the freedom of his slave-companions,
for whom he had conceived a lasting attachment.
He succeeded in winning to his scheme five trusted
confidants. These were John and Henry Harris,
Sandy Jenkins, the footman ; Charles Roberts, and
Henry Bailey. Young Douglass impressed them
with the perils of the undertaking. His knowledge of the difficulties of a successful escape, little
as it actually was, surprised and awed them.

When he had fully determined upon his plans, he
found that it would perhaps require many weeks
to perfect them. His first task was to study the
character, the temperament, and the various personal qualifications of the men whom he proposed to
make his partners in this dangerous undertaking.
He must learn whether they were proof against the
sin of betrayal under all possible circumstances.
Each man must cultivate an unhesitating faith in
the others. Each must have unlimited courage,
both physical and moral. All must learn the tricks
of self-concealment, and of assumed indifference
and deception. They must understand the various
kinds of perils they were likely to encounter. The
kidnapper, the slave-catcher, the black and white
detectives, and the whole range of restraints that,
like a continuous wall, hemmed in a slave, must be

considered and understood. If he had hope in his heart, he must not betray it by so much as a look, in manner or in speech. Overseers were all eyes and ears and quick to suspect something was wrong if a slave seemed unusually thoughtful, sullen, or happy. They were by no means easily deceived as to the real intention of a slave planning to run away. To become an object of suspicion was merely to insure that the suspected slave would be the more closely guarded. Young Douglass fully realized the severity of the penalty that must follow failure, but he never wavered in his determination to make a dash for liberty, at any cost.

Having satisfied himself that his companions were proof against treachery and were of the right sort of mettle, he began to study the practical means of escape. There were no well-marked routes from slavery to freedom, no highways, byways, or "underground railways," known to him at that time. Such knowledge belonged wholly to the region north of the boundary line of freedom. He had heard of slaves escaping, but how they got away and by what route was always a mystery. He had heard that there was a region called North, and that in this far haven, white and black people alike were free. He had heard of a land called Canada, but its location on maps and charts was unknown to him. He had no conception of the physical size of the world. He had seen Baltimore, St. Michaels, and the adjoining plantations; beyond this all was blank. He knew something of theology, but nothing of geography. He did not know that there were states called New York and Massachusetts. New York City was the northern limit of his knowledge. He had received vague hints that the dominion of slavery was without boundary and that even in New York, there were slave-catchers and kidnappers. But it was at this time an unknown land.

In these difficulties, young Douglass looked steadily North in the direction of the free states, seeking some chance guidance. His habit of reasoning out things that in any way affected his status as a slave and as a man, has already been noted. Everything that he saw, or heard, or read enlarged his knowledge of life and its meaning. His stay in Baltimore had been a sort of school to him. Here for the first time, he had seen free colored people ; the coming and going of ships gave him his first ideas of direction and distance ; the Chesapeake Bay was a thing of wonder ;—all of which awakened in him many thoughts that led him away from bondage.

While young Douglass was secretly working out his plans for escape, one of his confidants, Sandy, the footman, said to him : "I dreamed last night that I was roused from sleep by strange noises, like a swarm of angry birds ; looking to see what it was, I saw you, Frederick, in the claws of a large bird surrounded by a large number of birds of all colors and sizes. They were all picking at you. Now I saw that as plain as I see you now, and honey, watch the Friday night dream ; there is

sump'n in it, sho's you born, dere is indeed, honey."
Douglass confessed that the dream related to him
by old Sandy disturbed him for awhile. He felt
sure that his plans were seriously handicapped by
unseen forces of some sort, but he soon regained his
usual courage and overcame his superstitious apprehensions. The Saturday night before Easter had
been fixed upon as the time for flight. A large
canoe, owned by a Mr. Hamilton, had been seized
and made ready for the confederates. They were
to paddle down the Chesapeake Bay to its head.
Douglass had already written out passes for each
of the fugitives in the following form :—

"This is to certify that I, the undersigned, have
given leave to the bearer, my servant, John,
full liberty to go to Baltimore to spend the Easter
holidays.—W. H.

"*Near St. Michaels, Talbot Co., Md.*"

On the night before the proposed flight, every
possible detail had been rehearsed and arranged.
The resolution of each party to the conspiracy
was tested and proved firm, except that of Sandy,
who, much to the disgust of Douglass, backed out.
Early Saturday morning, they were all at work in
the usual way. Douglass was the only one who was
troubled with a presentiment of evil. He turned
abruptly to Sandy, who was working near him,
and said : "We are betrayed !" Within a short
while his worst fears were being realized. Looking
toward the "big house," he easily discerned a
stranger on horseback and an unusual stir. It was

not long before he was abruptly accused of plotting
to run away, and taken into custody. Thus it
turned out that at the very time he had planned to
be on the road to freedom, he was a prisoner bound
for Easton, to be examined by a magistrate.

His companions, the two Harris brothers, were
likewise accused. Henry, however, was the only
one who did not tamely submit to being arrested
and handcuffed. When a revolver was pointed at
him by the officer, he knocked it from the man's
hands and dared any one to shoot him. The recal-
citrant slave was soon overpowered, however, and
all were led away.

The excitement caused by Harris's daring revolt
served one purpose, of which young Douglass's alert-
ness enabled him to take advantage. He adroitly
threw his pass, the only incriminating evidence
against them, in the fire, and by some secret sign
advised the others to eat theirs with their bread
on the journey, which they did.

When they were examined, each stoutly dis-
claimed all knowledge of plans for running away
and denied that they had any intention of doing so.
Notwithstanding the total lack of evidence against
them, the officers and Douglass's master were thoroughly convinced that they were plotting some wickedness. There was always something so mysterious,
as well as commanding in the manner of young
Douglass, that he was naturally regarded as the
ringleader, when any misconduct of the slaves was
complained of. His fellows in bonds treated him
with a deference never shown toward any but white

people. As a slave he worked well and did his full duty, but his masters always regarded him with suspicion, and something akin to fear.

The examination of the four culprits must have afforded an interesting scene. Young Douglass, though a slave in chains, as well as a prisoner at the bar, had the temerity to assume the rôle of attorney and to attempt the defense of his comrades, for whose present predicament he felt himself responsible. When Thomas Auld insisted that the evidence in hand, showing the intention to run away, was strong enough to hang in case of need, Douglass promptly replied : "The cases are not equal. If murder were committed, the thing is done, but we have not run away. Where is the evidence against us? We were quietly at work." Douglass was confident that the only tangible evidence against them had been skilfully destroyed, and he knew also that his companions had been slyly but effectively coached as to what to say and how to act when they came before the examining magistrate.

So completely had they failed to make young Douglass and his companions convict themselves, that very shortly Mr. Freeland came to the jail and took home his own slaves, leaving Douglass still in confinement. He was glad to know that his companions had escaped punishment, but by this last separation from them he seemed to have reached the very depths of the desolation which it was the lot of a slave to experience.

Through the bars of his imprisonment, he could watch the slave-traders from Georgia, Alabama,

and Louisiana apparently eager to get hold of him.
He could even hear them pass comments upon his
size, strength, and general appearance, and make
guesses as to his age.   For the first time since he left
Covey's, he felt both hopeless and helpless.   If he
should be sold and sent down into the far South, he
well knew that all chances for escape would be cut
off forever.

While in this condition of dejection and hope-
lessness, the unexpected happened. His owner,
Thomas Auld, who, in spite of Douglass's rebel-
liousness, always cherished a peculiar fondness for
him, ordered his release from jail, and at once
decided to send him back to Baltimore to live with
Mr. and Mrs. Hugh Auld. In telling Fred what
he intended to do, he said that he wanted him to
learn a trade, and that if he would behave himself
and give him no more trouble, he would emancipate
him when he became twenty-five years old.

The happy assurance that he was not to be punished and that he was again to have the privileges
of the city, was at first almost too much to be
believed. All of his hopes for ultimate freedom
were revived and his confidence in himself, which
had been severely shaken by his recent failure and
disgrace, was renewed. Under the circumstances,
it seems to have been the only wise and practicable
course his master could pursue.   Mr. Freeland
would not again allow him to come upon his plantation ; Covey had failed to break his spirit ; and
his reputation as a would-be runaway and a
"smart nigger" made him a desperate asset in the

slave-market of Talbot County. In sending him to
Baltimore to learn a trade, with a possibility of
ultimate freedom, it was thought that he would be
more serviceable and more tractable. Then, again,
the most threatening aspect of young Douglass's
attempted flight was the daring plot to use the
Chesapeake Bay. Heretofore the slaves who had
succeeded in making good their escape were compelled to find a path through deadly swamps and
woods, other avenues being so carefully guarded
that a successful runaway was very rare. Every
effort, therefore, must be made to keep the Douglass
venture a secret; he must be removed as far as
possible from his old plantation-life. If he had had
a different master, nothing could have saved him
from the slave-traders. The good-heartedness of
Thomas Auld was the only thing that preserved our
young hero for that larger life which he was to make
for himself, and help to make for so many others
of his race.

When, through the kindness of Mr. Auld, Douglass again turned his face toward Baltimore, he
fully realized that the change was fraught with importance to him. He remembered that it was in
this city he had caught the first suggestion that
there was a life to be lived above the low levels of
a slave. There, in the family of Hugh Auld, he
had learned to wear clothes, had acquired good manners and the ability to read, and, for the first time,
had felt, in the person of his teacher and benefactor,
Mrs. Sophia Auld, the civilizing and softening
touch of a superior woman's kindness.

To his alert and observing mind, Baltimore again became a real school. It quickened his perception, and fired his imagination, and was the place, above all others, short of a free state, where he most longed to live. Hugh Auld easily succeeded in getting young Douglass apprenticed to a calker, in the extensive ship-yards of William Gardiner, on Fell's Point. The conditions under which he had to work were very trying ; he did not mind the severe labor, but he was much disturbed by the intense prejudice existing among the white boys and mechanics. During the six months that he worked with this firm, every one seemed to have license to make use of and abuse him. He was not a coward, and would quickly strike back at a man who insulted or attempted to maltreat him. Finally, however, he was assaulted by a crowd of ruffians and frightfully beaten. His face was swollen and he was covered with blood. In this condition, he reported himself to Mr. Auld, who was furious when he beheld the pitiable state of his slave. Mrs. Auld took pity upon him and kindly dressed his wounds, and nursed him until they were healed. In the meantime he was angrily withdrawn from Mr. Gardiner's employ, and it was sought to bring to punishment the perpetrators of the assault. Auld appeared with Douglass before a magistrate, and explaining how his slave had been attacked without provocation, demanded a warrant for the guilty parties, but both were surprised and chagrined when the magistrate replied : " I am sorry, sir, but I cannot move in this matter except upon the oath of a white man." This incident made a deep impression on Douglass. It gave him a new and vivid sense of his helplessness and dependence, and measurably increased his determination to be free at any cost.

Hugh Auld soon after became foreman in the ship-yards of Walter Price, of Baltimore. He took Douglass with him and, under his protection, Fred finished learning his trade and within one year became able to command and receive from seven to nine dollars per week, the largest wages at that time paid for such labor. All of his earnings, of course, were turned over to his master. From now onward he had no trouble in securing work. He was permitted to find his own employment and make his own arrangements or contracts for pay. This was a distinct advancement over his former condition of servitude, and was his first experience of self-direction and self-dependence.

He was soon known among the colored people of the city as a young man of singular power. His superiority of mind was recognized and, almost without being conscious of it, he became a leader. There was at that time an organization of free colored people, known as the East Baltimore Improvement Society. Although membership in this exclusive body was limited to free people, young Douglass was eagerly admitted. This was the first organization of any kind, outside of the church, to which he had ever belonged. It is probable that he had here his first opportunity to exercise his natural gift of eloquence.

But with all these improvements in his conditions
of life, he was not happy. A sense of bondage,
however slight, made him restless and impatient.
" Why should I be a slave ? " was the question that
went with him night and day. He has truly said :
" To make a contented slave, you must make him a
thoughtless one."

Kind treatment, liberty to come and go as he
pleased and to make his own contracts for employment ; mingling with freemen, as if he himself
were free ; the high esteem in which he was held
by fellow workmen and employers, and by free
people ; and the promise of emancipation at twenty-
five years of age, were no consolation to the heart
that panted to be its own. He had already become
too much of a man to remain a willing slave !

CHAPTER III

ESCAPE FROM SLAVERY ; LEARNING THE WAYS OF FREEDOM

FOR the second time in his life, Frederick Douglass now began earnestly to study the possible means of permanently breaking his fetters. At the end of every week, when he turned his entire earnings over to his master, his sense of injustice and indignation increased. He was scarcely able to conceal his discontent. His intense longing to be free must have betrayed itself in his countenance, for very soon he noticed that he was being closely watched. The fact that he had at one time made an attempt to run away caused more or less uneasiness.

Young Douglass soon found that the difficulties of escape were quite as great in Baltimore as on the Freeland plantation. The railroads running from that city to Philadelphia were compelled to enforce the most stringent regulations with reference to colored people. Even free Negroes found it difficult to comply with them. Every one applying for a railway ticket was required to show his "free papers " and to be measured and carefully examined before he could enter the cars. Besides this, he was not allowed to travel by night. Similar regulations were enforced by steamboat companies. In addition to all these difficulties, every road and turnpike was picketed with kidnappers on the lookout for fugitive slaves. Douglass found it much easier to learn the obstacles than the aids to successful escape. The former were many and obvious; the latter were few and difficult to discover. It was impossible to profit by the experience of those who had run the gauntlet successfully, and whenever it was learned that some keen-scented slave had found a pathway to freedom, the information was carefully concealed from those in bonds. Every slave preparing to escape his fetters must act without guide or precedent, and form his own plan of deliverance.

Douglass was now convinced that he must hereafter be the arbiter of his own fortunes. He at once decided that his great need was money. The problem was how to get the necessary sum. His whole time and all of his earnings belonged to his master, and so long as this was the case the funds must still be a long way off. He finally determined to propose to his owner, Master Thomas Auld, that he be allowed to have his own time. In other words, he would agree to pay him so much a week, and all in excess of that sum he would keep as his own. This proposition merely angered Mr. Auld, who accused young Douglass of scheming to run away, and threatened him with severe punishment, if he ever mentioned such a thing again. But Douglass had too much at stake to give up. He made the same proposition to Master Hugh Auld and it was accepted. By the terms of this agreement young Douglass was to be allowed all of his time, and to make his own contracts and collect his own wages; while in return for these privileges, he was to pay his master three dollars each week, board and clothe himself, and buy his own tools.

This was a pretty hard bargain, but it meant his first step toward freedom, so he entered upon it cheerfully. From May until August, 1838, he worked for himself under the above conditions, kept all his obligations, and was able to save out of his earnings a neat sum of money. In the month of August occurred an unfortunate interruption of his plans. One Saturday night, instead of taking his wages to his master, he was persuaded to go out of town to a camp-meeting. He convinced himself that there could be no objection to this, since he had the money and purposed turning it in early Monday morning. Owing to some misunderstanding, however, he was compelled to remain one day longer than he had intended. On coming back to the city, he went directly to his master and made his payment. Instead of being indifferent to his absence, Hugh Auld was almost beside himself with rage. Addressing Douglass, he said : "You rascal, I have a good mind to give you a sound whipping. How dare you go out of the city without my leave ? Now, you scoundrel, you have done for yourself; you shall have your time no longer. The next thing I shall hear of you, will be your running away. Bring home your tools at once ; I will teach you how to go off in this way."

Poor Douglass was for the moment dismayed by this very serious consequence of an innocent error of judgment. He had had his own way so long, he

had begun to feel that his master's only interest in
him was the regular payment of the three dollars per
week which he had been receiving during the previous four months. All his hopes for liberty had
been staked on the continuance of this arrangement
for a few months longer. Douglass understood the
man who was now his master. He had lived with
him long enough not to take his threats too seriously. Mr. Auld would have been indeed short-
sighted if he had not used an occasion of this kind
to impress his slave with the seriousness of taking
such a liberty. Douglass did not, therefore, lose
heart and as a result of this episode, he made two
important resolutions. One was to go out in search
of work and return to the old contract; and the
other was to fix September 3, 1838, as the day of his
flight from slavery.

He soon found good employment in the Butler
ship-yards. Mr. Butler thought much of the young
slave calker and gave him every opportunity to
earn good wages. At the end of the first week, he
presented to his master the whole of his earnings,
amounting to nine dollars, which was accepted with
evident satisfaction. For the moment Master Hugh
seemed entirely to have forgotten the reprehensible
conduct of only a few days before. Having thus
shrewdly helped his master to recover his good temper and natural kindness, Douglass took special pains
to keep him pleased and unsuspicious. The second
week of his employment, he again turned over the
whole amount of his wages, nine dollars. Mr. Auld
was overjoyed at this earning capacity of Douglass

and as an evidence of it made him a present of,
twenty-five cents. In the last week he worked as a
slave, he gave his master six dollars.

Ever since the first trouble with Auld, he had
been pushing his plans to redeem his pledge to himself that he would run away on Monday, September
3, 1838. These were anxious days and many small
details had to be mastered. He must carefully avoid
anything in manner or word which could excite the
slightest suspicion. He had to test the fidelity of a
number of free colored people whose aid, in secret
ways, was very essential to him. Who these persons were, has never been revealed and in fact, it
was not until many years after emancipation that
Mr. Douglass disclosed to the public how he succeeded in making his daring escape. "Murder itself," he says, "was not more severely and surely
punished in the state of Maryland than aiding and
abetting the escape of a slave."

Young Douglass's flight had not outward sem-
blance of dramatic incident or thrilling episode and
yet, as he modestly says, "the courage that could
risk betrayal and the bravery which was ready to
encounter death, if need be, in pursuit of freedom,
were features in the undertaking. My success was
due to address rather than to courage, to good luck
rather than bravery. My means of escape were
provided by the very means which were making
laws to hold and bind me more securely to slavery."

By the laws of the state of Maryland, every free
colored person was required to have what were
called "free papers" which must be renewed fre-

quently, and, of course, a fee was always charged
for renewal. They contained a full and minute
description of the holder, for the purpose of iden-
tification. This device, in some measure, defeated
itself, since more than one man could be found to
answer the general description; hence many slaves
could get away by impersonating the real owners of
these passes, which were returned by mail after the
borrowers had made good their escape. To use
these papers in this manner was hazardous both for
the fugitives and for the lenders. Not every freeman was willing to put in jeopardy his own liberty that another might be free. It was, however,
often done and the confidence that it necessitated
was seldom betrayed. Douglass had not many
friends among the free colored people in Baltimore
who resembled him sufficiently to make it safe for
him to use their papers. Fortunately, however, he
had one who owned a "sailor's protection," a document describing the holder and certifying to the
fact that he was a "free American sailor." This
"protection" did not describe its bearer very
accurately. But, it called for a man very much
darker than himself, and a close examination would
have betrayed him at the start. In the face of all
these conditions young Douglass was relying upon
something beside a dubious written passport. This
something was his desperate courage. He had
learned to act the part of a freeman so well that
no one suspected him of being a slave. He had
early acquired the habit of studying human nature.
As he grew to understand men, he no longer

dreaded them. No one knew better than he the
kind of human nature that he had to deal with in
this perilous undertaking. He knew the speech,
manner, and behavior that would excite suspicion ; hence he avoided asking for a ticket at the
railway station because this would subject him to
examination. He so managed that just as the train
started he jumped on, his bag being thrown after
him by some one in waiting. He knew that scru-
tiny of him in a crowded car *en route* would be
less exacting than at the station. He had borrowed
a sailor's shirt, tarpaulin, cap and black cravat,
tied in true sailor fashion, and he acted the part
of an "old salt" so perfectly that he excited no
suspicion. When the conductor came to collect
his fare and inspected his "free papers," Douglass,
in the most natural manner, said that he had none
but promptly showed his "sailor's protection,"
which the railway official merely glanced at and
passed on without further question. Twice on the
trip he thought he was detected. Once when his
car stood opposite a south-bound train, Douglass
observed a well-known citizen of Baltimore who
knew him well, sitting where he could see him
distinctly. At another time, while still in Maryland, he was noticed by a man who had met him
frequently at the ship-yards. In neither of these
cases, however, was he interfered with or molested.
When he got into the free state of Pennsylvania,
he felt more joy than he dared express. He had
by his cool temerity and address passed every sen-
tinel undetected and no slave, to his knowledge,

he afterward said, ever got away from bondage on
so narrow a margin of safety.

After reaching Philadelphia, he hurried on to
New York. It took him just twenty-four hours to
make the run from the slave city of Baltimore to
the free city of New York. Measured by his intense anxiety, the distance and time must have
seemed without end. For fifteen years he had been
patiently planning to get his feet upon free soil and
breathe the air of a free state. No one ever did
more to free himself or to deserve the liberty into
which he was now about to enter. He came to New
York, his pulses throbbing with high hopes. He
soon learned, however, that his stay there was not
safe and that the slave-traders plied their vocation
even in the free states.

Douglass's instinct for right action seldom failed
him. Although he was totally ignorant of New
York and its people, and had never heard of a
"Vigilance Committee," he had managed, in a few
days after his arrival, to put himself under the
protection and guidance of such influential friends
of the Negro race as Lewis and Arthur Tappan,
Thomas Downing, and Theodore Wright, who were
at that time high officials in that extensive Underground Railway system which had already safely
carried thousands of passengers from bondage to
freedom.

He retained a keen remembrance of his former
experiences in Baltimore and was conscious of a
sense of protection in his Abolition friends ; yet at
the age of twenty-one years, in this new environ-

ment of freedom, he was in many respects as ignorant as a child. To what was north, or east, or west of New York, he was entirely oblivious neither did he know the kind and the condition of the people among whom he was to live and work out his destiny. Where to go, what to do, and how to use his freedom, were questions he could ask, but could not answer. It was enough, now, just to know that he was free. What was to be his relationship to these non-slave-holding people was yet . to be discovered.

It is an evidence of his self-reliance and honor, as well as his loyalty to his past, that, almost the first step in his new life, was to send for his promised wife. She came to New York at once, and they were wedded by Rev. J. W. C. Pennington, a Presbyterian minister of that city. The early marriage of the young man must be regarded as an important event in his career as a freeman. It was a marriage for love and, as his wife was a woman of strong character and determination, she was able actively to assist her husband while he was seeking to establish himself in a new country. The act also made him at once a home-builder and the head of a family. Though he was poor almost to the very limit of poverty, without work, without habitation, and without friends or relationships, having nothing, in fact, but himself, which included a sound body and strong will, he went about planning and doing things as if certain that all must come out as he wished.

His newly discovered friends decided it was best

for him not to stay longer in New York, and that
New Bedford, Mass., was a much safer place. There
he could work at his trade without danger of re-
capture. He cheerfully started on his journey,
though he had not enough money to pay his way.
The stage-driver, plying between Newport and New
Bedford, held a part of his baggage as security for
his unpaid passage and when he and his wife arrived at their destination they had nothing to live
on except faith. In this New England town everything was strange to Douglass, but he was not long
in finding a friend, a colored man named Nathan
Johnson. The latter, the first important acquaintance the refugee made among Northern colored people, had a good home, good standing in the community, and more than ordinary intelligence. He
very soon discovered that Frederick Douglass was
a man of superior fibre and became his firm friend.

Johnson's house was well furnished with books
and music, and bore other evidences of good taste
and a cultivated mind. He was in a position to
render just that kind of help which the young fugitive and his new wife needed at this time. He at
once redeemed the baggage held by the stage-driver,
and gave Douglass needed directions and advice as
to how to get work and to establish himself.

Nathan Johnson had the further distinction of
being the man who gave to the Maryland slave the
name he ever afterward bore. Douglass left the
South as Frederick Augustus Washington Bailey.
His new-found friend had just been reading Scott's
Lady of the Lake, and persuaded the young man that

Douglas was a name of poetic and historical significance; he was sure it would be further glorified by its new owner. With so auspicious a beginning, the refugee started out bravely to seek work and make a living for himself and his wife.

As he moved about in the New England town, he was much impressed by Northern civilization, and was greatly surprised to see white people, who while rich, educated, and powerful, were yet not slave-holders. Up to this time he had known but two classes of white people, slave-holders and non-slave-holders. The non-slave holding white people of the South, he knew, were generally ignorant, despised, and poor; while those who owned slaves seemed to own everything else worth having. Here in New England he observed that white people were high or low according to their character, ability, and possessions. Life appeared to him larger, wider, and fuller of possibilities than he had dreamed, even in his more hopeful days down on the Eastern Shore. These impressions and the better understanding of his own condition gave him courage and made him feel equal to any task or problem. His first occupation, as a free man, was putting away some coal for Ephraim Peabody, for which he was paid two dollars. He cherished this "free money," for it was the first he had ever earned that he could call his own. He cheerfully went from one job to another, proud as a bank president in the new dignity which freedom seemed to have conferred upon him. He accepted any kind of task he could find to do, such as sawing wood, digging cellars, removing rubbish, helping to load cargoes on ships, scrubbing out ship cabins, and the rough work in a foundry. The employment was hard and the pay small, yet it did not seem so to this newly emancipated slave. The right to dispose of his own labor, and to have and to hold all that he made was a profound and unceasing satisfaction to him.

His spare moments were given to studying and reading everything he could lay hold of. He saw from the first that his freedom could not be profitably used and protected without knowledge and the mental discipline that comes with the effort to acquire it. He was liked by everybody who employed him, because he made it a matter of principle to do all and more than his full duty in every occupation. He put as much zeal, intelligence, and cheerful industry into these common tasks as he later gave to pursuits of a more dignified character.

Young Douglass was cheered and heartened in this wholesome atmosphere of freedom,—free schools, free labor, and general fair play, to such a degree that it was a long time before he began to feel the presence and trammels of race prejudice as they existed in New Bedford and elsewhere in the North in that day. That there was a feeling against his color he learned when he attempted to follow his trade as a calker. When he sought to hire himself to a certain ship-owner at New Bedford, he was told to go to work, but when he went to the boat with his tools, the foreman informed him that every white man would quit if he struck a blow at his trade. This unexpected *dénouement* drove Douglass back to common labor, at which he could earn less than one-half of what he could have made as a calker. He accepted the situation in good spirit, however, feeling that the worst possible treatment in freedom was infinitely better than slavery.

He met his next rebuff when he attempted to attend one of the lectures under the auspices of the New Bedford Lyceum Association. He was refused a ticket on the ground that it was against the policy of the society to admit colored people to the lecture-room. It was not long, however, before this discrimination was done away with, since men like Charles Sumner, Emerson, Horace Mann, and Garrison, refused to speak before the organization unless the restriction was removed. The privilege of attending these meetings and hearing some of the great anti-slavery leaders was a matter of great import to Douglass. Indeed, it was the very thing he needed as a part of his education in preparation for his life work. He heard for the first time white men who were taking strong positions on the question of the abolition of slavery. The existence of an anti-slavery society and an anti-slavery movement of ever-widening extent and influence in the nation impressed him as nothing had done since he came from the South. The things for which he had secretly dreamed and yearned and struggled in Maryland were now becoming great national issues, with men of might behind them, pushing them on and seeking to make them the foremost questions of the day.

Quite as important as the privilege of hearing

slavery discussed was the chance he obtained of
reading William Lloyd Garrison's paper, *The Liberator*. Garrison's direct and uncompromising
words came to him like a trumpet call. He began
to cherish each number as second only in importance to the Bible. Heretofore he had had no one
to help him reason out the philosophy of the question. What the facts of slavery were he knew by
actual and bitter suffering. The words of no one
could make him feel their injustice and pain more
than his own experiences had made him feel them,
but here, behold, was a mighty man, a prophet in
his moral earnestness—a sort of Isaiah, who with
inspired fervor, predicted the ultimate downfall of
slavery.

The Liberator and Mr. Garrison's words were as
important to young Douglass and his intellectual
development as was the *Columbian Orator*, which
had inspired him while a slave in Baltimore. Those
who knew him at once recognized his intelligence.
The colored people of New Bedford were the first
to discover his fluency as a speaker and to give
ear to his original ideas on the question of freedom
for their race. He was often called upon to speak
in meetings held by colored men in the town, and in
colored churches. As far as the masses of the
people were concerned, however, he was still an
obscure Negro laborer. There was no one except,
perhaps, Nathan Johnson, who saw in this patient
and cheerful toiler the promise of a public career.
No men of African descent had up to this time
achieved anything like distinction. A colored man

might now and then be smart as a freak of nature ; no one was prepared to think of his becoming great by sheer force of mind and character. But the power within this young fugitive slave and the forces without him were fast shaping themselves to call him forth and hold him up as an example to all the world.

CHAPTER IV

BEGINNING OF HIS PUBLIC CAREER

YEARS had passed and great changes had taken place since Uncle Lawson, the old colored preacher, who had been Frederick Douglass's first spiritual teacher and comforter, had solemnly told him that "the Lord had a great work for him to do," and that he must prepare to do it. These words were spoken at a time when the boy was just beginning to awaken to the vast possibilities of human life, and, dimly conscious of his own powers, was groping to find his place in the world. Douglass had never forgotten this speech. It seemed now that the prophecy of the old colored man was to be fulfilled. During the first years at New Bedford, he had been industriously preparing himself to perform the task that destiny apparently had assigned him. He had no teachers to help him in his studies, or direct him in his reading. He had no definite notion of what the future had in store for him, nor of how he was to be used "to perform the great work," of which Uncle Lawson had spoken. The latter believed that his young *protégé* was to become a preacher of the Gospel, because that seemed the only possible future of the slave upon whom unusual gifts had been bestowed. But Douglass had reached the conclusion that, if any great work had been assigned him, it was in the direction of securing the freedom of the members of his race in bonds. He was faithfully preparing himself to meet the emergency that should call him into the service of that cause.

In the summer of 1841, the opportunity, long waited for, came. A great anti-slavery convention was called by William Lloyd Garrison and his friends, to meet at Nantucket. We have already seen how deeply young Douglass was impressed with Mr. Garrison's writings in *The Liberator*, and it can be easily inferred that the word "anti-slavery" should have stirred him as no other word in the language of freedom. For the first time since he came to New Bedford he determined to take a holiday for the purpose of going to Nantucket and becoming as much as possible a part of the anti-slavery meeting. However ardent others might be in their interest for the convention, to him it meant everything worth living for and dying for to find the white people in a free community taking hold of the question of abolition as if their own kith and kin were in chains.

Douglass went to see, listen, and learn. This was privilege enough for one occasion. When he was sought out by a citizen of New Bedford, who had heard of him, and was asked to say a few words, he was quite startled. So frightened was he, "it was with much difficulty," he says, "that I could stand erect or could command or articulate two words without hesitation and stammering. I trembled in every limb. I am not sure that my embarrassment was not the most important part of my speech, if speech it could be called. The audience sympathized with me and at once, from having been remarkably silent, it became much excited."

But his embarrassment soon subsided. Parker Pillsbury, an eye-witness, says : " When the young man, Douglass, closed late in the evening, none seemed to know or care for the lateness of the hour. The crowded congregation had been wrought up almost to enchantment as he turned over the terrible apocalypse of his experience in slavery."

If Abolition was a great cause in the minds of those astonished auditors, it became more sincerely so after the young fugitive from bondage had concluded. William Lloyd Garrison followed, and of him Pillsbury says : "I think that Mr. Garrison never before, nor afterward felt more profoundly the sacredness of his mission. I surely never saw him more deeply and divinely inspired. He said among other things, ' Have we been listening to a thing—a piece of property, or a man ? ' ' A man,' shouted the audience. ' And should such a man be held a slave in a republican and Christian land ? ' ' No, no. Never, never ! ' was the fervent response. ' Shall such a man be sent back to slavery from the soil of old Massachusetts ? ' Almost the whole assembly sprang with one accord to their feet and shouted, ' No, no ! ' long and loud."

Measured by its effect on the audience and by its importance to himself and the Abolition cause, this first speech was one of the greatest Mr. Douglass ever made. Only three years out of bondage, never having been at school, wholly self-taught and coming direct from hard toil to a platform, he had been invited to speak before an audience of proud and cultured New Englanders !

The whole thing seemed so incredible and was so unexpected that those who heard him never ceased to wonder how such wisdom and eloquence could come from a slave. It was by far the most dramatic and important incident that had occurred in the anti-slavery fight up to this time.

William Lloyd Garrison was quick to discern that the cause needed this fugitive slave, more than any other man or thing, as an argument and an illustration in the further work of the anti-slavery society. Others spoke from knowledge and conviction gained by reading and study ; Douglass spoke from twenty years' experience of all the phases of slave-life. His words had the charm born of things seen, felt, and suffered. His presentation of the subject was more than argument; it was a transcript from actual life.

Immediately after the convention, John A. Collins, then the general agent of the Massachusetts Anti-Slavery Society, went to Mr. Douglass and urged him to accept a position as one of his assistants, publicly to advocate its principles. This unexpected offer was quite as embarrassing as was the request for him to speak at the meeting. Acting upon an impulse of self-mistrust, and a sense of unfitness, he tried to refuse, but all excuses were swept aside by Mr. Collins, and finally Douglass decided to make a trial for three months.

After recovering from his first timidity, he entered the fight with enthusiasm. No one was more surprised than he at his ability to meet the expectations of the people. In the early part of his work he was accompanied by George Foster. They traveled and lectured from the same platform through the eastern counties of Massachusetts. He was frequently introduced to the audiences as a "chattel," a "thing," a "piece of property," and Mr. Collins invariably called their attention to the fact that the speaker was a "graduate from an institution whose diploma was written upon his back."

A great deal of interest was excited in the meetings that he was invited to address. Many of those who came out of curiosity to see and hear a fugitive slave went away convinced and converted to the anti-slavery cause. Douglass soon persuaded his friends and associates to think that he was too much of a man to be employed as a mere "exhibit." At first his eloquence and success with the public both delighted and alarmed them. There began to arise a fear that his power as an orator would prove too great. It seemed well enough for him to tell the story of his servitude, but when he indulged in logic and flights of fancy and invective, it was feared that he would be considered an impostor. If slavery was such a degrading thing as this man said it was, the question naturally arose, How, then, did he acquire his accomplishments? Besides, Douglass did not give the name of his master, or the state from which he came.

All this was true enough, and the truth was somewhat embarrassing, but the people did not stop to consider the omission. Douglass was now a resident of Massachusetts; he was a slave, owned in Maryland. To state the facts about his identity would be to invite slave-catchers to New Bedford to reclaim strayed property. There was nothing for him to do but to keep the dangerous secret securely locked in his own bosom and talk down the doubts and suspicions that were now and then expressed. George Foster, Mr. Garrison, Mr. Collins, and other friends. who happened to be on the same platform with him, were always admonishing him not to appear too intelligent, too oratorical, or too logical, lest his claim of having been a slave be discredited. "Give the facts," they said, "and we will take care of the philosophy." "Let us have the facts only." "Tell your story, Frederick; people will not believe you were ever a slave, if you go on in this way." "Be yourself." "Better have a little plantation dialect than not." "It is not best that you should seem so learned."

Such were the complaints and warnings that came to him from those who most admired him, during the first few months of his career as an orator. The young man could scarcely curb his impatience, so great was his moral earnestness. The thoughts which he uttered flowed so spontaneously and uncontrollably from his lips, that it seemed to him he could no more limit himself than he could stop the force of gravitation. Speaking of this embarrassment he says: "It was impossible for me to repeat the same old story month after month and keep up

my interest in it.   I could not follow the injunction
of my friends, for I was now reading and thinking.
New views of the subject were being presented to
my mind : I could not always curb my moral indignation."

In order to remove all doubts as to whether he
was a slave, he put the facts, including the name of
his master, in the possession of the Anti-Slavery
Society. As soon as Phillips and Garrison knew
the truth, they advised him to go on as before, for
if he gave his name and that of his master, he would
be in danger of recapture,—even in Massachusetts.
When he showed to Wendell Phillips a manuscript
detailing the facts of his slave-life, he was advised
"to throw it in the fire"; but so straightforward
and earnest and effective was his work, and so
rapid his development as an orator, that he soon
overcame all doubts, and those who had once urged
him to curb his intellectual flights learned to admire
his courage, and to put a higher value on his services to the cause of Abolition. Whenever there
was serious work to be done, and the best men and
women were needed to combat pro-slavery policies
and measures, he was eagerly sought. His name now
began to be announced with those of the foremost
advocates of freedom.

In the latter part of the year 1841, and in the
early months of 1842, the Abolitionists were called
upon for a show of strength. The appeal came from
Rhode Island. The people of that state were
aroused to a high pitch of interest in an effort to
adopt a new constitution in place of the old colo-

nial charter that had been in use since the Revolution. Making a new constitution was a political question and every political contest, however local in concern, afforded occasion for the pro-slavery and anti-slavery people to clash. In this Rhode Island contest, interest centred on the proposition to restrict the right of suffrage to white citizens only. The pro-slavery sentiment of this, as of other Northern states, was so strong, that there seemed to be a great likelihood of the " color line " being fixed in the supreme law of the commonwealth. To combat this danger, the anti-slavery societies massed their forces and went into the little state to dispute every inch of the ground. Stephen S. Foster, Parker Pillsbury, Abby Kelley, James Monroe, and Frederick Douglass were the advance guard. The contest here was somewhat different from the more or less peaceful work of holding public meetings in Massachusetts to create public opinion. Here was a clean-cut issue in which was involved the right of free Negroes to be full citizens in a Northern state. Under the leadership of Thomas W. Dorr, the pro-slavery forces had to be opposed by strong arguments and not by mere sentiment. There was also a decided feeling against "intermeddlers," as Douglass and his associates were called. Meetings were held all over the state, and soon it was plain to be seen that the anti-slavery people were making progress in overcoming the "Dorrites." It was a picturesque and dramatic campaign, the chief features of which were the conspicuous parts taken by Frederick Douglass, the fugitive slave, and

Abby Kelley. Mr. Douglass says that she "was perhaps the most successful of any of us. Her youth and simple Quaker beauty, combined with her wonderful earnestness, her large knowledge and great logical powers bore down all opposition to the end, wherever she spoke, though she was before pelted with foul eggs, and no less foul words, from the noisy mobs which attended us."

Mr. Douglass speaks in generous praise of the effectiveness of other anti-slavery advocates, who were associated with him in this campaign. He himself made a multitude of friends and added immensely to his prestige as an orator. He was received by many of the leading citizens of the state, almost as a brother. Among these new friends he gratefully mentions the Clarks, Keltons, Chases, Adamses, Greens, Eldridges, Mitchells, Anthonys, Goulds, Fairbanks, and many others.

Yet it was not all smooth sailing for the colored orator. He was frequently dragged from the cars by mobs, though his associates were always loyal to him, many of them refusing to go where he could not. This was especially the case with Wendell Phillips, James Monroe, and William A. White.

The result of the battle in Rhode Island was a complete triumph over those who had sought to abridge the suffrage. The victory was not only important, as a show of strength of the Abolitionists, but it prevented the establishment of a dangerous precedent which might have had its influence upon other states.

From Rhode Island, Mr. Douglass was called to

speak in various places. At first he was not always well received, but in nearly every case, after he had once appeared, converts were made and opposition ceased. At one time when he, with Garrison, Abby Kelley, and Foster, attempted to speak in Hartford, Conn., the doors of every hall and church were closed against them, but they spoke under the open sky, to so much effect that some of their opponents had the grace to confess to a sense of shame for such action.

At Grafton, Mass., Douglass was advertised to speak alone. There was no house, church, or market-place in which he was permitted to appear. Not to be outdone, he went up and down the streets ringing a dinner-bell that he had borrowed, announcing that "Frederick Douglass, recently a slave, will lecture on Grafton Common this evening at seven o'clock." As a result of this notice, he spoke to a great concourse of people, and as usual advanced the cause of Abolition.

In the year 1843, the movement had so far progressed that a great undertaking was announced. It was proposed to hold one hundred conventions under the auspices of the Massachusetts Anti-Slavery Society in such states as New Hampshire, Vermont, New York, Ohio, Indiana, and Pennsylvania. Mr. Douglass was selected as one of the agents to assist in the work. This was regarded as an ambitious scheme on the part of Mr. Garrison, and attracted a great deal of public attention. Among the speakers associated with Mr. Douglass in this tour were George Bradburn,

John A. Collins, James Monroe, Sidney Howard Gay, and Charles Lenox Remond, the last-named a colored man of unusual eloquence.

Mr. Douglass felt very proud, as well he might, of being given so prominent a part in this important enterprise, and of being associated with men of such distinction. The wisdom of holding these conventions was soon made manifest, when it was discovered how ill-informed were the masses of the people as to the nature of the issue the Abolitionists were seeking to force upon the attention of the country.

The crusade received rather a chilly reception in the Green Mountain State. Along the Erie Canal, from Albany to Buffalo, it was more than difficult to excite any interest or to make converts. In Syracuse, the home of Rev. Samuel J. May, and where such men as Gerrit Smith, Beriah Green, and William Goodell lived, Douglass and his friends could not obtain a hall, church, or market-place to hold a meeting. Everybody was discouraged and favored "shaking the dust from off their feet," and going to other parts. But Frederick Douglass did not believe in surrender. He was determined to speak his word for the gospel of Abolition here, even if he must do so under the open sky, as in Connecticut and Massachusetts. In the morning he began in a grove with five people present. So powerful was his appeal that in the afternoon he had an audience of five hundred and in the evening he was tendered the use of an old building that had done service as a Congregational church. In this house the convention was organized and carried on

for three days. The seeds of Abolition were so well
sown in Syracuse, that thereafter it was always
hospitable ground for anti-slavery advocates. Mr.
Douglass had a more friendly reception in Rochester,
which was to be his future home. Here he found a
goodly number of Abolitionists and his words made
a lasting impression.

The next meeting of importance was in Buffalo.
The outlook for a convention in this western New
York city was so discouraging that Mr. Douglass's
associates turned on their heels and left him to "do
Buffalo alone." The place appointed was a dilapi-
dated old room that had once been used as a post-
office. No one was there at first except a few hack-
drivers who sauntered in from curiosity. But Mr.
Douglass went at them with great earnestness, as if
they could settle all the problems that were over-
burdening his heart. Out of this small and unsym-
pathetic beginning, grew a great convention. Every
day for nearly a week, in the old building, he spoke
to constantly increasing crowds of people who were
worth talking to, until finally a large Baptist church
was thrown open to him. Here the size and character of the audience were flattering. So great was
the eagerness to hear him that on Sunday evening
he addressed an outdoor meeting of five thousand
people in the park.

At this Buffalo meeting Mr. Douglass called to
his assistance a number of prominent colored
speakers, such as Henry Highland Garnet, Theodore
S. Wright, Amos G. Bearman, Charles M. Ray, and
Charles Lenox Remond, all of powerful speech and

growing influence, who held a convention of their own, at which the ex-slave made an eloquent address.

From this city Douglass continued on his way into Ohio and Indiana. The Ohio meeting, held in Clinton County, was a notable event. This was the farthest west Mr. Douglass had been as yet and he now went into the state of Indiana. This was dangerous ground, as he soon learned when he attempted to deliver his message. Here he found a mob spirit harder to resist than any he had encountered in the East. In attempting to speak at Richmond, Ind., where Henry Clay had been heard shortly before, he received a shower of "evil-smelling eggs." From this place he went to Pendleton, where he could find no hall or church in which to speak ; but, not to be outdone, he attempted what he had successfully accomplished at Syracuse, and at other places. He had a platform erected in the woods. A large assembly of people came out to hear the colored orator, but the Hoosiers, in this part of the state, were determined not to be persuaded.

It was, as one of them rudely expressed it, a case of "no nigger speaker for us." As soon as the meeting began, a mob of fifty or sixty rough-looking men ordered Douglass to stop. An attempt to disregard this threatening command, maddened the rioters. They tore down the platform and violently assaulted the orator and his associate, Mr. White. Seeing the danger, Douglass began to fight his way through the crowd with a club. The sight of a weapon in the hands of a Negro angered the mob still more, and they set upon him with such fury that he was felled to the ground, being beaten so fiercely that he was left for dead. Having dispersed the meeting, the men mounted their horses and rode away. Mr. Douglass's right hand was broken, and he was in a state of unconsciousness for some time. He was unable to speak for several days, being tenderly cared for by a Mrs. Neal Hardy, a member of the Society of Friends, until his wounds were healed, but he never recovered the full use of his right hand.

Notwithstanding this rough treatment, Mr. Douglass would not allow himself to be frightened out of the state. He continued his work for a long time, and compelled a respectful and peaceful hearing. He was no coward and was not afraid of mobs. He did not stop until, according to the plans determined upon by the Anti-Slavery Society of Massachusetts, the one hundred conventions had been held. The work was accomplished, in spite of indifference, contemptuous criticism, and sometimes violent and bloody opposition.

Although it seemed at the time that not much had been achieved, the seed sown was to bear fruit when a few years later the South and North were arrayed against each other in the great struggle for the preservation of the Union.

CHAPTER V

SLAVERY AND ANTI-SLAVERY

FREDERICK DOUGLASS was so much a part of
the Abolition movement from 1838 to the final
overthrow of slavery in the United States, that his
career will be the better understood after a brief review of the condition of the country as affected by
the evil during those years.

At the time of Douglass's escape from bondage
in 1838, slavery was the one great and overshadowing fact in our national life. According to the
census of 1840, the number of slaves in the United
States was about 2,500,000 and the number of
free colored people about 300,000. The value of
slave-property was upward of two billions of dollars. No other interest in the United States at
that time approximated in the amount of its invested capital the sum represented in these human
chattels. The labor of these slaves was to a very
considerable extent the basis of American commerce
and credit. Not the South alone, but the entire
nation, was interested directly or indirectly, in
preserving the integrity and maintaining the economic value of slave-labor. The mining, the manu-
facturing, and the great grain interests of the present time were unknown and scarcely dreamed of in
those early days of the nation's industries. Cot-

ton was "king," and its dominion affected in some way, and to some degree, the social, political, and economic life of the republic.

The results of Whitney's invention of the cotton gin were such as to check the current of sentiment in favor of emancipation, which had found expression in the sayings of Thomas Jefferson, Madison, and other Revolutionary leaders. In his great speech of March 7, 1850, Daniel Webster said : "In 1791 the first parcel of cotton of the growth of the United States was exported and amounted to 19,200 pounds. It has gone on increasing rapidly until the whole crop may now, perhaps, in a season of great product and great prices, amount to $100,-000,000." According to the estimates of the United States Census Bureau in its census of 1900, cotton production increased from 2,000,025 pounds in 1790 to 987,637,200 pounds in 1849, and 2,397,238,140 pounds in 1859. The enormous capital invested in this industry created a close community of interest between the planters of the South and the capitalists of the North; hence the influence of the cotton trade was felt in both sections.

This enormous interest easily dominated the politics of the times, North and South. The most prominent statesmen of the nation, after 1850, were either openly committed to policies and measures to protect and extend the power of slavery, or were silent, since to oppose these policies and measures meant, in many instances, political extinction. The trend of all legislation in our national government at this period was directly opposed to emancipation.

Meanwhile, the evil flourished and became more and more a part of the spirit and blood of our national life. If there were no slavery in the Northern states, one reason was that slave-labor had proven unprofitable. In the early days of the institution, the North was quite as willing to legalize and protect slavery as the South, and continued to do so as long as it paid and was practicable. The mere fact that slavery was profitable where climatic conditions were congenial to cotton raising, increased the demand for both slaves and territory. The pressure for more slaves and more territory for slavery, was so persistent, that it constantly became easier to ignore moral and religious precepts, to set aside the national maxims, and to override the laws that stood in the way of its extension and power. For example, the slave-trade was prohibited by national law, yet so little effort was made to enforce this law, that importations kept the market well supplied. The acts of Congress, the messages of our presidents, the utterances of our cabinet ministers, and correspondence with the representatives of the nation at foreign courts, contain abundant evidences of the constant concern of our government that nothing should be done to impair the security of slave-property in the United States. The acts of Congress by which every addition to our national domain south of the Ohio River became slave-territory, clearly show this. When in 1855, a "slaver" was driven by storm to seek refuge in Bermuda, our Minister at the Court of St. James was instructed that, "in the present state of diplomatic relations with the government of his British Majesty, the most immediately pressing of the matters with which the United States Legation at London is now charged, is the claim of certain American citizens against Great Britain, for a number of slaves wrecked on the island in the Atlantic." The message contains a polite hint that "neglect to satisfy these demands might possibly tend to disturb and weaken the kind and amicable relations that now so happily subsist between the two countries."

By sanction of the national government, slavery was legalized and protected at the national capital. The war with Mexico, which resulted in the annexation of Texas, was followed by the establishment of slavery in the territory so acquired. It was fostered and defended as a national institution not only by numerous acts of the government, but by public sentiment in the Northern states. It had existed before the foundation of the Union. It had been accepted as a fact by the framers of the Constitution. As such, it had a legitimate claim, it was urged, to the protection of the government. It was generally assumed that, on the whole, the Negro was better off in slavery than as a free man. Though the Northern people did not favor the extension of slavery, they were disposed to meet in a spirit of conciliation every demand for more protection, more power, and more territory for this traffic.

When opposition, not on grounds of expediency but of fundamental right, began to manifest itself in Northern states by the circulation of Abolition papers, the alarm of slave-owners was expressed in no uncertain tones. Some of the governors of slave-states and their legislatures made urgent demands that such publications be suppressed. The following is a sample of some of the resolutions passed by the legislatures: "Resolved that our sister states are respectfully requested to enact penal laws prohibiting the printing, within their respective limits, of all such publications as may have a tendency to make our slaves discontented."

The messages of the governors of two Northern states, William L. Marcy of New York, and Edward Everett of Massachusetts, aptly illustrate sentiment in the North at this time. Governor Marcy said: "Without the power to pass such laws, the states would not possess all the necessary means for preserving their external relations of peace among themselves." Governor Everett said: "Whatever by direct and necessary operation is calculated to excite an insurrection among slaves, has been held by highly respectable legal authority an offense against the peace of this commonwealth, which may be prosecuted as a misdemeanor at common law."

In the same year, 1836, the Rhode Island legislature reported on a bill in conformity with the demands of the slave-states. The significance of this action is that it was taken fully two months prior to the request of the Southern states. Thus it appears that the idea of the suppression of free speech and free publication against slavery was first broached in a Northern state.

President Jackson, in his annual message to Congress, in 1835 suggested "the propriety of passing such laws as will prohibit, under severe penalties, the circulation in the Southern states, through the mail, of incendiary publications, intended to instigate the slaves to insurrection."

The Postmaster-General, a Northern man, serving under Jackson, refused to "sanction" or condemn the acts of certain postmasters in arresting the circulation of Abolition circulars, characterized as "incendiary matter."

The state of public feeling at this time fully justified the government and its officials in everything they did to protect slavery, since their action was sanctioned by a sentiment national in extent and character. Just how strong was this public opinion in the North may be further illustrated by the spirit of mob-violence that forms one of the darkest chapters in the struggle to make this country, in deed as well as in name, "the home of the free." William Lloyd Garrison and Benjamin Lundy, were repeatedly assaulted while they were running a paper in Baltimore in 1827. The gentle and pious young Quakeress, Prudence Crandall, of Canterbury, Conn., was arrested and sent to jail for allowing colored children to attend her school. Her brother, Dr. Reuben Crandall, was arrested in the city of Washington, thrown into prison on August 11, 1833, and held there for eight months on the charge of circulating incendiary publications with the intent of inciting slaves to insurrection. The only evidence against him was that he had in his trunk some anti-slavery circulars. He died from the effects of his imprisonment soon after his release.

On the 4th day of July, 1834, an anti-slavery meeting in New York was made the occasion of a frightful riot. At Worcester, Mass., in 1835, an anti-slavery speaker, Rev. O. Scott, son of an ex-governor, was forcibly prevented from delivering a lecture, and his notes were torn up. On the same day at Canaan, N. H., an academy was demolished, for the reason that it was designed for the instruction of colored youth. At Boston, on October 21, 1835, a mob of "five thousand gentlemen" attacked the Boston Female Anti-Slavery Society and dispersed one of its meetings while its president was at prayers. At Syracuse, N. Y., in October, 1833, a crowd of "prominent" citizens broke up a meeting called by Gerrit Smith to form an anti-slavery society ; and in December, 1836, an anti-slavery meeting at New Haven, Conn., was dispersed by students of Yale College. At Alton, Ill., on the 7th day of November, 1837, Rev. Elijah P. Lovejoy was shot and killed and his printing press destroyed by a mob. At Cincinnati, O., in 1836, and again in 1840, mobs of citizens demolished the printing press of the *Philanthropist*, owned by James G. Birney, an ex-slaveholder from Kentucky. Pennsylvania Hall, in Philadelphia, built for the free discussion of all questions interesting to the American people, was burned by a mob in May, 1838, because Abolitionists had been allowed to hold a meeting there.

But what was perhaps the most heartless of all instances of violence occurred on the 1st of August, 1842, at Philadelphia. The colored people of that city had built a fine church and hall in which they were holding a temperance celebration on the day of the anniversary of British emancipation. A mob was formed which burned the building, demolished the homes of the participants, and in a most savage and brutal manner, beat and maltreated its innocent victims. This riot lasted two days and the city authorities offered but feeble protection.

Many other incidents of violence directed against attempts to discuss the slavery question might be recited, but enough have been mentioned to indicate public feeling in almost every community in the non-slave-holding States. All these manifestations of opposition to anti-slavery agitation and action were at first and for a long time very generally sanctioned by the churches, the schools and colleges, and by the politicians of the free North. All the forces of conservatism in the country were, as might have been expected, in favor of preserving the *status quo*, and scarcely any cause in the whole history of our country has ever been so unpopular as this Abolition movement. It seemed that the slave-holders might rest perfectly secure in the assurance that their interests would be well guarded by their friends in the free-states, assisted by the natural inertia of the great mass of the Northern people, who were instinctively opposed to any sudden or violent change such as the agitation of the Abolitionists seemed to portend.

The inherent weakness of slavery in this country appeared when the very laws that were passed to sustain and support it served merely to arouse the public to a real comprehension of its evils. Grad-

ually it became clear to an ever increasing number
of citizens that it had no place in a republic. It
was out of harmony with the doctrines and principles fought for in the Revolutionary War, and it
did violence to the consciences of large numbers of
men and women, North and South, who, uncon-
trolled by prejudice, were free to think and act for
themselves. Thousands of Southern people who
felt that slavery was a wrong, emancipated their
slaves; others were moved to treat them with unusual kindness, and still others held them because
they could not help themselves.

Many influences were at work to arouse and
quicken the moral sense of the public and to make it
conscious of the issues involved in the question.
Such agencies as the missionary movement, in its
effort to "evangelize" the world; the work of the
Bible, tract and educational societies, the religious awakening of the masses, in response to the
appeals of such eloquent preachers as Beecher,
Rice, and Summerfield; and the new interest in the
former teachings of Hopkins and Edwards:—all
these forces, along with the new enthusiasm for
social and political reform, which found expression
in the work of temperance and peace societies and
the fight against the cruel treatment of the Indians,
especially the Cherokees, aroused the people and
prepared them to take part in the discussion of
public questions, giving them a new sense of the
significance and the responsibility of self-government. This revived public spirit was aided and
advanced by the growing influence of the modern

newspaper press, and of journals dealing with a variety of subjects other than politics. Each moral and social question came to have an organ to spread its views. Every one who had a gift for writing had the opportunity to impress his opinions upon the public, if he could but get hold of a press and printing outfit. A noted author of that period says : " No one can comprehend in their real and distinctive characteristics, the existing agitations of America, if he does not take into account the new power and changed direction of the public press constituting a new era in human history."

With these agencies for the education of the masses, there came into being the lecture platform. Any man or woman with a talent for fluent speech and a " cause," was at liberty to take the rostrum and attempt to get a hearing. The same writer, above quoted, says : " The railway car of 1838, and the electric telegraph ten years after, were scarcely greater innovations or greater curiosities than were the voluntary lectures, free public conventions, and the moral and religious weekly journals with their correspondence from 1825 to 1830."

The development of these moral and religious agencies furnished the masses of the American people with the means of creating a more active interest in public affairs. Out of these grew that broader knowledge and more acute moral sense which led them to inquire into the sanctions that seemed to hedge about and protect the institution of slavery.

It was in such an atmosphere, in which religious

enthusiasm touched and quickened the sense of responsibility of the people in social and political conditions, that the Abolition spirit grew and became a power in public affairs. The question of slavery was definitely put before the people as a political issue in the Missouri Compromise in 1820. During the debate that followed they heard for the first time, the doctrine of "immediate and unconditional emancipation of the slave." Interest in this new and radical doctrine was immediate and wide-spread. To those who owned slaves, and indeed to the vast majority of the people, North and South, who accepted slavery as an established institution with a legitimate claim to protection from attack, this new doctrine seemed at once revolutionary and dangerous.

The cry at once went up, "Put down the discussion and silence the agitation!" It was indeed a question that could not survive debate. As a matter of fact, the opposition which Abolition aroused was the one thing that insured its final triumph. Men felt instinctively—it was the republican habit of mind—that there must be something essentially unsound in a system that could not tolerate open and free discussion. Hence it was that every attempt to suppress the agitation defeated its own purposes. The characters who now began to push to the front in the ranks of the Abolitionists were men of stern American fibre. Facts, figures, and arguments began to pile up which showed that this country could not long exist "half-slave and half-free." The terms "pro-slavery" and "anti-slavery " came into the vocabulary of political discussion during this new conflict. The breach between the forces represented by these names grew wider and wider as the strife continued. The very nature of the issue caused a degree of bitterness that has never before or since been equaled in political argument in the United States. There could be no such thing as compromise. A test of moral and physical strength was sooner or later inevitable.

The issues of the contest may be summarized with advantage.

Pro-Slavery

The powers and privileges the conservative party sought to maintain and defend were :

The unlimited authority of the master or owner of slaves.

Abrogation of marriage and the family relation among slaves.

The power to enforce labor without wages.

Incapacity of the slaves to acquire and hold property.

Incapacity to enjoy civil, domestic, and political rights.

Incapacity to make contracts or bargains.

The liability of the slave to be sold like other chattels, and separated from relatives.

The authorized prosecution of the inter-state slave-trade.

The power of the master to forbid education, and to permit religious gatherings at his own discretion.

The power of the legislatures of slave-states to prohibit education of slaves by their masters.

ANTI–SLAVERY

The principles for which the Abolitionists contended were the following :

All men are created equal and are endowed by their Creator with certain inalienable rights among which are life, liberty, and the pursuit of happiness.

Slavery, or more properly, the practice of slaveholding, is a crime against human nature and a sin against God.

Like all other sins, slavery should be abolished unconditionally, repented of, and abandoned. It is always safe to leave off doing wrong and never safe to continue in wrong-doing.

It is the duty of all men to bear testimony against wrong-doing, and consequently to bear testimony against slave-holding.

Immediate and unconditional emancipation, is preëminently safe and beneficial to all parties concerned.

No compensation is due to the slave-holder for emancipating his slaves ; and emancipation creates no necessity for such compensation because it is of itself a pecuniary benefit, not only to slaves, but to masters.

There should be no compromise in legislation, jurisprudence, or the executive action of the government, any more than in the activities and responsibilities of private life.

No wicked enactments can be morally binding. There are at the present time the highest obligations resting upon the people of the free states to remove slavery, by moral and political action, as prescribed in the Constitution of the United States.[1]

Societies were formed on all sides. On the 10th day of January, 1832, the New England Anti-Slavery Society was established in Boston. In 1833, another society was organized in New York City. A call was issued for a national anti-slavery convention, to be held in Philadelphia, December 4th, 5th, and 6th, in 1833, for the purpose of forming a National Anti-Slavery Society. Upward of sixty delegates came to this meeting from Maine, New Hampshire, Vermont, Massachusetts, Rhode Island, Connecticut, New York, New Jersey, Pennsylvania, and Ohio. This was the beginning of the national anti-slavery movement. Arthur Tappan, a well-known merchant of New York City, was chosen president. Among the delegates in attendance were such distinguished men as John G. Whittier, the poet ; Beriah Green, William Lloyd Garrison, Elizur Wright, A. L. Cox, and William Goodell. After this time anti-slavery societies were formed in every Northern state, men and women alike being eligible to membership.

The Quaker element in this anti-slavery move-

[1] See William Lloyd Garrison—"The Story of His Life Told by His Children," vol. 1, p. 408, *et. seq.*, where the full text of the Declaration of Sentiments of the Anti-Slavery Convention of 1833 is given.

ment was strong and important. Benjamin Lundy
was the pioneer Abolitionist and no single American ever did more for emancipation. In an appeal
to the public in 1830, he said : " In a period of ten
years prior to 1830, I have sacrificed several thousand dollars of my own hard earnings ; have traveled upward of five thousand miles on foot and
more than twenty thousand miles in other ways ;
have visited nineteen states of this Union and held
more than two hundred public meetings, and have
performed two voyages to the West Indies, by
which means the liberation of a considerable number of slaves has been effected."

The anti-slavery movement was a warfare, but
its weapons were those of peace. Appeal to the
people by public addresses and through the medium
of the press, constituted the only method of fighting. Agitators in behalf of this cause flooded the
country with facts, figures, and arguments. They
brought the republic back to the principles of liberty and justice upon which it was founded. They
urged this issue so persistently that no other question was permitted to equal it in public interest.
They set out with the determination that there
was to be no peace, no ease of conscience, no
further prosperity, no national glory until this
question of slavery was settled and settled right.
As the subject grew in interest and importance, it
attracted to itself some of the brightest minds of
the country ; men who afterward became distinguished as statesmen, poets, authors, orators.
Even men of wealth, whose natural interest would

have inclined them to aid in preserving existing conditions, joined the ranks. They gave to the movement a character for respectability and made it a power that must be reckoned with. The new party demanded a new dispensation, and with such persistency, upon grounds which appealed so directly to the fundamental political beliefs of the people, that finally there was not enough inertia in the nation to oppose its demands.

While these revolutionary forces were gathering strength, the great mass of the Negro people in the United States were dumb. In the plantation states, the black man was a chattel; in the Northern states, he was a good deal of an outlaw.

He was not permitted to share in the responsibilities and benefits of citizenship sufficiently to be able to make his abilities known and his purposes respected. "A man without force," to use Mr. Douglass's words, "is without the essential dignity of humanity. Human nature is so constituted that it cannot honor a helpless man, though it can pity him, and even this it cannot do long, if signs of power do not arise; you can put a man so far beneath the level of his kind that he loses all just ideals of his natural position."

CHAPTER VI

WHEN Frederick Douglass had concluded his remarkable tour from Vermont to Indiana in the interest of the anti-slavery conventions, he was one of
the most popular and widely talked of men on the
American platform. The public everywhere was
eager to learn everything possible about the " runaway slave " who was winning his place among the
foremost of American orators. Interest in him was
further enhanced by the publication of his " Narrative," in 1845. Its issue was made necessary by
the demand for something definite concerning the
antecedents of this "alleged slave." His accomplishments as a speaker and as a reasoner seemed inconsistent with the representation made by him, that
he had had no schooling, and that he had been a
slave until he was twenty-one years of age. There
was a desire for the exact facts. Yet to give them
was dangerous. His growing popularity was likewise a peril. The possibility of his capture and return to slavery increased with his influence as an
orator and agitator.

After this publication, Douglass's personal friends
and the leaders of the anti-slavery cause became
more and more apprehensive. It would have been
regarded as little less than a calamity to have had
Frederick Douglass, the incomparable orator, the

man in whom almost for the first time, the silent, toiling slaves had found a voice, dragged back into bondage. Under the circumstances it was deemed expedient for him to go to England. Douglass himself was less anxious than his associates. He was willing to continue to run any risk, if thereby he might serve the cause of emancipation. His objections, however, were overruled, and he was obliged to depart. He sailed on the steamer *Cambria* of the Cunard Line, Saturday, August 16, 1845, and James N. Buffum, of Lynn, Mass., accompanied him.

Though an English boat, Douglass was not allowed cabin accommodations upon it. This aroused the indignation of a large number of the passengers, among whom were many anti-slavery people,—notably the Hutchinson family, the sweet singers of the Abolition cause. Mr. Douglass by this time had become so used to such humiliations that he easily made himself at home in the steerage. Within a few days, however, he was the most popular person on the boat. Cabin passengers came into his dirty quarters to see and talk with him. And presently all restrictions were removed and he was welcomed and honored in every part of the great steamer. A short speech which he delivered *en route* aroused the resentment of some who were on the ship and a group of young men threatened to throw him overboard. It was only by the interference of the captain that Mr. Douglass was saved from violence. On reaching Liverpool Thursday, August 28, 1845, these young men attempted to forestall any possible influence he might try to exert, by the publication of statements derogatory to his character and standing ; but such statements, instead of having the desired effect, served but to arouse great interest in him.

In going to Great Britain, Mr. Douglass had no fixed plan or program. He was merely fleeing to a land of safety to escape capture and a return into slavery. He soon found, however, that he was almost as well-known in England, as he was in New England. The remarkable story of his life had been widely read by the British public, especially by those interested in the anti-slavery cause. They had just passed through an anti-slavery agitation which had resulted in emancipation in the West Indies. Many of the most distinguished men in public life in Great Britain were Abolitionists, and they took an active and eager interest in the question. All attention was now centred upon America, and the men and women there who were leaders in the Abolition movement, were well-known. Douglass found a hospitable public awaiting him. It was the time of the great political struggle for the repeal of the Corn Laws and the dissolution of the union between England and Ireland. Some of the greatest orators and statesmen in English history were on the stage of action at this period. The black leader was stirred and inspired by the debates in which such men as Cobden, Bright, Disraeli, Lord Brougham, Sir Robert Peel, Daniel O'Connell and Lord John Russell took part. He met all of them personally, was received cordially by them, and treated with much deference. He dined with

Bright and O'Connell, and in Belfast was tendered a breakfast, at which a member of parliament presided. While in Edinburgh he was entertained by the eminent philosopher, George Combe. Thomas Clarkson, who had assisted in inaugurating the anti-slavery movement in England, and who was at that time the most distinguished Abolitionist in the world, was deeply affected by meeting Mr. Douglass, of whom he had heard much. Taking both of his hands he feelingly said: "God bless you, Frederick Douglass; I have given sixty years of my life to the emancipation of your people, and if I had sixty more, they should all be given in the same way."

Mr. Douglass cherished a peculiar liking for Daniel O'Connell at that time the incomparable orator and leader of the Irish people. He had a genuine and lovable personality and was a powerful advocate. He had an intense hatred for slavery, as for all forms of oppression and injustice. He introduced Mr. Douglass always as the "Black O'Connell." His fondness for the "Maryland slave" made the latter's tour through Ireland a continuous ovation. At Cork, a public breakfast was tendered him and the mayor presided at the first meeting he addressed. On October 4th, Father Mathew devoted an evening to him and Mr. Buffum. The British and Foreign Anti-Slavery Society presented Douglass with a Bible splendidly bound in gold. In response to this gracious act, he made the following acknowledgment:

"I accept thankfully this Bible, and while it shall

have the best place in my home, I trust also to give. its precepts a place in my heart. Twenty years ago while lying, not unlike a dog, at the feet of my mistress, I was roused from the sweet sleep of childhood to hear the narrative of Job. A few years afterward found me searching for the Scriptures in the muddy street gutters to rescue its pages from the filth. A few years later, I escaped from my chains ; gained partial freedom, and became an advocate for the emancipation of my race. During this advocacy, a suspicion obtains that I am not what I profess to be, to silence which, it is necessary for me to write out my experiences in slavery and give the names of my enslavers. This endangers my liberty ; persecuted, hunted and outraged in America, I have come to England, and behold the change. The chattel becomes a man. I breathe : I am free ! Instead of culling the Scriptures from the mud, they come to me dressed in polished gold, as the free and unsolicited gift of devoted hearts."

Shortly after this happy occurrence, Douglass, with his associate, Mr. Buffum, left Ireland. He had spoken about fifty times to the people in various parts of the island. Everywhere he had made a deep impression and intensified the interest in the American struggle for emancipation.

In carrying the campaign into Scotland, he met for the first time something in the nature of an opposition or pro-slavery sentiment. William Lloyd Garrison had already arrived there. It was during the great excitement, in consequence of the position taken by the " Free Church " of Scotland in accepting money from slave-holders to be used in spreading the Gospel. In the cities of Glasgow, Greenock, Edinburgh, and other places were seen such sensational placards, as, "Send Back the Money." These posters fairly indicated the state of public feeling upon this subject, which was intensified by the presence of Frederick Douglass, J. N. Buffum, William Lloyd Garrison, and George Thompson, and by their terrible arraignment of slavery. At one of the great meetings held at Cannon Mills, Edinburgh, Mr. Douglass was a speaker. It seemed to be a test of strength between the friends and foes of the policy of the "Free Church." Doctors Cunningham and Candlish, men powerful in influence, learning, and eloquence, championed the cause of the "Free Church." Mr. Douglass's part in the meeting, was, as usual, a striking one. His facts and figures and actual experiences as a slave, silenced all arguments of a mere academic sort.

In one of his addresses in Scotland, when he was charged with being in the pay of some rival religious sect, he said : "I am not here alone : I have with me the learned, wise and revered heads of the church. But with or without their sanction, I should stand just where I do now, maintaining that man-stealing is incompatible with Christianity ; that slave-holding and true religion are at war with each other, and that a Free Church should have no fellowship with a slave church. The Free Church, in vindicating their fellowship of slaveholders, have acted on a damning heresy that a man may be a Christian, whatever may be his practice, so his

creed is right.   It is this heresy that holds in chains
three millions of men, women, and children in the
United States.''

Each of his Scotch addresses was of this uncompromising and stirring character.   It was a matter
of surprise and wonder to his associates to witness
his resourcefulness and readiness to meet all arguments and to sweep aside all half-truths, uttered in
behalf of slavery.   Summing up his work in Scotland, one who had followed him and studied its effects, wrote :   '' He has divided the Free Church
against itself on account of slavery.   He has gained
the admiration and esteem of all the friends of the
slave in this country.   He has always kept an open
platform, yet none of the rabbis have been found
gallant enough to break lance with him.   He completely exposed their miserable attempts to recon-
cile slavery with Christianity.''

While in England and Scotland a man named
Thompson, who formerly lived in St. Michaels, and
who pretended to have known Douglass on the Freeland and Covey plantations, published a letter that
tended to discredit some of his assertions.   The ex-
slave met these charges in a straightforward manner, which must have left no doubt of his truthful-
ness.   In his reply to the Thompson letter, he said :
'' You have completely tripped up the heels of your
slave-holding friends and laid them flat at my feet.
You have done a piece of anti-slavery work which
no anti-slavery man could do again.   If I could see
you now, amid the free hills of Scotland, where the
ancient 'black Douglas' once met his foes, I presume

I might summon sufficient courage to look you in the face ; and were you to attempt to make a slave of me, it is possible you might find me almost as disagreeable a subject as was the Douglas to whom I have just referred.''

The several months spent by the traveler in England were filled with interesting incidents. His oratorical triumph was complete, and the attentions accorded him by many prominent people, unusually flattering. Indeed, it can be said that he was positively lionized in London, but he bore it with becoming dignity and the grace of a man born to high conditions.

Perhaps special mention should be made of his address at the World's Temperance Convention, held in Covent Garden, August 7, 1846. A large delegation from the United States was present and some prominent Americans were on the program. The meeting was an immense affair and, in point of interest, the number of delegates, and the countries represented, genuinely international in character. Mr. Douglass was asked to address the convention and his speech was looked forward to with great interest. He rather anticipated a sensational outcome of his attempt to make himself heard, because he was not called upon until the delegates had spoken, and what they had said furnished him with the very text that appealed most strongly to his convictions and feelings. As he rose, the convention was in a quiver of excitement, for it was the first time that this much-talked-of fugitive from slavery had had a chance to stand up in the presence of men and women representing all shades of party opinion, and say the word that concerned the destiny of himself and his people. He began :

"Mr. Chairman, Ladies and Gentlemen—I am not a delegate to this convention. Those who would have been most likely to elect me as a delegate could not, because they are to-night held in abject slavery in the United States. Sir, I regret, that I cannot fully unite with the American delegates in their patriotic eulogies of America and American societies. I cannot do so for this good reason : there are at this moment three millions of the American population, by slavery and prejudice, placed entirely beyond the pale of American temperance societies. The three million slaves are completely excluded by slavery, and four hundred thousand free colored people are almost as completely excluded by an inveterate prejudice against them on account of their color. [Cries of "Shame! Shame!"]

"I do not say these things to wound the feelings of the American delegates ; I simply mention them in their presence and before this audience that, seeing how you regard this hatred and neglect of the colored people, they may be inclined, on their return home, to enlarge the field of their temperance operations and embrace within the scope of their influence my long-neglected race. [Great cheering, and some confusion on the platform.]

"Sir, to give you some idea of the difficulties and obstacles in the way of the temperance reformation of the colored population of the United States, allow me to state a few facts. About the year 1840, a few intelligent, sober, and benevolent colored people of Philadelphia, being acquainted with the alarming ravages of intemperance among a numerous class of colored people in that city, and finding

themselves neglected and excluded from white societies, organized societies among themselves, appointed committees, sent out agents, built temperance halls, and were earnestly and successfully
rescuing many from the fangs of intemperance.

"The cause went on nobly, until August 1, 1842,
the day when England gave liberty to one hundred
thousand souls in the West Indies. The colored temperance societies selected this day to march in procession through the city, in the hope that such a
demonstration would have the effect of bringing
others into their ranks. They formed their procession, unfolded their teetotal banners, and proceeded
to the accomplishment of their purpose. It was a
delightful sight. But, sir, they had not proceeded
down two streets before they were brutally assailed
by a ruthless mob; their ranks broken up; their
persons beaten and pelted with stones and brickbats.
One of their churches was burned to the ground,
and their best temperance hall utterly demolished."
["Shame! Shame! Shame!" from the audience
and cries of "Sit down" from the Americans on
the platform.]

A tremendous commotion was caused by this
speech. The American delegation was alarmed and
indignant. One member wrote an account of the
event for the New York *Evangelist*, from which the
following extracts will serve to gauge the feeling :

"They all advocated the same cause, showed a
glorious union of thought and feeling, and the effect
was constantly being raised—the moral scene was
superb and glorious—when Frederick Douglass, the
colored Abolitionist, agitator and ultraist, came to
the platform and so spoke *á la mode* as to ruin the
influence almost of all that preceded ! He lugged
in anti-slavery or Abolition, no doubt prompted to

it by some of the politic ones who used him to do what they would not themselves venture to do in person.   He is supposed to have been well paid for this abomination.

"What a perversion, an abuse, an iniquity against the law of reciprocal righteousness, to call thousands together and get them, some certain ones, to seem conspicuous and devoted for one sole and grand object, and then all at once, with obliquity, open an avalanche on them for some imputed evil or monstrosity, for which, whatever be the wound or injury inflicted, they were both too fatigued and hurried with surprise, and too straitened for time, to be properly prepared.   I say it is a streak of meanness ; it is abominable.   On this occasion Mr. Douglass allowed himself to denounce America and all its temperance societies together as a grinding community of the enemies of his people ; said evil with no alloy of good concerning the whole of us ; was perfectly indiscriminate in his severities ; talked of the American delegates and to them as if he had been our schoolmaster, and we his docile and devoted pupils ; and launched his revengeful missiles at our country without one palliative word, and as if not a Christian or a true anti-slavery man lived in the whole United States.

"We all wanted to reply, but it was too late. The whole theatre seemed taken with the spirit of the Ephesian uproar ; they were furious and boisterous in the extreme, and Mr. Kirk could hardly obtain a moment, though many were desirous in his behalf, to say a few words, as he did, very calmly and properly, that the cause of temperance was not at all responsible for slavery, and had no connection with it."

At a Peace Convention held in London, Douglass made an address from which the following excerpt is given to show to what an extent he at this time shared the illusions of the Abolitionists, who, while preaching the doctrine of non-resistance, were steadily feeding the passions that made war eventually inevitable :

"You may think it somewhat singular, that I, a slave, an American slave, should stand forth at this time as an advocate of peace between two countries situated as this and the United States are, when it is universally believed that the war between them would result in the emancipation of three millions of my brethren, who are now held in the most cruel bonds in that country. I believe this would be the result; but such is my regard for the principle of peace ; such is my deep, firm conviction that nothing can be attained for liberty universally by war, that were I to be asked the question whether I would have my emancipation by the shedding of one single drop of blood, my answer would be in the negative."

Thus he spoke in 1846, but by the time Lincoln was nominated for President, and war was actually impending, Douglass was prepared to welcome it as a part of the price to be paid for justice, progress, and freedom.

His ability to discuss any of the live questions of the day was a matter of genuine surprise to the English people. At a farewell entertainment, given to him, March 30, 1847, just before leaving London, William Howitt, the author, said : "He [Douglass] has appeared in this country before the most accomplished audiences, who were surprised, not only at his talents, but at his extraordinary information ; and all I can say is, I hope Americans will continue to send such men as Frederick Douglass, and slavery will soon be abolished."

Mr. Douglass had now spent about twenty-three months in England, Scotland, Ireland, and Wales. Like every other new experience, this opportunity fôr travel in foreign lands was an education, and those who had watched and heard him most often in his lecture-tours and in social intercourse, could easily note his progress in breadth of sympathy and intellectual grasp. He learned some things in England that he never could have learned in his own country. The possibility of a perfect comradeship between people of differing nationalities, creeds, and colors was a fact that deeply impressed him. He learned that the great men of the times, who had the power to make and unmake international law as well as to mould and express public opinion, all regarded slavery as a blight on civilization. He learned to have a new and stronger faith in the ability and disposition of the white race to deal fairly with his race. If he hated slavery more because of what he had seen, heard, and experienced in England, he had gained a new strength of heart and mind to battle for its extinction in America.

It would have been pleasant for him to have remained abroad and have become a citizen of free Britain. No colored man had ever been more flattered and fêted by the public. His friends and admirers multiplied everywhere. Many of his oversea friends urged him to surrender his American allegiance, but no inducement, however alluring, could cause him to desert his fellow-men in bonds. In fact, when it was given out in the United States that an attempt would be made by his old masters, the Aulds, to arrest him on his return and carry him back to a Maryland plantation, Douglass wrote : " No inducement could be offered, strong enough to make me quit my hold upon America as my home. Whether a slave or a freeman, America is my home, and there I mean to spend and be spent in the cause of my outraged fellow countrymen."

As the time approached for him to leave England, a deep concern for his safety began to be felt and expressed by his British friends. As an outcome of this feeling, a proposition was made by Mrs. Ellen Richardson, belonging to the Society of Friends, that a fund be raised to purchase his freedom and thus remove all possibility of danger of re-enslavement. The proposition was at once accepted, and gladly acted upon by Mrs. Richardson and her sister-in-law, Mrs. Henry Richardson. As the result of correspondence, the purchase price, £150, was named and the sum was raised. The following is a true copy of the legal papers by force of which Frederick Douglass became free :

" Know all men by these presents, that I, Thomas Auld, of Talbot County and State of Maryland, for and in consideration of the sum of one hundred dollars [1] current money, to me paid by Hugh Auld

---

[1] The £150 were paid to Hugh Auld who had previously obtained his $100, which seems to have been a sort of quit claim deed from his brother Thomas.

of the city of Baltimore, in the said state, at and
before the sealing and delivery of these presents, the
receipt whereof I, the said Thomas Auld, do hereby
acknowledge, have granted, bargained, and sold,
and by these presents do grant, bargain, and sell
unto the said Hugh Auld, his executors, administrators, and assigns, one Negro man, by the name
of Frederick Bailey or Douglass, as he calls himself
—he is now about twenty-eight years of age—to
have and to hold the said Negro man for life.   And
I, the said Thomas Auld, for myself, my heirs, executors and administrators, all and singular, the
said Frederick Bailey, alias Douglass, unto the said
Hugh Auld, his executors, and administrators, and
against all and every person or persons whatsoever,
shall and will warrant and forever defend by these
presents.   In witness whereof, I set my hand and
seal this thirteenth day of November, eighteen hundred and forty-six.   (1846.)   THOMAS AULD.

"Signed, sealed and delivered in presence of
Wrightson Jones, John C. Lear."

"To all whom it may concern : Be it known that
I, Hugh Auld of the city of Baltimore, in Baltimore
County, in the State of Maryland, for divers good
causes and considerations me thereunto moving,
have released from slavery, liberated, manumitted,
and set free, and by these presents do hereby release
from slavery, liberate, manumit, and set free, my
Negro man, named Frederick Bailey, otherwise
called Douglass, being of the age of twenty-eight
years or thereabouts, and able to work and gain a
sufficient livelihood and maintenance ; and him, the
said Negro man named Frederick Douglass, I do
declare to be henceforth free, manumitted and discharged from all manner of servitude to me, my
executors and administrators forever.

"In witness whereof, I, the said Hugh Auld, have

hereunto set my hand and seal the fifth of December, in the year one thousand eight hundred and forty-six.　　　　　　　　　　HUGH AULD.

"Sealed and delivered in presence of T. Hanson Belt, James N. S. T. Wright."

This purchase of Mr. Douglass's freedom was not approved by some of the ultra-Abolitionists in the United States. A contributor to *The Liberator* said : "Let us beg of you never to publish another word in your paper about the ransom of Douglass. I am quite ashamed that our American Abolitionists should expose their narrowness in expressing so many regrets at their loss of slave-property in Douglass. They seem to feel that he was their property, and not his man."

Many Abolitionists thought it a violation of anti-slavery principles and a waste of money. Mr. Douglass's own feelings in the matter are stated by himself in the following language : "For myself, viewing it in the light of a ransom or as money extorted by a robber, and regarding my liberty of more value than one hundred and fifty pounds sterling, I could not see in it either a violation of the law of morality or economy."

In still another practical way did his English friends show their affection for Douglass before he left them. Having learned upon his return to America that it was his desire to publish a newspaper, in the interest of his people, the sum of $2,500 was without difficulty raised and presented to him for that purpose.

The contrast between the conditions of his coming to England and those of his returning to the United States affords an interesting evidence of his power of conquest. He went to England knowing no one, and personally known by no one ; he returned to his own country carrying with him the friendships of men and women whose acquaintance but few Americans, at that time, could have obtained. He went to Great Britain a slave in danger of re-capture and re-subjugation ; he returned, freed from his master by the bounty of English friends. He was empowered and equipped to publish the gospel of immediate and unconditional emancipation.

Douglass arrived home in the spring of 1847. He sailed early Sunday, April 4th. The last night of his stay abroad was spent as the guest of John Bright and his sisters. From no one in England could Douglass have received a more gracious welcome and friendly benediction than from this great commoner. The only incident that in any way clouded his departure was the act of the officers of the steamer *Cambria* in refusing to let him have the berth previously engaged for him. When the English people heard of this, great indignation was voiced in the press and from the platform, in every part of the United Kingdom. The result was that Mr. Cunard in an open letter expressed his regrets, and Mr. Douglass was given a stateroom ; but he was not permitted to leave it or to place himself in view of the other passengers during the sixteen days he was upon the sea.

CHAPTER VII

HOME AGAIN AS A FREEMAN—NEW PROBLEMS AND NEW TRIUMPHS

FREDERICK DOUGLASS returned to American shores on the 20th day of April, 1847. The date and fact of his coming marked the beginning of a new chapter in his career. To be free and feel free was a great source of strength both to himself and to his friends, in renewing the struggle for emancipation. He had not only a bracing sense of security against the dangers of capture and return to slavery, but he had gained wonderfully in mental and spiritual equipment. The two years in England were years of education and inspiration. During that time he had met and mingled freely with large men who were dealing successfully with large problems. Emancipation had acquired a broader meaning for him as a consequence of his visit. In America he had not been able to free himself from the conviction that emancipation, confused as it was with all the interests of daily life, was a sectional or at most, a national question. Looking back, from this distance, upon his own life and the great struggle of which it had become a part, he was able to realize more fully than before the truth of what Garrison long had taught, that slavery was a world question,—a question not of national or sectional expediency, but of fundamental human right.

With this larger vision gained by European experience and study, he was the better prepared to take up the old battle-cry of "Unconditional Emancipation." His trip abroad had not merely widened his vision and deepened his sense of the moral significance of the struggle in which he was engaged; it had measurably increased his prestige with the American public. The fact that Europe had recognized his talents and had honored, in him, the race and the cause he represented, strengthened his position as a speaker, and lent a new importance to the things he had to say. Before he went to England, he was seldom noticed or referred to in any of the great pro-slavery newspapers of the country, except as a "runaway-nigger" and a "freak," "preternaturally clever." After his return, allusions to him were frequent and more abusive. In giving notice of a public anti-slavery meeting in Boston, one of these papers said: "The Abolitionists headed by William Lloyd Garrison, and tailed by Mr. Frederick Douglass, the fugitive slave, are in full blast. He, Douglass, elaborates very eloquently and fearfully, and is a good deal of a demagogue in black."

These newspaper attacks on Mr. Douglass were largely due to the resentment aroused in this country because of the way in which he had, in England, denounced America for its slave-holding policy. This feeling was not confined to the newspapers, but was shown at several large gatherings that Mr. Douglass addressed in company with William Lloyd Garrison.

In Boston an attempt was made to "silence" him. Stones were thrown in the meeting at Norristown, Pa., and at a very large assembly held in the court house at Harrisburg, Pa., on the 9th of August, 1847, after Mr. Garrison had spoken without molestation, Douglass was violently interrupted when he tried to speak, and was not allowed to continue. But such disturbances were not general, nor did they have the effect of shaking the eloquent apostle's determination to be heard. During the same month he and Garrison held numerous anti-slavery meetings in Massachusetts, Pennsylvania, and Ohio. There was in these meetings abundant evidence that the cause of Abolition was gaining ground. The gatherings in Oberlin and Cleveland were especially notable for the interest manifested. One of the Cleveland papers had the following notice of the meeting : "The Menagerie Company, Garrison, Douglass, Foster (and we expect Satan) are to be here on Saturday next and open at seven o'clock in the evening in the big tent, and continue their harangues over the Sabbath. This trio has made sale for a great many unmerchantable eggs in other places." It was evident, from the size of the Cleveland meeting, and from the interest aroused in the addresses of Douglass, Garrison, and Foster that this newspaper did not reflect the popular feeling.

In the early part of September, 1847, Mr. Douglass was the presiding officer of a colored convention held in Cleveland. His address upon this occasion was a notable departure from all former models. It showed that he had been giving a great

deal of thought to the needs of his people. It was
a powerful plea, "that the doors of the schoolhouse, the workshop, the church, and the college
shall be open as freely to our children as to the children of other members of the community." The
following extract is especially important, and prophetic of the present-day needs of the colored race :
"Try to get your sons into mechanical trades;
press them into blacksmith-shops, the machine-
shops, the joiner's-shops, the wheelwright-shops,
the cooper-shops, and the tailor-shops. Every blow
of the sledge-hammer wielded by a sable arm is a
powerful blow in support of our career. Every
colored mechanic is, by virtue of circumstances, an
elevator of his race. Every house built by black
men is a strong tower against the allied hosts of
prejudice. It is impossible for us to attach too
much importance to this aspect of the subject.
Trades are important. Wherever a man may be
thrown by misfortune, if he have in his hands a
useful trade, he is useful to his fellow-men, and will
be esteemed accordingly, and, of all men who need
trades, we are the most needy."

It was advice of this kind, in which the passionate controversialist displayed from time to time
something of the foresight and the constructive
ability of the statesman, as well as his growing popularity with the wiser and more influential class of
the white people, that gave Douglass high place,
and made him the undisputed leader of the free colored element of the country.

Two things, above all others, were at this time

pressing themselves upon his thought and attention : one was his cherished project of establishing a news-paper of his own ; and the other, the preservation of his friendly relations with William Lloyd Garrison.

He had long looked to Garrison and his associates for advice and direction in everything of impor-tance, and in an enterprise of such moment as this newspaper, he naturally felt that their opinion was indispensable. The money was raised, as we have already seen, by English friends, and sent over to Mr. Douglass within three months after he reached America, with the understanding that the use of it was to be left wholly to his discretion. It was clearly stated that, if he thought it inexpedient to invest the funds in a newspaper, he could use them, under trustees of his personal choosing, for the ben-efit of himself and his children. But he wanted an "organ" of his own. As time went on he believed that he perceived the need of it more and more.

"I already saw myself," he said, "wielding my pen as well as my voice in the great work of reno-vating the public mind and building up a public sentiment which should send slavery to the grave, and restore to 'liberty and the pursuit of happi-ness' the people with whom I suffered."

Among other considerations that moved him to establish his own paper was the conviction that the example of a well-managed and ably edited organ would be a powerful evidence that the Negro was too much of a man to be held a chattel.

Another side to this question had not occurred to

him until this time. His attention was called to the fact that he was more than Frederick Douglass, the individual. What he did and said, and what he was and was to be, were of so much concern to his associates and co-workers that, when it became known that he intended to start a newspaper, difficulties of all kinds arose. Douglass knew that Garrison opposed his enterprise. Could he ignore that leader's advice? Clearly, his first impression was that he could not. He felt then and ever afterward that he owed everything to Mr. Garrison. It was the latter who had discovered and brought him to the attention of the people. The word of such a man must be law to him. Garrison's philosophy of this whole slavery question was accepted by Douglass without an "if." He was so completely under the spell of the great Abolitionist's personality that, when he learned of the opposition to the newspaper project, he was overwhelmed with surprise and disappointment.

Various reasons were given for this attitude. Mr. Garrison thought it quite "impractical to combine the editor and the lecturer without either causing the paper to be more or less neglected, or the sphere of lecturing to be seriously circumscribed." It was further urged that the publication was not needed, that it would diminish the support of the papers already in existence, and that it could not succeed. Some of Douglass's other friends advised him, that being a man without any education and without any literary training, he would make himself ridiculous as an editor. These counselors

wished to save him from the humiliation of an ig-
nominious failure, and cautioned him against the
mistake of allowing his ambition to bring him into
ridicule and contempt. This opposition coming
from his former advisers and associates caused him
to hesitate, and, for a time, to give up the scheme;
so, instead of starting the paper as soon as he received the money to be devoted to that purpose, he
postponed the project for nearly a year, out of deference to the judgment of these wise and close
friends.

During the interval, Mr. Douglass had time to
examine into the merits of the advice against his
becoming an editor. He had a further opportunity
to feel the public pulse and learn something more
definite in regard to the prospects for good or
evil of a newspaper, such as he had in mind. He
was much in demand on the lecture platform. His
vogue was growing all the time, and with increasing
popularity and power, he saw the possibility of a
reading constituency large enough to support his
publication and widen his influence.

But other considerations intervened to widen the
breach between himself and Garrison. The Abolition movement, as planned and carried on by the
outspoken leader and his followers, was non-polit-
ical. It sought to effect a revolution, but by the
moral regeneration of the people. Slavery, as Garrison conceived it, was a national sin which could be
reached only by an appeal to the national conscience; but the effect of the anti-slavery agitation
had not been confined to those who accepted his

revolutionary doctrines.   Many persons who were
unable to follow the relentless logic of Mr. Garrison
to its revolutionary conclusions were roused to opposition to slavery by the sting and fire of his
sermons.   The number of people who were disposed
to do something to check its extension was rapidly
increasing.   This wider anti-slavery movement was
fast drifting from a mere unorganized sentiment,
without force sufficient to compel resistance, into a
political party with a definite platform.   Those who
could not follow the "disunion" and "non-resistance" principles of Garrison, but began to fear the
aggression of the slave-power, joined the "Free
Soil" and "Liberty" parties.   The issue raised by
the Abolitionists was daily becoming less a question
of the right or wrong of slavery and more a question
of how, under the actual circumstances in which
the institution existed, it might best be gotten rid of.

Garrison and his followers, supported by the in-
fallible logic of their leader, still clung to the disunion policy, which was primarily a discharge of
conscience from all complicity with slavery and
only secondarily a means to the abolition of slavery.

Frederick Douglass, with less consistency, perhaps, and a keener sense for the practical exigencies
of the situation, was undoubtedly influenced by a
desire to get into close touch with this larger
audience.   The sequence of events, and Douglass's
position in relation to them, tended to convince him
that he was justified in his desire to found a newspaper.   A colored periodical would be no new
thing.   As early as 1827 the *Ram's Horn*, pub-

lished by and for Negroes, had been started in the North. Other papers conducted by colored men were, *The Mystery*, *The Disfranchised American*, *The Northern Star*, and *The Colored Farmer*. Opportunity and duty seemed to combine in urging him to do the thing that he had abandoned in deference to the advice of Mr. Garrison and at length he reached the point where he no longer feared failure, every objection urged against his purpose seeming to be overcome.

Being thus convinced, he heroically set himself to the task. The first duty was to select a field sufficiently removed from New England not to compete with *The Liberator* and *The Anti-Slavery Standard*. Rochester, N. Y., was the place chosen. This was good anti-slavery territory, but it was of the Gerrit Smith kind as distinguished from the Garrison kind. Both of these men were towers of strength in the cause of Abolition, and both were lavish in the expenditure of time and means for the cause of freedom.

On the 3d day of December, 1847, appeared the first issue of the *North Star*. The name was afterwards changed to *Frederick Douglass's Paper*, in order to avoid all possible confusion with other anti-slavery organs with similar names. It was issued weekly, and had an average circulation of 3,000 subscribers, with a maximum of 4,000. A colored man named Delaney, who afterward distinguished himself as a Union soldier in the Civil War, had had some experience in newspaper work and aided Mr. Douglass in the publication. Financially the paper soon proved to be more of a sacrifice than a money-making venture, but in this there was no disappointment, for its purpose was to make public opinion rather than money.   It took everything that Mr. Douglass had and could obtain to keep the *North Star* in the newspaper firmament. He became deeply in debt and was compelled to mortgage his home to meet the heavy demands upon him.   His old friends and many new ones came repeatedly to his rescue.   The most important of these was Mrs. Julia Griffith Crofts, a gracious woman who took hold of the business management herself.   After a year's effort the circulation increased from 2,000 to 4,000, and enough money was realized to pay off all indebtedness and lift the mortgage from Mr. Douglass's home.   The paper grew in popularity and influence, and its patrons and financial helpers included such men as Gerrit Smith, Horace Mann, Salmon P. Chase, Joshua R. Giddings, Charles Sumner, William H. Seward, and John G. Palfrey.   Support came from these leaders, not in a patronizing way to help a "poor, struggling colored man's paper," but rather as a tribute to the high merit of the publication.   Those who were sure that Mr. Douglass could never write as well as he could speak were surprised at this new evidence of his versatility and resourcefulness.

In an issue of Mr. Garrison's paper, dated January 28, 1848, these flattering words appeared: "The facility with which Mr. Douglass has adapted himself to his new and responsible position is another proof of his genius and is worthy of especial praise. His editorial articles are exceedingly well written; and the typographical, orthographical, and grammatical accuracy with which the *North Star* is printed surpasses that of any other paper ever published by a colored man." Edmund Quincy, commenting on the *North Star*, paid a high tribute to the new editor and said that its "literary and mechanical execution would do honor to any paper, new or old, anti-slavery or pro-slavery, in the country." The ease with which Mr. Douglass adapted himself to his new responsibility, and the high praise that came to him from all parts, added immensely to his influence and prestige. What the *North Star* said editorially on the many live questions of the day was liberally quoted and widely discussed.

The successful carrying out of this enterprise was a distinct advantage to Mr. Douglass as a vindication of his own individuality. It is a good thing for a man to have an idea, but it is a better thing for him to have sufficient force of character to put his idea into effect. A man stands or falls by what he is able to do rather than by what he is able to say. Mr. Douglass was told that the responsibility was too great. It is always at this point that the strength of a man is tested. Frederick Douglass rose above the fears of his friends and took the first step that led him to a more commanding position. The determination to have his own way in this newspaper enterprise was his first "declaration of independence." While Mr. Douglass tells us that he felt an abiding gratitude toward William Lloyd Garrison for what that man had done in giving him a start in his upward career, he had reached the point where he must cease to rely upon the initiative of others. He must begin to trust himself and his own powers, and cease to be a burden upon those who had been his guides and teachers.

The anti-slavery cause was assuming large proportions. Every event in the social, economic, and political life of the nation pushed this question into prominence. All sorts of people were becoming interested in the slavery issues, but there were so many sides to the problem that it was not always easy to see the right. There was for a time a growing confusion of ideas, policies, doctrines, and a puzzling division and subdivision of forces, both in the pro-slavery and anti-slavery ranks. There were those who thought and asserted that the Federal Constitution was a "pro-slavery instrument," and others who were equally insistent that it was anti-slavery. There were those who were Abolitionists in doctrine, but in politics voted with one or the other of the old parties, both of which were pro-slavery in their policies. There were those who, while believing in the equality of the Negro, were extreme in their opposition to the admission of women into membership in anti-slavery societies. A large number of liberty-loving people could go no further in their hostility to slavery than to oppose its extension into new territory. These made a partial trial of their anti-slavery feelings in the Free Soil and the Liberty parties.

Only two classes of people in the country oc-

cupied fixed positions on the great question.
These were William Lloyd Garrison and his associates, and the slave-holders and their followers.
Mr. Garrison's famous utterance that "the United
States Constitution was a covenant with death and
an agreement with hell," and his declaration of "no
union with slave-holders," constituted his unvarying platform. The slave-holding interests were
equally tenacious of their creed and quite as fixed
in their determination to risk everything rather
than yield an inch to the anti-slavery clamor.

Enough has been said to show that the time had
come when the man who wished to be respected, believed in, and followed, must be strong enough to
have convictions of his own and be responsible to
himself and the public for these convictions. It
was now incumbent upon Mr. Douglass to find solid
ground on which, amidst so many conflicting
opinions, to oppose slavery. The conclusions of his
studies and thinking had the disagreeable effect of
leading him away from Garrison's doctrine of "non-
resistance" and "disunion." From his first reading
of *The Liberator* he held firmly to Garrison. What
that leader said or believed on the question, Mr.
Douglass accepted without reservation. It is well
that he did. No one could be a weakling who
lived and labored under so stimulating a guide.
There was something sublime in his moral courage,
and something extraordinary in the steadiness with
which, unswerved by the changing circumstances
about him, he pursued his fixed purposes. It was
this quality of soul in him that made him always

the dominant figure and influence in the contest. Abolition had become so closely identified with his name that the question could scarcely be discussed without some reference to him. It is no wonder that Frederick Douglass was so completely under his spell, but it must certainly be counted an evidence of the ex-slave's intellectual sincerity and strength of mind that when he could in practice no longer follow the disunion theory, he had the courage and ability to frame a clear and logical statement of the grounds for his own action.

His explanation of his change of position is best told in his own words :

"My first opinions were naturally derived and honestly entertained. Brought directly, when I escaped from slavery, into contact with Abolitionists, who regarded the Constitution as a slave-holding instrument and finding their views supported by the united and entire history of every department of the government, it is not strange that I assumed the Constitution to be just what these friends made it seem to be. I was bound, not only by their superior knowledge, to take their opinions in respect to this subject, as the true ones, but also because I had no means of showing this unsoundness.

"But for the responsibility of conducting a public journal, and the necessity imposed upon me of meeting opposite views from Abolitionists outside of New England, I should in all probability have remained firm in my disunion views. My new circumstances compelled me to re-think the whole subject, and to study with some care, not only the just and proper rules of legal interpretation, but the origin, design, nature, rights, powers, and duties of civil government, and also the relations which human beings sustain to it.   By such a course of thought and reading, I was brought to the conclusion that the Constitution of the United States, inaugurated 'to form a more perfect union, establish justice, insure domestic tranquillity, provide for the common defense, promote the general welfare and secure the blessings of liberty,' could not well have been designed at the same time to maintain and perpetuate a system of rapine and murder like slavery, especially as not one word can be found in the Constitution to authorize such a belief.   Then again, if the declared purposes of an instrument are to govern the meaning of all its parts and details, as they clearly should, the Constitution of our country is pure warrant for the abolition of slavery in every state of the Union."

Having thus, and by other reasonings convinced himself of the unconstitutionality of slavery, the editor of the *North Star* voiced the conviction in and out of season, until it was overthrown.   In thus separating from the Garrisonian Abolitionists, there was much heart-burning on both sides, but nothing of the nature of rivalry or jealousy, as some writers have attempted to show.   Both Garrison and Douglass were manly in their attitude toward friend and foe, and too sincere in their convictions to be otherwise than high-minded in their differences on matters of principle.

It has been charged against Mr. Douglass, and not without reason, that he was ungrateful in turning upon the men who had made him what he was ; that it was ambition and the desire for success in a wider field which prompted him to independent action.   No doubt there were, and are,

those to whom his course during this period seemed
then and still seems unwise, mistaken, and directed
rather by selfish interests than by the lofty idealism
that guided the labors of the Abolitionists, from
whom he at this time parted company. However
this may be, it is likely that the differences which
sprang up between Garrison and Douglass at this
period were due, in great part, to certain fundamental differences of mind and temperament making this divergence of views inevitable.

The power which Garrison exercised over his
contemporaries was due, to a considerable degree,
to the clearness and vigor of his intellect and the
unflinching fidelity with which he followed its de-
crees. The first thing that he demanded of himself
and of others was that they should think and feel
rightly in regard to this question of slavery. The
revolution he sought to effect was a purely spiritual
one : he aimed to change men's minds and hearts.
The power he desired to overthrow was a state of
mind—a state of mind which permitted slavery to
exist.

Douglass, on the contrary, was destined, by natural disposition, for a different field of action. He
was by temperament a politician, and, like all politicians, more or less of an opportunist. He was
less interested in the theory upon which slavery
should be abolished than he was in the means by
which freedom could be achieved. No doubt he
was influenced to a considerable degree, in the for-
mulation of his views in regard to the Constitution,
by his practical sense of what the situation de-

manded, and, even if these views have not been upheld by subsequent interpretation of that document,
they still appeal strongly to common sense.

Whatever motives may have influenced Douglass
in taking the position that he did, there seems to be
no reason for doubting their sincerity. Though
drawn into different fields of endeavor in the cause
of anti-slavery, the importance of Garrison and his
work was in no wise diminished in Douglass's eyes.
In 1860 he wrote to *The Liberator* concerning the
anti-slavery society : "So far from working for the
annihilation of that society, I never failed, even in
the worst times of my controversy with it, to recognize that organization as the most efficient generator
of anti-slavery sentiment in the country." And in
September, 1890, he said in Boston : "It was they
[Garrison and Phillips] who made Abraham Lincoln and the Republican party possible. What
abolished slavery was the moral sentiment which
had been created, not by the pulpit, but by the
Garrisonian platform."

Finally, it seems clear that, through all this controversy, Douglass retained his affection for William
Lloyd Garrison, and that this feeling was honestly
reciprocal. There is, in the life of the great Abolitionist, as told by his children, a bit of correspondence that reveals the tender side of these two robust
human natures. It was at a time when Mr. Garrison was very much disturbed on account of the
Negro newspaper project. Mr. Douglass had accompanied him on a lecture tour as far west as
Cleveland, where Garrison became ill and his col-

ored colleague was compelled to leave him to meet other engagements. Letters were frequently exchanged, but for some reason they were not received. This mutual failure to hear from each other gave rise to many unpleasant misgivings. Samuel J. May, the friend of both, writing to Garrison under date of October 8, 1847, says : " Frederick Douglass was very much troubled that he did not get any tidings from you when he reached Syracuse on the 24th of September. He left reluctantly, yet thinking that you would be following in a day or two, and as he did not get any word from you at Waterloo, nor at Auburn, he was almost sure he should meet you at my house. His countenance fell and his heart failed him when he found me likewise in suspense about you. Not until he arrived at West Winfield did he get any relief, and then through *The Liberator* of the 23d."

Some days afterward, Mr. Garrison wrote as follows : " Is it not strange that Douglass has not written a single line to me or any one else in this place, inquiring after my health, since he left me on a bed of illness ? It will also greatly surprise our friends in Boston to hear that, in regard to his project for establishing the *North Star*, he never opened his lips to me on the subject, nor asked my advice in any particular whatever ! Such conduct grieves me to the heart. His conduct about the paper has been impulsive, inconsiderate, and highly inconsistent with his decision in Boston. What will his English friends say of such a strange somerset ? I am sorry that friend Quincy did not ex-

press himself more strongly against the project in
The Liberator. It is a delicate matter, I know, but
it must be met with firmness."

True to his own high sense of gratitude to Mr.
Garrison, and always deferential to the latter's position in the anti-slavery fight, Mr. Douglass never
permitted himself to utter a single word of criticism
or complaint. The field was large enough and the
work was great enough for each to display the full
measure of his respective powers toward the one
great object, the abolition of slavery. During this
period, Mr. Douglass always found time and opportunity for platform work. Every great gathering
of the anti-slavery forces was enlivened in interest
by his presence. His power as an orator did not
diminish, as was predicted, by his continued ascendency as an editor. On the contrary, his words
gained force as he became more confident of himself, and more clear in regard to his convictions.
In the great anti-slavery convention held in New
York, he made a speech which revealed remarkable
strength. The following extract from a report of the
meeting is worth quoting in proof of the stirring
quality of his address :—

" Frederick Douglass now takes the platform, and
is welcomed with applause. The assembly is now
fixed in its close attention, and Frederick is going
on to show up the cowardly and sneaking conduct of
John P. Hale in bringing in a bill to protect property, and not daring to stand up and fearlessly
advocate the right of slaves to run away, and the
right and duty of Abolitionists to protect them.

Frederick is describing *Punch's* portraits of Brother
Jonathan, with the devil hovering over him, eye-
ing with satisfaction passing events.   The audience
give him great applause.   He is speaking to great
effect, portraying the wrongs of the colored population of this nation.   His eloquence sways the great
assembly with him.   He denounces the Northerners,
who swear to support the Constitution, as the real
slave-holders of the country.   It is good to listen to
him.   He shows up the Northern apologists of
slavery as those whose smiles he does not want.   He
pledges himself to denounce those enemies of God
and man, who swear to support the Constitution, as
his enemies.   Frederick has got the audience into a
great state of glorification ; and he is now showing
that there is no way to abolish slavery except by the
dissolution of the Union.   There, he is done, and
the meeting is breaking up.   It has been a pleasant
and profitable time.''

In the course of his career as a public speaker,
Douglass developed a capacity for repartee that
made him the dread of any one who had the temerity
to interrupt him in a public discussion.   At the
convention to which I have just referred, he was
described as '' with brows knit, fiery eyes like dag-
gers, scorn upon his thick lips, and lurking in his
sable woe-begone visage the traces of malignity,
disappointment, and despair.''   By another paper,
when speaking on the same platform with Garrison,
Phillips, and Lucretia Mott, he was called the
''master-genius of the crowd.''

In 1848, Mr. Douglass took another step forward,

and became an advocate of female suffrage. He had had opportunity to judge of the worth of woman in the anti-slavery movement. The work done by Lucretia Mott, the Grimké sisters, Frances Wright, Ernestine L. Rose, and other forceful leaders, strongly impressed him with what seemed to him the great injustice of excluding such women from the benefits of those rights by means of which citizenship could be protected. On the 19th day of July of that year the Seneca Falls convention was held. The following extract from the *North Star* shows Mr. Douglass's position :

"We are free to say that in respect to political rights, we hold women to be justly entitled to all we claim for man. We go further and express our conviction that all political rights, which it is expedient for man to exercise, it is equally so for women. All that distinguishes man as an intelligent and accountable being is equally true of woman ; and if that government only is just which governs only by the free consent of the governed, there can be no reason in the world for denying to woman the exercise of the elective franchise, or a hand in making and administering the laws of the land. Our doctrine is that 'Right is of no sex.' We, therefore, bid the women engaged in this movement our humble Godspeed."

Mr. Douglass consistently held to these views ever afterward. He was one of the first of all prominent Americans to champion the cause of female suffrage, and the women in return esteemed him and accorded to him more honor than has been shown to

most men by their organizations.   He was always a
guest in any large gathering of woman suffragists.

In connection with the labor of running his newspaper and keeping up a strenuous interest in the
many public questions that appealed to his heart
and conscience, it is fitting to make some mention of
his early experiences in Rochester, N. Y., his home,
and the scene of his most important activities for
twenty-five years.   He became deeply attached to
the city and its people.   He said :   "I know of no
place in the Union where I could have located at
the time with less resistance, or received a larger
measure of sympathy and coöperation, and I now
look back to my life and labor with unalloyed satisfaction, having spent a quarter of a century among
its people.   I shall always feel more at home there
than anywhere else in this country."

When Mr. Douglass began the publication of the
North Star, there were people in the city who felt it
a sort of disgrace that a Negro paper should be established in their midst.   This was not surprising.
It is doubtful if, at that time, any inhabited spot in
the United States could have been found entirely
free from race prejudice.   So far as the Negro was
concerned, wherever he wished and tried to be a
good citizen, he found himself in the "enemy's country."   The most troublesome of Douglass's early
experiences in Rochester was the attempt to educate
his children.   They were not allowed to attend the
public school in the district in which he lived and
owned property ; and his young daughter, who was
the "apple of his eye," was so unkindly treated in

Tracy Seminary, a school for girls, that she had to leave it. This difficulty, like every other that he encountered in his career, served only to embolden him; it encouraged him to fight. He went at the question with his characteristic force, and before long every barrier was removed and the children of black parents were freely admitted to all the schools of the city. Indeed he conducted himself so well and was personally so interesting that he soon became a popular citizen of Rochester, and his friends were as numerous and cordial in pro-slavery as in anti-slavery circles. Among those mentioned in his biography, for whom he had a special fondness, are Isaac Post, William Hallowell, Samuel D. Porter, William C. Bliss, Benjamin Fish, Asa Anthony, and Myron Holley. From time to time he addressed the citizens in Corinthian Hall. His audiences were always composed of the best people in Rochester, and in this way he did much to break down the prejudice against his race. This hall was built and owned by a prominent pro-slavery man, but so great was his respect for Mr. Douglass that he cheerfully allowed it to be used for the propaganda of emancipation. Thus the black leader became proud of Rochester and in more ways than can well be recited, the city honored him as no other colored man has ever been honored by an American municipality.

CHAPTER VIII

FREE COLORED PEOPLE AND COLONIZATION

THE recognized leadership of Frederick Douglass among the colored people of the country may be dated from the publication of the *North Star*. Prior to that time he was regarded as an Abolition orator and a conspicuous example of the possibilities of the Negro race. He had not yet established his relationship with the free colored people of the North.

Douglass came from the South. His hardest experiences and bitterest memories were those of the Southern plantations. It was the toiling black masses, whose fortunes he had shared, that claimed his first and profoundest sympathy and interest. "Freedom first and rights afterward," was the precept that had thus far guided his efforts in behalf of his race. His position as the publisher of a colored newspaper brought him into closer touch with the interests and aspirations of the free colored people of the North. They had obtained freedom, but they were thus far in practice, to a large degree, without rights. Douglass seemed to feel that the work he was doing and the position he occupied gave him some special claim to the support and loyalty of these people. He sometimes complained of and took deeply to heart the criticism and petty fault-finding with which a few of his fellow freedmen followed his movements. But, on the whole, they gave him generous support, and accorded him grateful recognition for his services. The leading colored men of the period who, in various ways, were helping the cause of emancipation, rallied around him and lived and labored in intimate association with him.

At this time the free Negroes formed a considerable portion of the American population. In 1850 there were about 230,000 of them in the slave-states and about 200,000 in the free-states. The liberation from bondage of this nearly half-million of colored persons had been brought about in various ways. The larger portion of them in the Northern states became free through their emancipation by Northern slave-holders. Those in the slave-states were either manumitted by their former masters or had by personal enterprise bought their own freedom. Here and there were a few West Indian colored people who had come to the United States to find a home. An ever-increasing number in the North were runaway slaves who had gained their freedom in some such way as Frederick Douglass had gained his. These were for the most part a superior class of men and women. The fact that they had the courage and enterprise to win their own liberty is good evidence that they had personal initiative and ambition. Among their number were many who, like Douglass, had secretly learned to read and write while they were still slaves. Others were first-rate mechanics who, in spite of opposition, found good employment.

The attitude of the white citizens of the North toward the free people of color was, in almost every way, hostile. The slave-holders of the South were angered by the loss of their property and the Northern people were annoyed by the presence, in their midst, in ever-increasing numbers, of this class. In fact, prejudice against the free blacks in the Northern states came to be of the most uncompromising sort. In many sections the status of the free Negro was often little better than that of an outlaw. It was literally true that he had "no rights that a white man was bound to respect." Wherever the Negro turned his face for encouragement or for opportunity, he met with opposition and discouragement. His children were generally shut out of the public and private schools. In many instances those which would admit colored pupils, in defiance of public sentiment, were burned down or mobbed and the teachers ostracized. The case of Miss Prudence Crandall, in Canterbury, Conn., in 1833, is fairly illustrative of the public feeling in regard to Negro education. Miss Crandall was a beautiful young Quakeress of tender heart and great courage, who had opened a school for young women in the village of Canterbury. A chance admission of a colored girl raised such a storm of indignation among her neighbors that she was assailed by a mob and an attempt was made to burn the building. When she still persisted in having her way, she was arrested and sent to jail.

Other instances of this kind might be cited. In nothing were the Northern people more bitterly intolerant than in their opposition to the education of the children of free colored families. The same spirit that in the slave-holding states accounted it a crime to teach colored people to read and write, made it very dangerous for any man or woman to do, or attempt to do, the same thing in the free-states.

In some of the Northern commonwealths, as Illinois, for example, the term "black laws" was given to a code of special regulations which were applied to men and women of a dark complexion. In nearly all of the states north of the Ohio, the Negro was disfranchised either by constitution, statute, or public sentiment. In practice, he was not regarded as a member of political society and was, consequently, almost wholly without the guarantee of civil rights. The Christian people were often as hostile as non-church people. Mr. Garrison mentions "a certain Baptist church in Hartford, Conn., where the ' Negro pews' were boarded up in front so that only peep-holes gave an outlook; truly a human menagerie." In a Massachusetts town, the floor was cut out from under a colored member's pew by the church authorities, so that he could not occupy it. In all means of travel, either by rail or stage-coach, the Negro passenger was rigidly quarantined. His presence was everywhere frowned upon unless he appeared as a servant or a slave.

This anti-Negro feeling in the North was not a passing whim or sentiment; it was deeply rooted and constitutional. People, noble and ignoble, were alike influenced by race prejudice. Abolitionists found themselves swayed to such an extent by the sentiment about them that they often did not have the courage to act consistently with their principles. Mr. Douglass gives a very interesting incident in the early part of his career, which aptly illustrates how at times race feeling manifested itself in the most unexpected places. He had been invited to speak at Concord, N. H., by a subscriber of *The Liberator*. Arriving in the town, he went directly to the home of the Abolitionist, where it was expected he would be entirely welcome. He was received with anything but enthusiasm. When the good man got ready to go to the church, where the meeting was to take place, he drove off alone and left the orator of the occasion to walk and find the way—a distance of two miles—as best he could. Upon reaching the church, Mr. Douglass was obliged to introduce himself, as no one was willing to risk his reputation by standing sponsor for a Negro. After the address, the Abolitionists went to their several homes for lunch, but no one invited Mr. Douglass to eat, and the hotel did not entertain Negroes. Hungry, chilly, and desolate, he found his way to the graveyard, and while roaming among the graves and contemplating the equality of men in death, he was approached by a gentleman who proved to be a Democratic senator from New Hampshire. He took Mr. Douglass to his home and treated him with the greatest courtesy.

Another cause of racial antagonism was the dread, on the part of slave-owners, that the pres-

ence of an increasing number of free colored people
in the free-states would be an incentive to the more
enterprising slaves to run away. This fear was certainly justified by the constantly enlarging stream
of fugitives. The Negro's growing desire for freedom was the fundamental weakness of the slave-
system. When the veterans of the War of 1812
returned to the Southern states and told of the land
of Canada which was consecrated to free men, the
seed of discontent took root in slavery's soil. The
good news was passed along, and, as a result, thousands of slaves learned to associate the words Canada
and freedom. Many a one, ignorant of everything
except his master and the plantation, had received
tidings of the Haytian struggle for liberty; of the
Nat Turner uprising in Virginia; and of the success of those who had the courage and enterprise to
flee to Massachusetts, New York, and elsewhere
north of the Ohio River. Negroes who had dared
to emancipate themselves in the way Frederick
Douglass had done were a direct menace to the security of slavery. Every man who succeeded in
making his escape began at once to plan and plot
for the escape of those he had left behind. On the
border-land of freedom there was continuous skir-
mishing for friends in chains.

In spite of the humble position they occupied,
the free Negroes, in one way or another, helped to
make sentiment against the slave-power. Like
Douglass, they became "human arguments," at
once offering evidence as to the capacity of the
race and the limitations that slavery imposed

upon it. They were quickeners of the public conscience.

Since the Negroes were escaping from Southern
plantations, in spite of all precautions and every
kind of threat and punishment, an organized effort
was made to send all free colored people out of the
country and deposit them on the west shore of Africa. This movement found expression in the
American Colonization Society, which was organized in 1817. Its declared purposes were :

(1) "To colonize the blacks on the West Coast
of Africa."

(2) "To discourage manumission by slave-
holders."

(3) "To avoid insurrection."

An attempt was put forth to make this colonization scheme a national policy, and the general government, as well as the several states, was appealed
to for its support. In many of the slave-holding
states there were direct appropriations of money to
forward this enterprise. Ministers, statesmen, educators, slave-holders, and many who were not slave-
holders, endorsed the plan of the Colonization
Society as a most happy solution of the difficult
problem of dealing with the Negro question. It
met with popular favor throughout the country.
The Southern people saw in it the removal of a great
menace to slavery ; it appealed to the humane sentiments of the North for it seemed to say to
the free people, "Now we are going to give you
an opportunity, and will materially aid you to found
a government of your own on the soil of Africa."

To some of the Negroes this policy appeared fair and generous, especially when they considered the extent to which, by popular prejudice, they were shut out from the rights and benefits supposed to be the natural heritage of all American citizens. Certain it is that nothing concerning the Negro had, up to this time, been proposed in which men of the North and South met so nearly on common ground. In 1834, such names as James Madison, Chief Justice Marshall, General Lafayette, Henry Clay, Daniel Webster, and Gerrit Smith were enrolled among the officers of the society. But in spite of the distinguished character of those who were associated with the movement, it was thought by many that the propaganda carried on by the Colonization Society did much to increase the prejudice against the colored people. The following extracts from some of the speeches of its members and friends, and from its documents and publications, show the pro-slavery spirit of the society :

Henry Clay said : "The emancipated slave should be removed. This is a condition indispensable. Expense of expatriation is to be defrayed by a fund to be derived from the labor of each freedman."

Judge Bullock of Kentucky said : "He [the colored man] is an exotic that does not and cannot flourish on American soil. There is no place for him in this country. It is not their land, and they cannot be made at home here."

The Colonization Journal said : "You cannot abolish slavery, for God is pledged to sustain it."

"Policy, and even the voice of humanity, forbid the progress of manumission. It would be as humane to throw them from the decks in the Middle Passage as to set them free in this country. Free blacks are a greater nuisance than slaves. This class of persons is a curse and a contagion where they reside."—*Colonization Report*, iv, 261.

"An anomalous race of beings, the most depraved on earth."

"They constitute a class by themselves, out of which no individual can be elevated and below which none can be depressed. Even necessity places them in a class of degraded beings."

"Christianity cannot do for them here what it will do for them in Africa. This is no fault of the colored man, nor the white man, but an ordinance of Providence, and no more to be changed than the laws of motion."

"If the free people of color were generally taught to read, it might be an inducement for them to remain in this country. We should offer them no such inducement."

"It must appear evident to all . . . that measures calculated to bind the colored people to this country and seeking to raise them to a level with the whites, whether by founding colleges or in any other way, tends directly to counteract and thwart the whole plan of colonization."

Such were the teachings and spirit of the American Colonization Society at that time. The effect was naturally and necessarily brought home, in some form or other, to every colored man, woman, and child in the free-states. Justifying, as it did, an already existing prejudice, its tendency was, everywhere and in every direction, to bring about a narrowing of opportunities. Thus, there soon sprang up an active opposition to the society and its purposes. The anti-slavery members withdrew their support when they saw that the organization was almost wholly pro-slavery in spirit and purpose.

Meanwhile, the colored people began to show themselves worthy of respect in the efforts they were making to improve their own condition. It could not be denied that, in those Northern states where he was given an opportunity to work, the Negro was, on the whole, a peaceful, loyal, law-abiding, and industrious citizen. In spite of the might of all the forces against him, he doggedly persisted in his determination to be a man, to win a right to remain in this country, and to deserve the privileges of citizenship therein. No race under like conditions ever exhibited greater patience and faith in the ultimate triumph of right over wrong.

In times of war the Negro was instantly ready to sacrifice himself for the good of his country. As sailor or soldier, no commander ever had occasion to complain of his courage or lack of soldierly qualities. Just before the battle of New Orleans, in the winter of 1814, General Jackson, through his Adjutant General, made the following stirring address to his black soldiers:

"To the Men of Color—Soldiers: From the shores of Mobile I called you to arms, I invited

you to share the perils, and to divide the glory with
your white countrymen. I expected much from
you, for I was not unmindful of those qualities
which must render you so formidable to an invading
foe. I knew that you could endure hunger and
thirst and all the hardships of war. I knew that
you loved the land of your nativity, and that, like
ourselves, you had to defend all that was most dear
to man, but you surpassed my hopes. I have found
in you, united to these qualities, that noble enthusiasm which impels to great deeds.

"Soldiers! The President of the United States
shall be informed of your conduct on the present occasion and the voice of the representatives of the
American nation shall applaud your valor, as your
general now praises your valor."

The black heroes of New Orleans nobly won a
place on the roll of honor, among those who strove
for the protection and preservation of the American
republic.

In the arts of peace and in the every-day struggles to live and survive the forces that made for his
degradation, the Negro showed a courage and a disposition altogether creditable. While many were
thinking that the black people were hopelessly incapable of absorbing American civilization, the latter were building churches of their own and organizing the great African Methodist Episcopal Zion,
and the Colored Methodist Episcopal Church.
These have steadily grown in membership until they
have come to be numbered among the great religious bodies of the Christian world. They also
founded and developed a Baptist organization which,
with its schools, colleges, and missions, is regarded

as one of the important civilizing agencies of the country.

What the colored people accomplished for themselves, in their great religious associations and under so many hindering influences, is of far greater importance than is generally understood, or recognized by the American people. To the restraining and humanizing forces of these religious bodies, is largely due the peaceful and law-abiding character of the Negro population. In those critical periods of our history a race with passions less in restraint might have caused no end of trouble and bloodshed. These efforts of the free colored people of the North to improve their condition by means of religious training, were accompanied by endeavors to provide themselves with the facilities for secular education. There was never a time in the history of the American Negro when he did not show an eagerness to learn. Whether on the plantation in the far South, where ignorance in the slave was slavery's only security, or in the northern states, where schools were closed against him by popular prejudice, he was always struggling, by night and by day, to obtain an education. The most important and creditable thing in his career as slave or freeman, and the most striking thing in his achievements, is his passion and struggle to lift from himself and his race the dark mantle of ignorance. This persistent determination to be educated has won for him more consideration and more friends among the white race, than any other one trait.

When practically every school, public and pri-

vate, closed its doors against the admission of a
Negro child, these courageous people tried to establish schools of their own.   In every Northern
community where there were colored persons some
way was provided for their education.   Sometimes
classes would meet in a private house, like that of
Primus Hall in Boston ; at other times in a Negro
church, and often in a barn.   In these early efforts
to furnish means of education, in spite of the protest of white neighbors, there was exhibited fine
courage, impressive sacrifice, and rare consecration.
Here the Negro was always at his best.   Such men
as Primus Hall and the Ruffins in Massachusetts ;
Nelson Wells in Maryland ; John F. Ganes and
Peter H. Clark in Ohio ; John F. Cook in Washington ; John Peterson in New York ; Thomas and
Fannie Jackson Coppin in Pennsylvania, all noble
types of men and women, saw to it that ways
and means for the education of the children of their
day and generation should be provided.   Hundreds
of the best types of white men and women became
interested in the education of the Negro as a result
of his own persistent efforts in this direction.   Some
of these friends gave themselves as teachers, while
others gave money for the founding and sustaining
of schools and colleges.   A few of those started at
this early period, still live, many colored men and
women, who have since become prominent in public
affairs, having received their education in these es-
tablishments.

One of the most interesting of these schools that
have survived the revolution of conditions is the

"Institute for Colored Youth," founded in Philadelphia in 1837, from funds bequeathed for that purpose by Richard Humphrey. The trustees were instructed to establish an institution "for the education of the descendants of the African race in school learning, in the various branches of the mechanical arts and trades and agriculture."

In the preamble of the constitution, the following language is used :

"We believe that the most successful method of elevating the moral and intellectual character of the descendants of Africa, as well as improving their social condition, is to extend to them the benefits of a good education, and instruct them in the knowledge of some useful trade or business whereby they may be enabled to obtain a comfortable livelihood by their own industry ; and through these means to prepare themselves for fulfilling the various duties of domestic and social life with reputation and fidelity, as good citizens and pious men."

This school has recently been reorganized and considerably enlarged, and removed to Cheyney, Pa., near Philadelphia, the work being entrusted to Hugh M. Browne, an educator of proved worth and responsibility. It starts out upon a career of increased usefulness, with the express purpose of fitting teachers for their appointed work.

The men and women who have graduated from the Institute have more than justified the generosity of its founder, and they have likewise reflected the unexampled excellence as a teacher of Mrs. Fannie Jackson Coppin, an early graduate of Oberlin, and one of the first principals of this famous school in Philadelphia. Her influence on the lives and careers of many prominent men and women of the Negro race is quite beyond comparison with that of any other of our early Negro educators.

Charlotte L. Fortin, now Mrs. Frank J. Grimké, Frances Ellen Watkins Harper, and Mary Ann Shadd Carey must always be mentioned among the men and women whose devotion to the education of the members of their race has made the American people recognize the justice and the usefulness of giving the Negro the teaching he so earnestly desires.

The lack of economic and industrial opportunities of the free colored people, prior to the Civil War, can be easily inferred from what has already been said concerning the general sentiment of proscription that prevailed. As a general rule, they were not allowed to work at any of the trades and their children were not accepted as apprentices. It has already been noticed how impossible it was for Mr. Douglass, even in Massachusetts, to follow his occupation as a ship-calker, although, as we have seen, he had no trouble in obtaining good employment in Baltimore.

But the Negro, in this as in matters of education, persisted in his effort to learn trades and to work at them. There were in the free-states a considerable number of colored mechanics. Many of them had fitted themselves for their work while in slavery, and either by self-purchase or as runaways, had obtained their freedom. From these mechanics the

trades were passed along to others by apprentice-
ships. In this way colored men entered and main-
tained themselves in many employments. There
were always some people who were willing to hire
skilled Negro mechanics. In cities like Philadelphia, they were, for a time, important factors in the
industrial life. Indeed, long before slavery was
abolished, every large northern city had a certain
number of enterprising individuals who had succeeded in establishing themselves in some of the
trades. In many communities they were making
commendable headway as contractors, caterers, shop-
keepers, tailors, shoemakers, and barbers. Not a
few of them accumulated small fortunes. A number
too had built up enviable reputations in the professions, especially in medicine, the ministry, and
journalism. Some obtained their education in England, but most of them managed to get their training in this country.

In all this activity and enterprise they were not
without leaders of force and intelligence. In the period covered by the anti-slavery movement, there was
a remarkable group of aggressive and influential colored agitators. Without attempting to name all the
prominent men who coöperated with Mr. Douglass
in the anti-slavery warfare, we should mention a
few, in order to make complete any account of the
struggle in which their leader was so heroically
engaged. Henry Highland Garnet of New York,
was a gifted and thoroughly educated man. He was
a Presbyterian minister and as such held an influential position, being elected at one time as a dele-

gate to a Peace Conference at Frankfort, Germany. Charles Lennox Remond, Dr. James McCune Smith, Samuel R. Ward, H. Ford Douglass, Martin R. Delaney, John M. Langston, J. Howard Day, and Mifflin W. Gibbs, were men of rare oratorical gifts and were heard and admired on every great anti-slavery occasion. Robert Purvis, of Philadelphia, would have held a high place in any age, and the cause of freedom would have suffered without his aid. He was a man of patrician manners and had all the instincts of an aristocrat. He was for many years, vice-president of the National Anti-Slavery Society, and he enjoyed the intimate acquaintance and association of some of the most eminent men of his time.

It would scarcely be possible to write a history of the anti-slavery movement without mentioning the work of William Still. He had the rare powers of heart and mind that gave him an interest in and a large grasp of affairs. He was one of the original stockholders of *The Nation*, and a close friend of John Brown's. It was at his house that the latter's family were concealed after the Harper's Ferry tragedy. Mr. Still's contribution to the literature of the anti-slavery cause has a special value and is nowhere duplicated.

These colored men, who were associated with Mr. Douglass, got their training in the school of adversity. They were permitted to share few of the joys of life. Men of strong faith, they spent themselves in the service of their people. When the history of the Negro in America comes finally to be written and scholars seek to tell the story of the curious problem in civilization which his presence here creates, these dark-skinned heroes of an unpopular race may find their place in the ranks of those who helped to benefit the world.

CHAPTER IX

PRO-SLAVERY and anti-slavery were at this time the names of two sets of ideas and two states of mind that no longer admitted of compromise. The words meant immeasurably more in 1850 than they had in 1830. If they had ever been mere academic terms, they were fast becoming fighting terms,— the standards of two hostile camps. In the minds of the people, they stood, respectively, for irreconcilable principles. With every fresh event affecting either one side or the other, new and more intense animosities were engendered, and the two forces were driven farther and farther apart. Those who believed in the institution, became more and more firmly fixed in their determination not only to resist every attack upon it, but to give it the widest possible extension. Those who stood opposed to slavery were equally fixed in their determination that it should be destroyed.

The anti-slavery movement was fast becoming something more than a sentiment or an opinion with which one might try conclusions in the forum. It was fast becoming a revolutionary movement which meant force, more force, and, finally, the utmost force. All the time Frederick Douglass, like William Lloyd Garrison, was in the forward ranks.

The tone of "no compromise" rang out with increasing insistence.

"Come what will," said Douglass, "I hold it to be morally certain that sooner or later, by fair means or foul means, in peace or in blood, in judgment or in mercy, slavery is doomed to cease out of this otherwise goodly land, and liberty is destined to become the settled law of the republic."

"I am in earnest," said Garrison, "I will not equivocate, I will not excuse, I will not retract a single inch, and I will be heard."

These declarations by these two conspicuous Abolitionists are aptly expressive of the growing intensity of the anti-slavery feeling. Such words called more loudly for action than for argument. What was known in the United States during the anti-slavery struggle as the "Underground Railway," best represents all that was aggressive and militant in that contest. This so-called "railway system" was constituted and operated in defiance of law by the Abolitionists. It was Abolition in action.

But if the Underground Railway was conducted in defiance of law, it should be said that the law in its terms, spirit, and effects seemed to them who were engaged in operating the road to be in defiance of those principles of liberty and the rights of man, which they had been taught to think were higher than any positive enactment of a legislature.

The Underground Railway had none of the features of the modern railway, except the carrying of passengers, and these were limited in kind and in the direction of the travel. No one could obtain passage on this road, unless he or she were a slave, and wanted to be free. The trains ran in but one direction, and that was Northward. There were no "Jim Crow" cars, no sleepers and no smokers, and all passengers were carried free of charge. It was a railroad without stockholders, but it had innumerable directors. No dividends were paid except to passengers, and such dividends were in the form of certificates of freedom from bondage.

To be more explicit, the Underground Railway was a system of clandestine travel, extending from the borders of "Mason and Dixon's Line" through the North and West to Canada. The residence of Mr. Douglass was one of the last stations on the line before reaching British soil. Much has been written about this mysterious railway, but the details of its activities have never been told. From September 26, 1850, to the breaking out of the Civil War, the new and rigid Fugitive Slave Law was in active operation, and it was in open violation of this measure that the Underground Railway was conducted. A slave, and sometimes an entire family or body of slaves, would make the dash for liberty, escaping across the borders of Maryland into Pennsylvania. There they found themselves in the hands of friendly Quakers, who piloted them by night to other stations, where they were secreted until a favorable opportunity presented itself to push them along farther north.

Mr. Douglass's house in Rochester was a large three-story frame structure, situated in the centre of four acres of land on South Avenue, two miles from the business portion of the city. It stood out by itself, the ieares' residence being fully five hundred feet away to the north. This was the objective point, before reaching Canada, for many slaves fleeing from the South. The tales of privation and suffering told by these men, women, and children who escaped half-clad, encountering in the winter-time snow-drifts and zero weather, made a profound impression on the people of the North through whose towns they passed and in whose homes they constantly sought protection. Thus it was that many a Northern farmer, convinced, it may be, of the right or expediency of slavery, found himself compelled, from motives of common humanity, to open his doors to these refugees, and grant their appeals for food and shelter. Many a cold winter night has a knock come to Mr. Douglass's door, when a white-faced stranger, covered with frost and snow, would announce in whispered tones that he had a sleigh full of runaway Negroes *en route* for Canada. Mr. Douglass, or Mrs. Douglass in her husband's absence, calling the boys, Lewis, Fred and Charles, would have fires started in that part of the house where fugitives were hidden away, and at an opportune time they were taken to Charlotte, seven miles from Rochester, and placed aboard a Lake Ontario steamer for Canada. These friendly white farmers had to hasten on for fear of detection, which meant terrible penalties. Thus it will be seen that the risks which their sympathy for the slave led them to take were very serious.

It required large sums of money to keep this Un-

THE UNDERGROUND RAILWAY   161

derground Railway system in motion. The runaways must be fed, clothed, and their passage paid
across the lake to Canada. Mr. Douglass was in the
lecture-field most of the time to raise money to do
his part. The Female Anti-Slavery Society, with
its branches throughout the North, solicited funds
and clothing, and, as these unfortunate fugitives
were invariably destitute, means had to be supplied them until they could secure employment under the British flag.

Besides William Still of Philadelphia, among col-
ored people, Mr. Douglass had the active coöperation of Dr. James McCune Smith, of New York;
Stephen J. Myers, of Albany; William Rich, of
Troy, and Rev. J. W. Loguen, of Syracuse. Many
others actively assisted in the work, including
Charles Lennox Remond, William Whipper, of
Philadelphia; Thomas L. Dorsey, Rev. Henry
Highland Garnet, Anthony Barrier, of Brockport,
N. Y., and Thomas Downing, of New York. There
were not a few clashes with the law in efforts to capture and return escaping slaves, but only two or
three such attempts were successful.

Mr. Douglass' s home was always considered an
asylum for runaways, and was constantly under the
surveillance of the United States marshals; nevertheless, not a single fugitive, after reaching him,
was ever apprehended and carried back. The majority of the escapes were made in winter, when the
oversight on the plantation was less rigid than in
the working-season, and many who were given
passes during the Christmas holidays to visit neigh-

boring towns or plantations, seized that opportunity for a longer journey.

The western and southwestern branch of the Underground Railway was operated from Cincinnati, O., and through Michigan to Canada. Fugitive slaves from Kentucky, Tennessee, Mississippi, Arkansas, and Louisiana took this latter route. The whole number of slaves who successfully made their escape through the system has never been ascertained.

The thousands of men, women, and children, white and black, who had a hand in conducting this Underground Railway were less concerned about the statistics of their dangerous work than they were with results. That the number of slaves set free by the operation of the system ran up into the thousands, was evident from the vast army of people in all parts of the North engaged in the work, and the constantly increasing colored population in the free-states and Canada. There was scarcely a day or night when some black man or woman did not defy the perils of the journey and elude the vigilance of the law to find free-soil. So persistent were these enslaved people in running away from bondage that they excited not merely the sympathy but often the admiration of those not otherwise interested in their cause. The perils and adventures of these sombre fugitives stirred the blood and touched the heart. William Still's volume of nearly eight hundred pages, contains a carefully kept record of the experiences of those runaways who came under the immediate observation and direction of the "Vigilance Committee" of the Pennsylvania Anti-Slavery Society. Their resourcefulness, cleverness, and daring revealed to the Northern people an unsuspected quality in the Negro character.

The stories of these fugitives, told in their own simple-hearted way, and attested by the hardships that they had undergone, were, to those who heard them, a revelation of conditions in the South, of which they had hitherto known only at second-hand. They might still doubt the expediency of granting freedom to the slave but they could no longer question the sincerity of his desire for liberty and with that desire they were compelled to sympathize. As Douglass said : "Men were better than their theology, and truer to humanity than their politics or their offices."

The manner of Douglass's flight—riding out of Baltimore and Maryland in daylight and in sight of those who knew that he was a slave—is a good illustration of the boldness and ingenuity of some of the escapes. Among the hundreds of interesting cases cited by Mr. Still is that of William Crafts, who gained his liberty by acting the part of a valet or body-servant of his wife. She was of light brown complexion, and for this adventure wore men's clothing. Another case is that of a slave-woman who hitched up her master's horse and carriage and, taking her family of five children and several others, drove off to liberty. Box Brown was the name of a slave, who permitted himself to be nailed up in a box and sent by express to Baltimore. Two

colored women dressed themselves in deep mourn-
ing and rode Northward to freedom in the same
coach as their masters, who did not know them.
In some cases slaves secreted themselves for several
months and, when search for them had ceased, crept
off unsuspected. In hundreds of instances, the parts
were as cleverly played as if the fugitives had had
special training in the drama of running away from
their masters. In nearly all cases these black men
and women took desperate chances. The conductors of the Underground Railway were everywhere,
and at all times on the alert. They knew every
path, the byways and highways in which slaves
might hide or on which they might travel to reach
freedom. The stations were always ready and open
to receive them. It was never too late, or too early,
or too difficult, or too perilous to be on the lookout
to welcome, protect, and pass on fugitives to the next
place of safety. Clothing, food, shoes, carriages,
wagons, horses, and mules were always at hand.
No secret society has ever veiled its proceedings in
deeper mystery than this widely separated army of
determined conspirators and emancipators. The
secret-service men of the government tried to locate
the stations and the station-agents, but the more
they searched, the less they found. It is a curious
fact that the United States secret service men seem
to have had just as little success in uncovering the
systematic plans for aiding slaves to escape to the
Northern states as in preventing the smuggling of
slaves from Africa into the Southern states. The
traffic of the Underground Railroad continued to in-

crease in volume and the slave once off United States soil was beyond reach or recall.

Some of the men and women who were carrying on this clandestine work of delivering fugitives were people of much prominence. Among them were members of Congress, distinguished clergymen, editors, prominent merchants, doctors, lawyers, farmers, and tradesmen. From the slave-holders' standpoint, the situation was not encouraging. They rightly felt that unless something effective were done to stop this increasing loss, slave-labor would cease to be profitable. This condition of things required a remedy, a remedy more far-reaching than any guaranteed the slave-holding system under the law then existing. To meet these attempts of the Abolitionists to undermine the system, the pro-slavery leaders deemed it just and necessary to extend the arm of national power to reclaim and carry back to bondage every slave who reached a free-state in quest of liberty. The government that sanctioned slavery as a national institution ; that acquired new territory for the extension of slavery ; that derived a goodly part of its revenue from it, was bound, they believed, to do what was necessary to make slavery more secure. Until the Underground Railway began to do so large a business, there was thought to be enough law in the Constitution of the United States.[1]

---

[1] As provided in Article IV, Section 2 : "No person held to service in one state, under the laws thereof, escaping to another state, in consequence of any law or regulation therein, shall be discharged from such service or labor, but shall be delivered up on the claim of the party to whom such service or

The constitutionality of this law had been fully upheld by the Supreme Court in what was known as the "Prigg case," wherein Justice Story declared that it was self-executing, so that an owner could seize and carry away his runaway slave wherever he found him, providing he could do so without breach of the public peace. Those who desired and demanded more legal provisions for the better protection of slavery were in absolute power North and South. Daniel Webster of Massachusetts was as much in favor of it as Henry Clay of Kentucky and Calhoun of South Carolina ; and in response to popular demand, the new Fugitive Slave Law was passed on September 10, 1850, as a part of the great Compromise Measures of that year.

The instrument was most carefully drawn, and covered ten sections. Those who worked out its carefully-worded provisions had evidently studied the Underground System with considerable care, and this law was framed to meet the conditions that the railroad had created. Some of its main features were as follows :—

A United States Commission and a United States court should have concurrent jurisdiction in disposing of cases of fugitive slaves brought before them.

Any postmaster or clerk could be appointed a commissioner to hear cases under the law.

A United States marshal was under penalty of $1,000 for refusing or neglecting to make an arrest when called upon to do so.

labor may be due," supplemented by the statute giving force to its provisions in 1793.

Fugitive slaves could be arrested, with or without warrant and taken before a commissioner or judge, who was empowered to dispose of the case forthwith.

If a fugitive escaped from a United States marshal, the latter could be sued on his bond and the full value of the slave recovered.

There was a penalty of five years in prison or a fine of $5,000 for aiding or abetting a slave's escape.

The only proof needed was an affidavit by the alleged owner or some one acting in his behalf alleging right of property, escape or service due on escape, and a description of the person arrested, certified to by the magistrate.

There were provisions for military aid for the United States marshal in case of resistance.

The commissioner received a larger fee in case of extradition than he would obtain in case of discharge.

The slave thus arrested could not testify in his own behalf and was not allowed a jury trial.

The first effect of the law was to create a panic and stampede among the colored people of the free-states. It looked for awhile as if every Negro resident north of the Ohio had lost faith in the tenure of his own title to himself. There was wholesale emigration to Canada of colored people from every part of the United States. In his Life of Frederick Douglass, Mr. Holland gives an account of forty Negroes of Boston, who left home within three days after the Fugitive Slave Law was passed. The pastor of a colored church and his entire membership of 112 persons fled to British soil. A number of talented men who had done service in the anti-slavery cause, went to England.   Mr. Douglass, who was in close touch with every movement, every fear, and every secret purpose of his people, says:

" I was compelled to witness the terribly distressing effects of this cruel enactment ; fugitive slaves, who had lived for many years safely and securely in western New York and elsewhere, some of whom by industry and economy had saved some money and bought little homes for themselves and their children, were suddenly alarmed and compelled to flee to Canada.   Even colored people who had been free all their lives felt very insecure in their freedom, for under this law the oaths of any two villains were sufficient to confine a free man to slavery for life. . . .   Although I was now free myself, I was not without apprehension.   My pardon was of doubtful validity, having been bought when out of possession of my owner, and when he must take what was given or not at all. . . .   From rumors that reached me, my house was guarded by my friends several nights."

A much more serious consequence of the Fugitive Slave Law was the altogether unexpected feeling of resentment aroused in the North by its enforcement. There was abundant willingness among the Northern people that the slave-holders should have their slaves and that they should have everything needed to protect and make secure their property rights in them ; but when it came to pressing unwilling citizens into the service of men who were hunting slaves, there was a very natural revulsion of sentiment.   Just how intense was this feeling may best be illustrated in the history of three different cases that created wide-spread interest at the time. These were known respectively as the Burns, Shadrach, and Thomas Sims cases.

Anthony Burns had made his escape from his master in Virginia and in 1854 was living in Boston. In the month of May he was arrested under the provisions of the Fugitive Slave Law. At this particular time, Boston was aroused because of the passage of the Kansas-Nebraska Bill, repealing the Missouri Compromise, and thereby permitting the extension of slavery in the western territories. Burns was confined in the Boston court-house under strong guard. The people were in a mood to become profoundly interested in his case, which presented itself to them as an illustration of the cruelties of slavery and of the Fugitive Slave Law. Wendell Phillips, Theodore Parker, Richard A. Davis, Charles M. Ellis, Thomas Wentworth Higginson, and many others equally prominent, gave practical effect to this interest by securing a postponement of the hearing for a few days. In the meantime, a meeting was called in Faneuil Hall in which feeling ran high. While it was in progress, Colonel Higginson led in an attempt to rescue Burns. The door of the jail was battered in, the deputy was killed, and the Colonel and others were wounded. When the case came up for a hearing before Commissioner Loring, Burns had the best counsel that Boston could afford, but like all cases under the Fugitive Slave Law, there was no escape. After the formalities were complied with, he was ordered back to his master.

When this decision became known, many houses were draped in black and so intense was the public feeling against it, that the government directed that Burns should be returned in a United States revenue cutter. He was escorted to the wharf by a strong guard and the streets were thronged with Boston citizens in a great state of excitement. There seemed to be no possible escape from a bloody riot. When the water-side was reached and an outbreak was imminent, a minister named Foster cried out, "Let us pray," and with this call for prayer silence fell upon the excited throng; but the law had its way and Burns was sent back.

The case of Shadrach was less exciting, but is interesting as presenting another and different view of the sentiment excited by the Fugitive Slave Law. He was a fugitive and a resident of Boston. He had been arrested in February, 1851, and during a postponement of his hearing before the United States Commissioner, the Boston Abolitionists rescued him and got him into Canada, the land of safety. The government officials in Washington took serious notice of this rescue of a United States prisoner and the uproar that followed seemed altogether out of proportion to the incident. Commenting on the excitement at the capital at this apparent determination of Boston to defy the national government, Mr. Garrison wrote:

"The head and front of the offending in this instance—what is it? A sudden rush of a score or two of unarmed friends of equal liberty—an uninjurious deliverance of the oppressed out of the hands of the oppressor—the quiet transportation of a slave out of this slavery-ruled land to the free soil of Upper Canada . . . a solitary slave in Boston is plucked as a brand from the burning, and forthwith a Cabinet Council is held and behold a menacing proclamation!"

Senator Henry Clay was "horrified" and proposed an inquiry as to the expediency of passing an additional law making it a penal offense in the nature of treason for any one to interfere with the smooth and peaceful exercise of his pet measure in the Compromise Bill. Mr. Webster declared that the rescue of Shadrach was "strictly speaking" treason.

Scarcely had the United States grand jury finished its examination of the Shadrach case when Boston was again in the midst of an excitement over the arrest and extradition of another fugitive slave, Thomas Sims. Profiting by the failure to send Shadrach back to his master, the officials had taken extraordinary precautions to prevent a rescue by mob or otherwise. The court-house where Sims was imprisoned was surrounded by chains and guarded by a large part of the city police force. As a further precaution, the state militia was called out and kept in readiness to quell a possible riot. A part of this soldiery furnished an escort all the way to Savannah, where the prisoner-slave was delivered safely.

The bloody resistance on the part of runaways at Christiana, Pa., did more than anything else, in the opinion of Mr. Douglass, to put a check on the execution of the law.   At this place three colored men were pursued by officers, and, when hard-pressed, turned about, shot, and killed a Mr. Gorsuch, wounded his son, drove back the officers, and then made their escape to Rochester, where they were rescued and given shelter in Mr. Douglass's house. The latter, with his assistants, finally smuggled these fugitives to the Canadian shores, but in doing so he imperiled his own safety to a greater extent than ever before, because he was not only harboring fugitives from slavery, but fugitives from justice. After this experience, the law became a dead letter. It not only intended to put an end to the business of the Underground Railroad, but to make every community in some degree responsible for the return of runaway slaves, and it proved to be one of the most unpopular and irritating pieces of legislation enacted by the Federal Government.   This act, more than any other one thing, increased opposition to slavery.   Thousands of people who were either indifferent or hostile to the anti-slavery cause, flocked to the ranks of the Abolitionists when they saw what it meant and whither it was leading the nation.   The language used by the leaders, both in their publications and on the stump, became more bitter and defiant.

Mr. Douglass was always in the storm-centre of every movement to thwart the execution of this measure.   He was in Boston, and in continuous conference with Theodore Parker, Higginson, Garrison, and others belonging to the "vigilance" committees.   It was in these meetings that Douglass says

he "got a peep into Parker's soul." He characterized him as "a man who shrank from no opportunity to do his full duty when man's liberty was
threatened." Mr. Douglass's thorough and comprehensive understanding of each succeeding change in
the development of the slavery question was generally recognized by friend and foe. When he was
invited by the members of the New York state legislature to address them on the subject, he was selected because no man then living could speak with
a fuller knowledge of the great issue.

Belonging to this period of increasing antagonism between pro-slavery and anti-slavery parties
was the decision in the Dred Scott case. This, the
Fugitive Slave Law, and the Kansas-Nebraska Bill,
taken together, represent the sum of the conservative forces in the nation opposed to the Abolitionists and their cause. Douglass's opinion of the
situation, as it concerned himself and his people,
is voiced in the following extract from an address
delivered at New York in May, 1857 :

"I am myself not insensible to the many difficulties that beset us on every hand. They fling their
broad and gloomy shadows across the pathway of
every thoughtful colored man in this country. For
one, I see them clearly and feel them sadly. Standing, as it were, barefoot, and treading upon the
sharp and flinty rocks of the present, and looking
out upon the boundless sea of the future, I have
sought in my humble way to penetrate the interven-
ing mists and clouds, and, perchance, to descry in the
dim and shadowy distance the white flag of freedom."

CHAPTER X

DOUGLASS, HARRIET BEECHER STOWE AND JOHN BROWN

THE anti-slavery agitation made and revealed some of the most notable characters in American history. As it grew in extent and intensity, it attracted to itself men and women gifted with the powers needed to force great issues to a conclusion. Those who were already in the struggle, like Mr. Douglass, became more strongly committed to it, and those who were not yet enlisted, but belonged to it by right of individual temperament and spiritual inheritance, hurriedly took their places in the foremost ranks of responsibility and action.

There was no such thing as indifference in this matter. For those who understood the vast issue there were grave questions involved, and in some form or other the right or wrong of it knocked at the door of every one's mind and conscience.

To those who were sufficiently gifted to say and do anything great concerning this cause, the opportunity was now at hand. In the midst of the confusion and controversy, the public was ready to listen to some clear voice that would tell it the facts in regard to American slavery.

Harriet Beecher Stowe responded to this need and was inspired to recite the story of the Negro in

America.   This she did with a mastery and a fasci-
nation that commanded the widest reading ever yet
given to an American book.   She so stirred the
hearts of the Northern people that a large part of
them were ready either to vote, or, in the last ex-
tremity, to fight for the suppression of slavery.
The value of *Uncle Tom's Cabin* to the cause of Abolition can never be justly estimated.

Mrs. Stowe was a member of the great Beecher
family, and was by inheritance, as well as by special
inspiration, peculiarly fitted to perform this service.
She developed a concern in the slavery question in
the natural course of her interest in all questions of
the time.   She lived for awhile in Cincinnati,
where she was brought into close touch with some
of the most cruel incidents of slavery,—the flight
and capture of fugitives.   Her sensitive nature was
stung by seeing men hunted through the streets of
the city, and carried back into bondage.   She was
near the scene when Birney's anti-slavery press was
destroyed by the mob.   The whole atmosphere about
her was surcharged with the spirit of the controversy, and the more she learned of the issue,
the deeper became her interest in it.   Stirred by
sympathy for those whom she had come to regard
as the victims of a bad system, she determined to
know everything that was possible to be known
about it.

Crossing the Ohio River, Mrs. Stowe went down
into the land of slavery, to study the institution at
first hand.   When she left the South and returned
to New England with her husband, she saw and felt

the evil as few in the North had ever seen and felt it.

She soon discovered that the great mass of the Northern people were not able to share her views. She found most of them either indifferent or incredulous, and concluded that if they had had her experiences, they would also have her convictions. The immediate incentive to the writing of *Uncle Tom's Cabin* was the desire to arouse the national conscience and bring the people to a sense of their responsibility. This remarkable story first appeared in an anti-slavery newspaper, and proved so popular that it was soon issued in book form. The rapidity with which one edition after another was published and consumed at home and abroad, was without precedent. The Abolitionists were quick to recognize the story as the most powerful engine that had yet been employed against slavery. Frederick Douglass thus speaks of its influence :

"Nothing could have better suited the moral and humane requirements of the hour. Its effect was amazing, instantaneous, and universal. She [Mrs. Stowe] at once became the object of interest and admiration the world over."

The author was not only concerned for the well-being of those who were enslaved in the South, but was also intensely interested in those who were already free in the North. She looked to Mr. Douglass as the most eminent representative of the Negro race in the free-states, and before sailing for England, whither she had been invited by the people, who were anxious to show her some honors for what she had done, asked him to her home in Andover, Mass.   He gladly accepted the invitation, and, in his *Life and Times*, gives the following account of his visit :

"I was received at her home with genuine cordiality.   There was no contradiction between the author and her book.   Mrs. Stowe appeared in conversation equally well as she appeared in her writing.   She made to me a nice little speech in announcing her object in sending for me :   'I have invited you here,' she said, 'because I wish to confer with you as to what can be done for the free colored people of the country.   I am going to England and expect to have a considerable sum of money placed in my hands, and I intend to use it in some way for the permanent good of the colored people and especially for that class which has become free by their own exertions.   In what way to do this most successfully is the subject which I wish to talk with you about.   In any event I desire to have some monument rise after *Uncle Tom's Cabin*, which shall show that it produced more than a transient influence.' "

They discussed at some length the condition of his people in the Northern states, and as a result both concluded that there should be established an "Industrial College," where colored people could learn some of the useful handicrafts,—to work in iron, wood and leather—and where a good plain English education could also be obtained.   Their poverty kept them ignorant, and ignorance kept them degraded.   Mrs. Stowe became so much interested in

Mr. Douglass's educational purposes that she asked
him to submit his plans in writing, so that she
could take them to England with her and show them
to her friends. On his return to Rochester he
elaborated his views, as she had requested. The
plans were then shown to many of the leading
Negroes who worked with him, and they very
heartily approved. Later they were submitted to a
convention of representative colored people in
Rochester to receive the endorsement of that body.
In this educational scheme, Mr. Douglass has given
evidence of his understanding of the needs of the
Negro in our generation, as well as of those in his
own. The following is an extract from the statement which he sent to Mrs. Stowe in 1853 :

"The plan which I humbly submit in answer to
this query is the establishment in Rochester, N. Y.,
or in some other part of the United States, equally
favorable to such an enterprise, of an Industrial
College in which shall be taught several important
branches of the mechanic arts. This college shall
be open to colored youth. I will pass over the details of such an institution as I propose. . . .
Never having had a day's schooling in all my life,
I may not be expected to map out the details of a
plan so comprehensive as that involved in the idea
of a college. The argument in favor of an Industrial College, a college to be conducted by the best
men and the best workmen which the mechanic
arts can afford ; where the colored youth can be instructed to use their hands, as well as their heads ;
where they can be put in possession of the means of
getting a living, whether their lot in after-life may
be cast among civilized or uncivilized men, whether

they choose to stay here, or prefer to return to the land of their fathers, is briefly this : Prejudice against the free colored people in the North has nowhere shown itself so invincible as among mechanics. The farmer and the professional man cherish no feeling so bitter as that cherished by these. The latter would starve us out of the country entirely. At this moment I can more easily get my son into a lawyer's office to study law than I can into a blacksmith's shop to blow the bellows and to wield the sledge-hammer. Denied the means of learning the useful trades, we are pressed into the narrowest limits to obtain a livelihood. In times past we have been the hewers of wood and drawers of water for American society, and we once enjoyed a monopoly in menial employments, but this is so no longer. Even these employments are rapidly passing out of our hands. The fact is, that colored men must learn trades; must find new employments new modes of usefulness to society ; or they must decay under the pressing wants to which their condition is rapidly bringing them.

"We must become mechanics ; we must build as well as live in houses ; we must make as well as use furniture ; we must construct bridges as well as pass over them, before we can properly live or be respected by our fellow-men. We need mechanics as well as ministers. We need workers in iron, clay, and leather. We have orators, authors, and other professional men, but these reach only a certain class, and get respect for our race in certain select circles. To live here as we ought, we must fasten ourselves to our countrymen through their every-day cardinal wants. We must not only be able to black boots, but to make them. At present, in the Northern states, we are unknown as mechanics. We give no proof of genius or skill at the county, state, or national fairs.

"The fact that we make no show of our ability is held conclusive of *our inability to make any*, hence all the indifference and contempt with which incapacity is regarded fall upon us, and that too when we have had no means of disproving the infamous opinion of our natural inferiority. I have during the last dozen years denied before Americans that we are an inferior race, but this has been done by arguments based upon admitted principles rather than by the presentation of facts. Now, firmly believing as I do, that there are skill, invention, power, industry, and real mechanical genius among the colored people, which will bear favorable testimony for them, and which only need the means to develop them, I am decidedly in favor of the establishment of such a college as I have mentioned. The benefits of such an institution will not be confined to the Northern states nor to the free colored people. They would extend over the whole Union. The slave, not less than the freeman, would be benefited by such an institution. It must be confessed that the most powerful argument now used by the Southern slave-holder, and the one most soothing to his conscience, is that derived from the low condition of the free colored people of the North. I have long felt that too little attention has been given by our truest friends in this country, to removing this stumbling block out of the way of the slave's liberation.

"The most telling, the most killing refutation of slavery is the presentation of an industrious, enterprising, thrifty and intelligent free black population. Such a population I believe would rise in the Northern states under the fostering care of such a college as that proposed.

"Allow me to say in conclusion that I believe every intelligent colored man in America will approve and rejoice at the establishment of some such institution as that now suggested. There are many respectable colored men, fathers of large families, having boys nearly grown, whose minds are tossed by night and by day with the anxious query, What shall I do with my boys ? Such an institution would meet the wants of such persons. Then, too, the establishment of such an institution would be in character with the eminently practical philanthropy of your trans-Atlantic friends. America could scarcely object to it as an attempt to agitate the public mind on the subject of slavery, or to dissolve the Union. It could not be tortured into a cause for hard words by the American people, but the noble and good of all classes would see in the effort an excellent motive, a benevolent object temperately, wisely and practically manifested.''

It would hardly be possible to show in any better way the far-reaching and prophetic character of the mind of Frederick Douglass. This letter indicates very plainly that even before General Armstrong had formulated his plan of academic and industrial education, before Hampton Institute, and long before Tuskegee Institute was thought of, Frederick Douglass saw the necessity for just such work as many of the industrial schools are doing in the South at the present time.

It is thus most pleasant to have the name of Douglass linked with the cause of industrial education. He believed not only in academic and college training but also in agricultural and mechanical education. Hampton, Tuskegee and many other institutions are now putting his teachings into practice.

While in England, Mrs. Stowe was made the object of much abuse by certain American newspapers, which accused her of obtaining British gold for her own use. Douglass, through the *North Star*, defended her vigorously against these charges, and the malicious were silenced. For reasons which he could not ascertain, the plans for the industrial school were never carried out, and, so far as is known, Mrs. Stowe never again took up the project with him.

The period that discovered to America and the world Harriet Beecher Stowe, the writer of the Abolition movement, also revealed John Brown, the man of action. What Mrs. Stowe felt and wrote, John Brown attempted to carry into effect.

Mr. Douglass's relations with this man were more intimate and continuous than his associations with the author of *Uncle Tom's Cabin*. No one could be a part of the anti-slavery movement between 1849 and 1859 without knowing and being more or less influenced by the personality of John Brown. His opposition to slavery was like that of no other person. It was scarcely a compliment to him to say that he was highly regarded by the Abolitionists; their feeling toward him had in it more of awe than admiration. At all times he would rather fight than discuss slavery. He began to dislike it when he was twelve years of age. His business, his family, his patriotism were all subordinated to the one dominant purpose of hurling himself, and everybody else who would follow him, against the system. He would judge and estimate all persons by what they thought and felt about slavery. John

Brown early formed an attachment for Douglass, being, in the beginning of his career, better known by the Negroes than by the white people. He mingled with them continually, hearing over and over again the stories, sometimes thrilling, sometimes pathetic, of a dawning desire for freedom, and soon learned to know almost everything about their condition. He became one of the most active conductors of the Underground Railway system. Douglass says that when the slaves mentioned the name of John Brown, they dropped their voices to a whisper, as if it were a sort of profanity to speak of him as they would of any one else.

In 1847, Douglass received an urgent invitation from Brown to visit him at his home in Springfield, Mass. He responded to the call as if to a command, and he has given the following account of that visit :—

" At the time to which I now refer, this man was a respectable merchant in a populous and thriving city, and our first place of meeting was at his store. A glance at the interior, as well as at the massive walls without, gave me the impression that the owner must be a man of considerable wealth. My welcome was all that I could have asked. Every member of the family, young and old, seemed glad to see me, and I was made at home in a very little while. I was, however, a little disappointed with the appearance of the house and its location. After seeing the fine store I was prepared to see a fine residence in an eligible locality, but this conclusion was completely dispelled by actual observation. It was a small wooden building on a back street, in a neighborhood chiefly occupied by laboring men and mechanics, respectable enough, to be sure, but not quite the place, I thought, one would look for the residence of a flourishing and successful merchant. Plain as was the outside of this man's house, the inside was plainer. There was an air of plainness about it which almost suggested destitution. My first meal passed under the misnomer of tea, though there was nothing about it resembling the usual significance of that term. It consisted of beef-soup, cabbage and potatoes—a meal such as a man might relish after following the plough all day or performing a forced march, of a dozen miles, over a rough road in frosty weather. Innocent of paint, veneering, varnish, or table-cloth, the table announced itself unmistakably of pine and of the plainest workmanship. There was no hired help visible. The mother, daughters and sons did the serving, and did it well. They were evidently used to it, and had no thought of any impropriety or degradation in being their own servants. Everything implied stern truth, solid purpose, and rigid economy. I was not long in company with the master of this house before I discovered that he was indeed the master of it, and was likely to become mine too, if I stayed long enough with him. He fulfilled St. Paul's idea of the head of the family. His wife believed in him, and his children obeyed him with reverence. Whenever he spoke, his words commanded earnest attention. His arguments, which I ventured at some points to oppose, seemed to convince all; his appeals touched all, and his will impressed all. Certainly I never felt myself in the presence of a stronger religious influence than while in this man's house.

"In person he was lean, strong, and sinewy, of the best New England mold, built for times of trouble, and fitted to grapple with the flintiest hardships. Clad in plain American woolen, shod

in boots of cowhide leather, and wearing a cravat of
the same substantial material, under six feet high,
less than 150 pounds in weight, aged about fifty
years, he presented a figure straight and symmet-
rical as a mountain pine. His bearing was singularly impressive. His head was not large but com-
pact and high. His hair was coarse, his strong
spare mouth, supported by a broad and prominent
chin. His eyes were bluish gray, and in conversation they were full of light and fire. When on the
street, he moved with a long springing race-horse
step, absorbed by his own reflections, neither seeking nor shunning observation. Such was the man
whose name I heard in whispers ; such was the
spirit of his house and family ; such was the house
in which he lived ; and such was Captain John
Brown, whose name has now passed into history, as
that of one of the most marked characters and
greatest heroes known to American fame.

"After the strong meal described, Brown cau-
tiously approached the subject which he wished to
bring to my attention ; for he seemed to apprehend
opposition to his views. He denounced slavery in
look and language fierce and bitter ; he thought
that slave-holders had forfeited their right to live,
that the slaves had a right to gain their liberty in
any way they could ; did not believe that moral
suasion would ever liberate a slave, or that political
action would abolish the system. He said that he
had long had a plan which could accomplish this
end, and he had invited me to his house to lay that
plan before me. He said that he had been for some
time looking for colored men to whom he could
safely reveal his secret, and at times he had almost
despaired of finding such men ; but that now he was
encouraged, because he saw heads of such rising in
all directions. He had observed my course at home
and abroad, and he wanted my coöperation. His

plan, as it then lay in his mind, had much to commend it. It did not, as some suppose, contemplate a general rising among the slaves, and a general slaughter of the slave-masters. An insurrection, he thought, would only defeat the object; but his plan did contemplate the creating of an armed force which should act in the very heart of the South. He was not averse to the shedding of blood, and thought the carrying of firearms would be a good rule for the colored people to adopt, as it would give them a sense of their manhood. No people, he said, could have self-respect, or be respected, who would not fight for their freedom. He called my attention to the map of the United States. 'These mountains,' he said, 'are the basis of my plan. God has given the strength of the hills to freedom; they were placed here for the emancipation of the Negro race; they are full of natural forts, where one man for defense will be equal to a hundred for attack; they are full also of good hiding places, where large numbers of brave men could be concealed, and baffle and elude pursuit for a long time. I know these mountains well, and could take a body of men into them and keep them there, in spite of all the efforts of Virginia to dislodge them. The true object to be sought is first of all to destroy the money value of slave property; and that can only be done by rendering such property insecure. My plan, then, is to take, at first, about twenty-five picked men, and begin on a small scale; supply them with arms and ammunition and post them in squads of fives on a line of twenty-five miles. The most persuasive and judicious of these shall go down to the fields from time to time, as opportunity offers, and induce the slaves to join them, seeking and selecting the most reckless and daring.' "

From this time on the relationship between these

two Abolitionists grew in intimacy and thereafter
Mr. Douglass's Rochester home was John Brown's
headquarters whenever he was in that part of the
country.

In the Springfield conference, he related his daring plans for the rescue of the slaves in Virginia.
Mr. Douglass readily saw how impracticable and
certain of disastrous failure this project must be,
but John Brown could never be made to understand
the peril of anything that he thought it was right
to do.   The possibility of failure seemed never to
enter into his calculations.   Mr. Douglass said to
him at Springfield :

"Suppose you succeed in running off a few
slaves, and thus impress the Virginia slave-holders
with a sense of insecurity in their slaves, the effect
will be only to make them sell their slaves further
South."

Whereupon Captain Brown replied :   "That will
be just what I want first to do ; then I would follow
them up.   If we could drive them out of one county
it would be a great gain ; it would weaken the
system throughout the state."

"But," said Douglass, "they would employ
blood-hounds to hunt you out of the mountains."

"That they might attempt," was the answer,
"but the chances are that we should whip them, and
when we should have whipped one squad, they
would be careful how they pursued us."

Thus would Brown confidently meet all possible
obstacles to his plan of invasion.   If any other man
had urged such views about freeing the slaves with

a force of less than one hundred men in the Virginia mountains, he would have been regarded as ridiculous ; but John Brown was an advocate of such intensity of faith and readiness to put himself in front of every danger, that it required no little courage to oppose him.

Mr. Douglass was evidently much affected by this interview. He had never before seen courage and self-confidence so imperious, or a determination to do something large and terrible so absolutely regardless of consequences. After this conference he admits that his own "utterances became more and more tinged by the color of this man's strong impressions," and his conviction grew "that slavery could only end in blood."

Brown's influence was easily traceable in Mr. Douglass's subsequent utterances, both in the *North Star* and in his public addresses. During the fight for free soil and free men in Kansas, after the Kansas-Nebraska bill became a law, Mr. Douglass probably did more than any one to supply the militant captain with money and munitions. The full size of Brown as a man was revealed in Kansas when the struggle between pro-slavery and anti-slavery forces became actual war. His daring deeds in going into the state of Missouri, bringing out dozens of slaves and conducting them safely to the North ; and his fight to keep Kansas free, could not have succeeded, but for the support of such men as Frederick Douglass. Captain Brown's experiences and adventures here strengthened his conviction that his plans for the invasion of Virginia were right. He had studied the mountain ranges and was satisfied in his own mind that the "Almighty had raised those mountains for the very purpose of aiding him to strike a death blow to slavery." The correspondence between the two men continued and the black leader was well informed of every movement. Brown never ceased to urge the ex-slave to join him, both in drawing up a constitution for future use and in the actual fighting. Indeed he had so exalted an opinion of Douglass's influence that it was believed the slaves in Virginia and other parts of the South would rise *en masse* if they knew that he was a part of this rescuing army.

About three weeks before the assault at Harper's Ferry, while John Brown was at Chambersburg, making final arrangements for his attack, he sent an urgent letter to Douglass, begging a conference. The latter knew that this was a perilous step and would certainly implicate him in the conspiracy when the crash of failure came ; yet he ignored the danger and responded. He speaks of this last visit to the old warrior, in part, as follows :

"I approached the old quarry with a good deal of caution, for John Brown was generally armed and regarded strangers with suspicion. He was there under ban of the government and heavy rewards were offered for his arrest for several offenses which he is said to have committed in Kansas. He was then passing under the name of John Smith. As I came near him, he regarded me rather suspiciously, but soon recognized me and received me cordially. He had in his hand, when I met him, fishing tackle, with which he had been fishing in a stream hard by, but I saw no fish. . . . The fishing was simply a disguise and was certainly a good one. He looked in every way like a man of the neighborhood and as much at home as any of the farmers around there. His hat was old and storm-beaten and his clothing was about the color of the quarry itself, his present dwelling-place. His face wore an anxious expression and he was much worn by exposure. I felt that I was on a dangerous mission and was as little desirous of discovery as himself."

Captains Brown, Kage, Shields Green and Mr. Douglass sat down to hold a council of war. The whole scheme of the proposed attack on Harper's Ferry and its capture was gone over without the slightest hint of possible failure. Douglass opposed the plan as wholly impracticable and fatal to all who might engage in it, but his arguments were promptly set aside by Brown. "He was not to be shaken by anything I could say, but treated my views respectfully. The debate continued during Saturday and Sunday. Brown was for striking a blow that would arouse the country, and I, for the policy of gradually and secretly drawing off the slaves to the mountains, as at first suggested by Brown himself." In the most fervent manner he urged Mr. Douglass to remain and take part in the fight. Just before the latter's departure, Brown threw his arm around the black man's neck and said: "Come with me, Douglass! I will defend you with my life. I want you for a special purpose. When I strike, the bees will begin to swarm, and I shall want you to help hive them."

The colored leader did not yield to the entreaty. Brown was incapable of seeing the death-trap that he had set for himself and his followers, and even if he could have seen it, he would not have been moved from his determination. A thousand men might have followed him and all have perished, but there could have been but one martyr, and that was himself. Mr. Douglass's death would have been a wanton sacrifice, because it would have meant nothing to the cause for which he had contributed so much of his life during the previous twenty-five years. He had a right to feel, as his subsequent career so abundantly proved, that his work was not finished. Of all the Abolitionists he was the only one who followed Brown to the last with advice, money, and other assistance. Because of what he had already done, and especially in this final conference at Chambersburg, he became amenable, as afterward appeared, to the charge of treason.

When the news was flashed over the land that John Brown was captured, the whole country was thrown into a state of great excitement. In Virginia the conclusion was quickly reached that the raid was backed by a wide-spread conspiracy and that men high in rank were implicated. Mr. Douglass at the time was addressing a large audience in Philadelphia. If he had any fear for himself, he did not show it. By lingering in the state so near the borders of slavery, where he had just been in conference with the head and front of the movement, he was in imminent danger. Brown's satchel, now in the hands of the officials, contained much of Douglass's correspondence. His friends were apprehensive and insisted upon his immediate flight from Philadelphia to his home in Rochester, and thence to Canada. As a matter of precaution, the following telegram was sent by his friend, Miss Assing, to Rochester:

"B. F. Blackall, Esq. :   Tell Lewis [Douglass's eldest son] to secure all the important papers in my desk."

All the newspapers stated that the Federal Government would spare no pains to run down and arrest every one who was in any way connected with the conspiracy. It would have been gratifying to those in power to have laid hands on Frederick Douglass and to have made an example of him, because he was regarded as one of the most offensive of those who fought slavery. That his friends were not unduly anxious for his safety is also proven by the following copy of a letter signed by the Governor of Virginia and sent to the President:

"(Confidential.)
"RICHMOND, VA., Nov. 13, 1859.
"*To His Excellency, James Buchanan, President of the United States, and to the Honorable Postmaster-General of the United States:*
"GENTLEMEN :—I have information such as has caused me, upon proper affidavits, to make requisition upon the Executive of Michigan for the delivery up of the person of Frederick Douglass, a Negro man, supposed now to be in Michigan, charged with murder, robbery, and inciting servile

insurrection in the State of Virginia. My agents for the arrest and reclamation of the person so charged, are Benjamin M. Morris and William N. Kelly. The latter has the requisition and will wait on you to the end of obtaining nominal authority as post-office agents. They need to be very secretive in this matter, and some pretext for traveling through this dangerous section for the execution of the laws in this behalf, and some protection against obtrusive, unruly, or lawless violence. If it be proper to do so, will the Postmaster-General be pleased to give to Mr. Kelly, for each of these men, a permit and authority to act as detectives for the Post-office Department, without pay, but to pass and repass without question, delay, or hindrance?

"Respectfully submitted,

"By your obedient servant,

"HENRY A. WISE."

Mr. Douglass was fairly pushed into Canada by his friends, but the determination to get hold of him was so strong that he was not regarded as safe even there. It would not have been impossible to effect some plan for arresting him so long as he remained so close to his native land. It was decided therefore that he must again go to England. He had already planned this trip, but the interesting events that culminated in the Harper's Ferry tragedy had delayed his departure.

Mr. Douglass stated publicly that he would be perfectly willing to be tried anywhere in New York State, but not elsewhere. He took passage for England from Quebec on the 12th day of November, 1859, and was everywhere received with the old-time cordiality. As he was fresh from the scenes and events that had stirred the English almost as much as the American people, he was in great demand for more complete information. He had occasion to deliver many addresses and it was everywhere manifest that he had lost none of his former prestige. The only setback he suffered was when he applied to George M. Dallas, the American Minister to the Court of St. James, for a passport for the purpose of visiting Paris. He was refused on the ground that he was not a citizen of the United States. His visit was cut short by the distressing news of the death of his beloved little daughter, Anna, the delight and life of his home, his absence having covered only five months. He returned to find the public temper toward him mollified by the swift happenings of a season which was marked by incessant change in the currents of popular feeling.

CHAPTER XI

FOREBODINGS OF THE CRISIS

THE ten years from 1850 to 1860 were years of cumulative danger to the republic and to the principles of liberty and democracy upon which it was founded. For the Negro these years contained more of perils than of hopes. The great historical events growing out of the conflict between the pro-slavery and the anti-slavery parties appeared to have set the goal of emancipation ever farther out of the range of practical possibilities. The Fugitive Slave Law seemed for a time to put an end to all hopes for further rescues from bondage. The Dred Scott Decision made every Negro, free or slave, an outlaw. The Kansas-Nebraska Bill threatened to render slavery so thoroughly national that Abolition would be forever impossible. Finally, the John Brown raid intensified, for a time, the hatred toward the colored people and their friends in the North.

But the success of the pro-slavery party was more apparent than real. It had gained merely a tactical victory. All the deeper currents of the nation's life were running counter to it. The raid excited the horror of the people. Even men active as Abolitionists denounced the acts of John Brown as both foolhardy and wicked. It seemed for a time that every one prominent in social and political life in

the North was anxious publicly to disavow all
share in what was described as a "reckless and
fanatical" deed. But John Brown's raid did not
bring the people of the North and South any nearer
together. On the contrary, it merely widened the
breach between them. The North might disclaim
this act, but the people of the opposite section were
not satisfied with these disclaimers. It seemed to
them that behind John Brown was a great conspiracy, and that the North, having determined to
make a nullity of the Fugitive Slave Law, was preparing to follow it up with still more daring efforts
to free the slaves at any cost.

Brown was hurried to the gallows, but not before
an effort was made to implicate in his crime men
who were prominent as Abolitionists. It has already been shown what steps were taken to capture
Frederick Douglass. A Congressional committee
was appointed for the purpose of thoroughly inves-
tigating the whole matter, but it accomplished nothing. It is scarcely necessary to say that the death
of Brown produced an impression throughout the
country quite as profound as that already created
by his "raid." The execution changed public
sentiment at once. People now began to feel and
to say that the cause, and not the man, had been on
trial when he was found guilty. The sentence of
.death passed by the Virginia court transformed
Brown in the eyes of a great many Northern people
into a martyr and shed a halo over the cause for
which he gave his life. Emerson compared the
gallows of Virginia to the cross in Palestine. All

through the North the people began to sing the
song that continued to be a favorite throughout the
Civil War :

"John Brown's body lies a-mouldering in the grave,
But his soul is marching on."

The panic-stricken friends of freedom recovered
their spirits and renewed their attacks with increased vigor.   To quote from Frederick Douglass :
"John Brown's defeat was already assuming the
form of victory, and his death was giving new life
and power to the principles of justice and liberty.
What he had lost by the sword, he had more than
gained by the truth."

The people of the South all through this controversy had shown themselves correct interpreters of
public sentiment.   They clearly saw that the execution of John Brown did not put an end to the cause
of Abolition.   This reckless act of invasion was
merely typical of what was possible on a scale of
vaster proportions.   In spite of everything that had
been achieved by law and by decisions of the
Supreme Court, the trend of feeling in the North
was steadily against slavery.   In spite of the Fugitive Slave Law and an increasing vigilance on the
part of masters and their agents, the Underground
Railroad continued its business of carrying slave-
property to free-soil.   Charles Sumner's speech in
the Senate added fresh interest to the cause of emancipation, and the continued popularity of *Uncle
Tom's Cabin* was ominous.   All these disquieting circumstances boded some dreadful issue of the contro-

versy. The drift of events is best exhibited in the effects of the Kansas-Nebraska Bill, already referred to. When this bill became a law, as the consummation of the policy of Senator Stephen A. Douglas of Illinois, the physical boundary between slavery and freedom, which many had supposed to be fixed as firmly as the Declaration of Independence, was swept away and all the vast empire of the west and northwest became disputed ground between the forces of free-soil and slavery. This act gave effect to the new doctrines of state sovereignty. Whatever may have been its purpose, the result was to unite the forces of the North and South, pitting the two sections against each other in a struggle for supremacy in the new territory. In outward appearance this new doctrine was peaceful and sound, but it held dreadful possibilities. Expressed plainly, the Kansas-Nebraska Law said that whether these new states should be free or slave-states must be left to the people. It was for them to vote slavery "up" or "down." In other words, if the majority of the people of these territories voted for slavery, it became, by their sovereign will, an institution fixed and irrevocable ; if not, slavery was forever to be shut out, just as it was excluded from Massachusetts.

The intensity of public interest in and anxiety for the future status of these new states was shown in the instant rush into Kansas from New England of colonists favorable to the cause of free soil, and from the South of colonists favorable to the cause of slavery. Each side appreciated how momentous was the issue. The people of Missouri and other neighboring slave-states knew that it would be difficult, with a free-state adjoining them to hold their bond-servants in security. The people of New England and other Northern states understood that the political supremacy of the free-states would be forever lost if the South were able to make slave-ground out of the western territory.

It was an exciting contest and soon proved a gory one. Men from both sections were expecting that the struggle would be attended with bloodshed and they went out armed and prepared for it. Kansas, "bleeding Kansas," was a battle-ground. It is not necessary here to recount the sanguinary incidents between the cohorts of emancipation and slavery in this neutral territory. Suffice it to say that in the end the cause of freesoil triumphed and the contest was merely preliminary to a vaster conflict of which it was a premonitory token.

Before and during these stormy events in Kansas, there was in progress an intellectual conflict which was destined to have a more serious ending. This was the historic debates between Abraham Lincoln and Stephen A. Douglas, both of Illinois. More clearly, perhaps than any other one event, this round of speeches formulated the issue which divided the American people politically on the question of slavery. It revealed to the nation a man who gave to them, for the first time, a frank and clear-cut definition of the issue to which it had been brought by the struggle. Lincoln said in effect: "The Union cannot long endure,

half-slave and half-free.   It must be all one or all
the other, and the public mind can find no resting-
place but in the ultimate extinction of slavery.''

Of course, this was but a reiteration of what had
been repeatedly said by the Abolitionists during the
past twenty-five years, but coming now at a time
when there was an unconscious groping of the popular mind toward a definite issue for public action,
these clear words seemed to be charged with meaning of tremendous importance.   The people of the
whole country listened to these Illinois debaters
with an interest that seemed prescient of coming
events.   As the debate progressed, Mr. Lincoln
seemed to rise visibly and steadily from the western
provincial obscurity he had lived in up to this
point, to a prominence in which he appeared for the
time to overshadow every one else who had spoken
on the great question.   The immediate prize to be
won in the debate was a seat in the United States
Senate ; but before its close, this sank into insignifi-
cance, and the presidency of the United States, the
preservation of the Union, and the fate of slavery,
had become the stakes of the contest.

The issues in the coming election already began
to shape themselves along the lines enunciated by
Mr. Lincoln and Senator Douglas.   In due time new
political alignments were completed as follows :

(1)   The pro-slavery and Union Democrats of the
North stood for state sovereignty, or the right of
the people of a territory to admit or bar slavery as
they saw fit.   Senator Douglas was the unquestioned
leader of this wing of the Democratic party.

(2)   The pro-slavery people of the South stood for the bold declaration that the Constitution of its own force gave the right to carry slaves into any territory of the United States and to hold them there, with or without the consent of the people of the territory.   John C. Breckinridge was the leader of the Southern wing of the Democracy.

(3)   Abraham Lincoln was chosen to bear the standard of all the people who were opposed to both varieties of pro-slavery Democrats.   His doctrine was that the Federal Government had the right to exclude slavery from the territories of the United States, and that this right and power ought to be exercised to keep slavery within the confines of the then existing slave-states.

It will be seen that emancipation was not an issue on the surface of these declarations of principles. The whole question appeared to be : Shall slavery have the power of expansion ?   If this power were denied, could there be any doubt as to what must ultimately follow ?   If the people feared the power of slavery to such an extent that they would or could keep it within a restricted territory, would not this principle, when successful, be the first step toward its extirpation ?   The South more clearly than the North understood that the triumph of Mr. Lincoln would settle nothing.   Beneath these platform utterances was the unwritten issue :   Slavery's security of expansion, or its "ultimate extinction." If the South won in the impending contest, not only would slavery be secured by the right of its extension into the undivided territory west of the Mississippi, but political supremacy might pass permanently from the free-states.

The position of Stephen A. Douglas and his followers was rather anomalous. As the Senator at one time expressed it, he cared not whether the question of extending slavery into the territories was "voted up or voted down"; with him the important thing seemed to be that the people of the new territory should have the opportunity to vote on the question and decide for themselves the character of their institutions.

Mr. Lincoln's followers represented nearly everything left of the spirit that was glorified in the Declaration of Independence and the Revolution of 1776. Those who would preserve the soil of the West free; those who would not only restrict, but abolish slavery altogether; and those who would endow the Negro with all the proclaimed natural rights of man, supported Lincoln.

The situation was complicated as well as perilous. Heretofore, when the only question between the North and the South was slavery or the right to hold slaves, the people of the North were governed as much by their racial prejudices as the Southern people. Now, however, when other questions, incidental to slavery, as, for instance, the future political supremacy, were involved with the main issue, many men and women, who had heretofore been indifferent or silent, became actively concerned, and felt impelled to take a definite stand. There seems never to have been any possibility of the North and South going to war on account of Negro slavery. It was at this time clear from the whole history of the controversy that if the Negro were ever to be free, his freedom must come as a consequence and not as the cause of a conflict.

Probably no man in public life saw this more clearly than Frederick Douglass. He was just as much a part of the history in the process of making, all about him, as he was permitted to be. He had his say and was heard. He understood the trend of events and he was not swept away by merely transitory incidents. In all this controversy he sought constantly, in his speeches, and in his paper, *Douglass's Monthly*, to lift into clear view the paramount issue. The following extract from one of his speeches indicates the clearness with which he saw, and the definiteness with which he was able to foreshadow the events of the next succeeding years :

"The only choice left to this nation is abolition or destruction. You must abolish slavery or abandon the Union. It is plain that there can never be any union between the North and South, while the South values slavery more than nationality. A union of interests is essential to a union of ideas and without this union of ideas, the outer form of union will be but as a rope of sand."

During the Illinois debates, Frederick Douglass did all he could to enforce the arguments and extend the steadily growing influence of Mr. Lincoln. He made an extensive campaign in Michigan, Wisconsin, and Iowa. His audiences were large and interested, being eager to hear any man who could speak with the distinction, clearness, and frankness that characterized his public utterances. He had grown in esteem and the mob-spirit that tried to harass him in his earlier campaigns in the West had given way before his increasing influence and popularity. Once in Illinois he met Senator Douglas, who treated him with marked courtesy.

In 1854, Frederick Douglass delivered an address in Chicago which ranks as one of his greatest orations. Frederick May Holland, who has already been referred to as the author of a valuable biography of the Negro leader, has given to the public, for the first time, I believe, nearly all of this interesting speech. The reproduction of at least a part of it seems essential to this chapter :

"The Constitution knows no man by the color of his skin. The men who made it were too noble for any such limitation of humanity and human rights. The term ' white' is a modern term in the legislation of this country. It was never used in the better days of our republic, but has sprung up within the period of our national degeneracy.

"I am here simply as an American citizen, having a stake in the weal or woe of the nation in common with other citizens. I am not here as the agent of any sect or party. Parties are too politic and sects are too sectarian, to select one of my odious class and of my radical opinions, at this important time and place, to represent them. Nevertheless, I do not stand alone here. There are noble-minded men in Illinois who are neither ashamed of their cause nor their company. Some of them are here to-night, and I expect to meet them in every part of the state where I may travel.

"But, I pray, hold no man or party responsible

for my words, for I am no man's agent, and I am no
party's agent. . . . It is alleged that I came
here in this state to insult Senator Douglas. Among
gentlemen that is only an insult that is intended to
be such, and I disavow all such intention. I am
here precisely as I was in this state one year ago—
with no other change in my relations to you, or the
great question of human freedom, than time and
circumstances have brought about. I shall deal
with the same subject with the same spirit now as
then, approving such men and such measures as
look to the security of liberty in the land and with
my whole heart condemning such men and measures
as serve to subvert or endanger it. If Hon. S. A.
Douglas, your beloved and highly gifted senator,
has designedly or through mistaken notions of public policy, ranged himself on the side of oppressors,
and the deadliest enemies of liberty, I know of no
reason, either in this world or in any other world,
which should prevent me or any one else, from
thinking so or saying so.

" The people in whose cause I came here to-night
are not among those whose right to regulate their
own domestic concerns is so feelingly, and earnestly,
and eloquently contended for in certain quarters.
They have no Stephen A. Douglas, no General Cass,
to contend at North Market Hall for their popular
sovereignty. They have no national purse, no
offices, no reputation with which to corrupt Congress, or to tempt men, mighty in eloquence and
influence into their service. Oh, no ! They have
nothing to commend them, but their unadorned
humanity. They are human—that's all—only
human. Nature owns them as human ; but men
own them as property, and only as property. Every
right of human nature, as such, is denied them ;
they are dumb in their chains. To utter one groan
or scream for freedom in the presence of the

Southern advocate of popular sovereignty, is to bring down the frightful lash upon their quivering flesh. I know this suffering people; I am acquainted with their sorrows; I am one with them in experience; I have felt the lash of the slave driver, and stand up here with all the bitter recollections of its horrors vividly upon me.

"There are special reasons why I should speak and speak freely. The right of speech is a very precious one. I understand that Mr. Douglas regards himself as the most abused man in the United States; and that the greatest outrage ever committed upon him was in the case in which your indignation raised your voices so high that he could not be heard. No personal violence, as I understand, was offered him. It seems to have been a trial of vocal powers between the individual and the multitude; and as might have been expected, the voice of one man was not equal in volume to the voices of five thousand. I do not mention this circumstance to approve it; I do not approve it. I am for free speech, as well as free men and free soil; but how ineffably insignificant is this wrong done in a single instance, compared to the stupendous iniquity perpetrated against more than three millions of the American people, who are struck dumb by the very men in whose cause Mr. Senator Douglas was here to plead! While I would not approve the silencing of Mr. Douglas, may we not hope that this slight abridgment of his rights, may lead him to respect in some degree the rights of other men, as good in the eye of Heaven as himself?

"Let us now consider the great question of the age, the only great national question which seriously agitates the public mind at this hour. It is called the vexed question, and excites alarm in every quarter of the country.

"The proposition to repeal the Missouri Com-

promise, was a stunning one. It fell upon the
nation like a bolt from a cloudless sky. The thing
was too startling for belief. You believed in the
South and you believed in the North ; and you
knew that the repeal of the Missouri Compromise
was a breach of honor ; and therefore, you said that
the thing could not be done. Besides both parties
had pledged themselves directly, positively, and
solemnly against reopening in Congress the agitation on the subject of slavery ; and the President
himself had declared his intention to maintain the
national quiet. Upon these assurances you rested
and rested fatally. But you should have learned
long ago that men do not gather grapes of thorns or
figs of thistles. It is folly to put faith in men
who have broken faith with God. When a man
has brought himself to enslave a child of God, t
put fetters on his brother, he has qualified himsel
to disregard the most sacred of compacts ; beneath
the sky there is nothing more sacred than man, and
nothing can be properly respected when manhood
is despised and trampled upon.

" It is said that slavery is the creature of positive
law, and that it can only exist where it is sustained
by positive law—that neither in Kansas nor Nebraska is there any law establishing slavery, and
that therefore, the moment a slaveholder carries his
slaves into these territories, he is free and restored
to the rights of human nature. This is the ground
taken by General Cass. He contended for it in the
North Market Hall, with much eloquence and skill.
I thought, while I was hearing him on this point,
that slaveholders would not be likely to thank him
for the argument. It is not true that slavery cannot exist without being established by positive law.
The instance cannot be shown where a law was ever
made establishing slavery, where the relation of
master and slave did not previously exist. The law

is always an after-coming consideration. Wicked men first overpower and subdue their fellow men to slavery, and then call in the law to sanction the deed. Even in the slave states of America, slavery has never been established by law. It was not established under the colonial charters of the original states, nor the Constitution of the United States. It is now and has always been a system of lawless violence. On this proposition I hold myself ready and willing to meet any defender of the Nebraska bill. I would not hesitate to meet even the author of that bill himself.

"He says he wants no broad, black line across this continent. Such a line is odious, and begets unkind feelings between the citizens of a common country. Now, fellow citizens, why is the line of thirty-six degrees, thirty minutes, a broad black line? What is it that entitles it to be called a black line? It is the fashion to call whatever is odious in this country, black. You call the devil black, and he may be; but what is there in the line of thirty-six degrees, thirty minutes, which makes it blacker than the line which separates Illinois from Missouri or Michigan from Indiana? I can see nothing in the line itself which should make it black or odious. It is a line, that's all. It is black, black and odious, not because it is a line, but because of the things it separates. If it keep asunder what God has joined together, or separate what God intended should be fused, then it may be called an odious line, a black line; but if, on the other hand, it marks only a distinction natural and eternal, a distinction fixed in the nature of things by the eternal God, then I say, withered be the arm and blasted be the hand that would blot it out.

"Nothing could be further from the truth, then, to say that popular sovereignty is accorded to the people who may settle the territories of Kansas and

Nebraska. The three great cardinal powers of government are the executive, legislative and judicial.
Are these powers sacred to the people of Kansas and
Nebraska? You know they are not. That bill
places the people of that territory, as completely
under the powers of the Federal government as
Canada is under British rule. By this Kansas-Nebraska Bill, the Federal government has the substance of all governing power, while the people
have the shadow. The judicial power of the territories is not from the people of the territories, who
are so bathed in the sunlight of popular sovereignty by stump eloquence, but from the Federal government. The executive power of the territories
derives its existence, not from the overflowing
fountain of popular sovereignty, but from the Federal government. The secretaries of the territories
are not appointed by the sovereign people of the
territories, but are appointed independent of popular sovereignty.

"But is there nothing in this bill that justifies the
supposition that it contains the principle of popular
sovereignty? No, not one word. Even the territorial councils, elected, not by the people of the
territory, but only by certain descriptions of people,
are subject to a double veto power, vested, first in
the governor, whom they did not elect, and second
in the President of the United States. The only
shadow of popular sovereignty is the power given
to the people of the territories by this bill to have,
hold, buy, and sell human beings. The sovereign
right to make slaves of their fellow-men, if they
choose, is the only sovereignty that the bill se-
cures.

"But it may be said that Congress has the right
to allow the people of the territories to hold slaves.
The answer is, that Congress is made up of men, and
possesses only the rights of men; and unless it can

be shown that some men have a right to hold their fellow-men as property, Congress has no such right. There is not a man within the sound of my voice, who has not as good a right to enslave a brother man, as Congress has. This will not be denied, even by slave-holders.

"Error may be new, or it may be old, since it is founded in a misapprehension of what truth is. It has its beginnings; and its endings. But not so truth. Truth is eternal. Like the great God, from whose throne it emanates, it is from everlasting to everlasting, and can never pass away. Such a truth is man's right to freedom. He was born with it. It was his before he comprehended it. The title deed to it was written by the Almighty on His heart; and the record of it is in the bosom of the Eternal; and never can Stephen A. Douglas efface it, unless he can tear from the great heart of God this truth; and this mighty government of ours will never be at peace with God, unless it shall practically and universally embrace this great truth as the fountain of all its institutions, and the rule of its entire administration. . . .

"Now, gentlemen—I have done. I have no fear for the ultimate triumph of free principles in this country. The signs of the times are propitious. Victories have been won by slavery; but they have never been won against the onward march of anti-slavery principles. The progress of these principles has been constant, steady, strong and certain. Every victory won by slavery has had the effect to fling our principles more widely and favorably among the people. The annexation of Texas, the Florida war, the war with Mexico, the Compromise Measures, and the repeal of the Missouri Compromise, have all signally vindicated the wisdom of the great God, who has promised to over-ride the wickedness of men for His own glory—to confound the

wisdom of the crafty and bring to naught the
counsels of the ungodly.''

The nomination, in 1860, of Mr. Lincoln by the
Republican party, of Stephen A. Douglas by the
Northern Democracy, and of John C. Breckinridge
by the Southern Democracy, brought on that memorable campaign which preceded the final collision
between the North and the South.

''Into the fight,'' says Frederick Douglass, '' I
threw myself, with a firm faith and more ardent
hope than ever before, and what I could do by pen
and voice was done with a will.   The most memorable feature of the canvass, was that it was prosecuted under the shadow of a threat.''

The followers of Breckinridge had boldly announced that if they were defeated, they would not
submit to the rule of Abraham Lincoln, but would
proceed to take the slave-states out of the Union.
This threat of secession was not a new one, but,
coming, as it did, after the failure to make Kansas
a slave-state, it created something like a panic in
the North.   It served for the moment to divert public opinion from political issues to the very grave
possibility of national disruption.

In spite of this openly declared purpose on the
part of the Southern Democracy, the Republican
party, made up in part of Whigs, the old '' Liberty ''
and '' Free Soil '' parties, and a large number of the
Abolitionists, elected Abraham Lincoln as President of the United States.

It was a signal victory, but it brought with it

little comfort, more anxiety, and many grave responsibilities. The people of the North were desirous of peace, and so were the people of the South ; but to agree on terms was difficult. While the North, in the presence of a great triumph was worried and anxious, the South openly and resolutely began to prepare for secession and war. When, in the early part of the presidential canvass, the South notified the nation what it would do in case of defeat, the threat was generally accepted as mere bluster. No sooner was the result of the election known than there began to accumulate evidence which indicated that this threat was backed by a very positive determination to carry it out. The states south of the Ohio prepared to leave the Union in orderly procession, as if secession were a familiar and undisputed custom. The administration, under President Buchanan, saw the process of national dismemberment go on and merely declared that it could find no power in the Constitution to coerce a state. In the presence of this unchallenged dissolution of the Union, the North fairly quaked with fear. An opinion which favored almost any kind of compromise that would save the country from the horrors of civil war gained wide influence. While the South was confident of its strength to maintain itself in its present course, it did finally and with apparent reluctance, indicate a few of the conditions on which it would agree to remain in the Union. Among these were the following :

Each Northern state, through its legislature or in convention assembled, should repeal all laws which tended to impair the constitutional rights of the South.

It should pass laws for the easy and prompt execution of the Fugitive Slave Law.

Laws should be passed imposing penalties on all malefactors, who should hereafter encourage the escape of fugitive slaves.

Laws should be passed declaring and protecting the rights of slave-holders to travel and sojourn in Northern states, accompanied by their slaves.

Every state should instruct its representatives and senators in Congress to repeal the law prohibiting the sale of slaves in the District of Columbia, and pass laws sufficient for the full protection of slave property in the territories of the Union.

These conditions, offered by the South, could not be heartily approved by the people who had just won such a decided victory on an issue involving these very conditions. Yet there was a decided wave of popular feeling in favor of peace upon any terms. Men of positive convictions and eminent in all walks of life—William H. Seward, H. B. Anthony, and Joshua R. Giddings—were now ready to purchase it at almost any price. The enthusiasm for emancipation and free-soil that had so stirred the North during the presidential campaign, began to wane, and so serious a reaction set in that, for a time, it seemed likely to make barren the Republican victory. Not only so, but the mob-spirit of the '30's was reawakened, and Wendell Phillips, William Lloyd Garrison, Frederick Douglass, and their supporters were assaulted on the streets of

Boston.   The people of the North refused to tolerate
further agitation against slavery, and were desirous,
in every possible way, to appease the anger of the
other section.   Committees were appointed to confer with representatives of the South for the purpose of obtaining a better understanding of their
grievances.

Thus, while the North seemed anxious to recede
from almost every position it had won in the recent
election, the South was too confident of its strength
and of the justice of its cause to give much encouragement to the messengers of peace from the other
side.   The situation just described is an interesting
illustration of the characteristic difference between
the people of the North and the South on every
question in which the Negro was involved.   The
North was very reluctant to make slavery an issue ;
the South was always willing to be challenged on
that issue.   In the North, the Negro was a problem ;
in the South, he was property.   It is always easier
to deal with property than to deal with a problem.
For example : In the Kansas and Nebraska controversy, the South wanted territory for slave property,
and the North wanted it as an outlet for New England emigrants.   If the only question involved had
been to save the black man from further enslavement, the South would very possibly have won.   In
other words, interest in the Negro as a human being,
deserving a chance to live and grow, was not the
only and perhaps not the immediate motive behind
the men who fought for free-soil.   Slavery was fundamental and therefore, from the point of view of

party politics, a dangerous issue. There were men in the North and also in the South who for conscience' sake would like to have seen the Negro emancipated, but the nation was not yet ready for it. It involved consequences so vast and so far-reaching that the mass of the people hesitated and were afraid. In the state of the country at that time, the political parties of the North were anxious to make it appear to the South that they had little or no concern about the Negro, either as a freeman or a slave. Their great anxiety was to save the Union. Mr. Lincoln was politically wise enough to state that his administration was in no way committed to emancipation or to anything else that looked to a change in the condition of the Negro people. He would save the Union with or without slavery. He would very likely have found himself lacking in national confidence or support, had he failed to make this declaration.

When the South decided to go out of the Union, it furnished the President with the one thing needed and that was a platform on which he could unite the people of the North. When his policy was distinctly the preservation of the government, Free Soil Democrats, Abolitionists, and all believers in an undivided country, came at his call. All sentiment in favor of emancipation served only to swell the passionate appeal to the national feeling to save the Union. The Negro's only hope was that, in this threatened conflict to preserve intact the federation of the states, his emancipation might become an inevitable necessity.

Frederick Douglass expressed this hope in the following language : " I confess to a feeling allied to satisfaction at the prospect of a conflict between the North and South. Standing outside of the pale of American humanity, denied citizenship, unable to call this land of my birth my country, and adjudged by the Supreme Court to have no rights which a white man was bound to respect, and longing for the end of bondage for my people, I was ready for any political upheaval that would bring about an end to the existing condition of things."

CHAPTER XII

DOUGLASS'S SERVICES IN THE CIVIL WAR

THE Civil War came on as the direct result of the irreconcilable sentiments of the North and the South on the question of slavery and the political conflicts already mentioned. On the part of the South, it was begun and waged with marvelous courage and intelligence to preserve slavery and to establish the right of secession; and on the part of the North, to preserve the Union, and the right of Congress to deal with slavery as a national issue. During the first two years of the war, the Federal Government did and said everything possible to convince the people of the South that the new Republican party had no intention, near or remote, of interfering with slavery. At the very beginning of hostilities, William H. Seward, Secretary of State, declared to the nations of the world that "terminate however it might, the status of no class of people of the United States would be changed by the Rebellion; that the slaves would be slaves still and that the masters would be masters still." This policy was consistently followed in the field of military operations, as well as in the civil administration of the government.

General McClellan, Commander-in-Chief of the Union Army, early in the conflict, warned the slaves that "if any attempt was made by them to gain their freedom, it would be suppressed by an iron hand." In many places Union soldiers were detailed to guard the plantations of Southern slave-owners. In parts of the South in possession of the Federal army, black fugitives, who had found their way into the lines, were returned to their masters by order of the commanding officers. The following is a copy of the proclamation issued by General T. W. Sherman at Port Royal in November, 1861:

"In obedience to the order of the President of these United States of America, I have landed on your shores with a small force of national troops. The dictates of duty which, under the Constitution, I owe to a great sovereign state, and to a proud and hospitable people, among whom I have passed some of the pleasantest days of my life, prompt me to proclaim that we have come among you with no feelings of personal animosity ; no desire to harm your citizens, destroy your property or interfere with your lawful rights or your social and local institutions beyond what the cause herein briefly attended to, may render unavoidable."

This proclamation is typical of those issued by General John A. Dix, General Burnside, and other Union commanders in different parts of the South. All this was in perfect accord with President Lincoln's oft-repeated declaration, that his paramount object was to save the Union and not to save or destroy slavery. "If I could save the Union, without freeing the slaves, I would do it," said he. "If I could do it by freeing some and leaving others alone, I would also do that. What I do about

slavery and the colored race, I do because I believe
it helps to save the Union, and what I forbear, I forbear because I do not believe it would
help to save the Union. . . . I have here
stated my purpose according to my views of official
duty, and I intend no modification of my oft-ex-
pressed wish that all men everywhere could be
free.''

This declaration of President Lincoln was reflected
in every act of every agency of his administration.
It gave the cause of the Union a spirit and character wholly apart from the cause of Emancipation.
It is needless to say that this attitude of the Federal
government was not pleasing to the Abolitionists,
and the colored people in the free-states were much
disheartened. Horace Greeley voiced the impatience of this element when, in a letter of complaint
to the President, he said : '' Every hour of defense
of slavery is an hour of added and deepened peril to
the Union ;'' and asked, '' if the seeming subserv-
iency of your policy to the slave-holding, slavery-
upholding interests, is not the perplexity and the
despair of statesmen of all parties ? ''

In spite of the seeming pro-slavery policy of the
national administration, Frederick Douglass was
earnestly consecrating every energy of his being to
the President's support. He was wise enough to
understand that if Lincoln in the beginning, had
stated his policy to be, not only to save the Union,
but also to free the slaves, all would have been lost.
While other Abolitionists were impatient and
doubtful of Mr. Lincoln's course, Douglass declared

himself convinced that the war, even though it be called a "white man's war," was nevertheless the beginning of the end of the nation's great evil. He still believed, and so declared in his public speeches, that "the mission of the war was the liberation of the slaves as well as the salvation of the Union." "I reproached the North," he said, "that they fought with one hand, while they might strike more effectively with two ; that they fought with the soft white hand, while they kept the black iron hand chained and helpless behind them ; that they fought the effect, while they protected the cause ; and said that the Union cause would never prosper until the war assumed an anti-slavery attitude and the Negro was enlisted on the side of the Union."

It required time and the cumulation of events to bring about a state of feeling that would tolerate the suggestion of using colored men in the Union army. Mr. Douglass more than any other one man, helped to bring about this change. It finally became evident that if the Negroes were good enough to be employed in the Confederate ranks, as laborers, they ought to be good enough for like service in the Union lines. In the South, thousands of Negroes were at home, protecting the families of the men who fought in the field, and raising crops as subsistence for the Confederate soldiers and their wives and children ; thousands more were employed in building fortifications, digging trenches, and doing work which otherwise would have had to be done by the men who were needed at the front ; and, anomalous as it may seem, a few colored men, it is said, were actually enrolled and enlisted as soldiers in the Confederate army, fighting for their own continued enslavement. The following account was published of a procession of Southern troops in New Orleans in November, 1861 : "Over 28,000 troops were reviewed by Governor Moore, Major-General Scoville, and Brigadier-General Ruggles. The line was over seven miles long. One regiment comprised 1,400 free colored men." [1]

It was expedient that the government, in enlisting Negroes, should move with extreme caution, not only to prevent undue irritation of Southern feeling, but what was more serious, to avoid offending the deep-seated prejudice against colored people in the North. It was rightly believed that thousands of white men would refuse to enlist if Negroes were to serve in the army on an even footing with them. Then again, the border states, which were more or less favorable to the Union, would be irrevocably lost to it. In due time, however, all objections were swept aside by the pressure of black men themselves and by the needs of the government.

Correspondents from the seat of war began to tell how a Negro regiment at Port Royal, and certain Negro companies in Louisiana had conducted themselves in battles for the Union, and these accounts dispelled all doubts as to their fighting capacity. The early orders by the government to return all fugitive slaves to their masters were no longer issued. General Benjamin F. Butler announced that

[1] Greeley : *The American Conflict*, Vol. II, p. 522.

he would regard all fugitive slaves, finding their way into his lines, as "contraband of war." Colored men were being employed extensively as laborers in building fortifications, roads, entrenchments, and as cooks and other necessary workers in support of the army. Their usefulness was so manifest that prejudice gradually gave way to a more kindly feeling of respect. When the white Union troops thus recognized the services, kindness, and faithfulness of these black men, they were soon willing to tolerate them in their ranks.

Mr. Douglass eagerly assisted in the formation of the first regularly organized regiments of United States colored troops, the Fifty-fourth and Fifty-fifth Massachusetts Infantry Volunteers. Governor Andrew, an ardent Abolitionist, was justly proud of this important experiment, and said : "I stand or fall as a man and a magistrate with the rise or fall in the history of the Fifty-fourth Massachusetts." Colonel Robert Gould Shaw, who commanded the regiment, was one of the noblest sons of this freedom-loving commonwealth.

In order to satisfy any lingering misgivings that the people might have concerning this step by the government, it was stated that the regiments to be enlisted would not be put into active service, being held for garrison duty in districts where yellow fever was prevalent. It was also decided not to give them the same pay as that allowed to the white troops. Negro soldiers were to receive only seven dollars per month. At Fort Wagner the Fifty-fourth Massachusetts soon had an opportunity to show what it could do.   The conduct of the men was so brave that it put an end to all further opposition to Negro enlistment.   These colored soldiers refused to accept any reward for their services until the government was ready to pay them what it gave to other troops.   They continued to serve and fight for the honor of the flag and the preservation of the Union until in the following year the country voted full pay to its black defenders.   The Massachusetts volunteers, and all Negro regiments subsequently enlisted, were officered by white men.

Mr. Douglass rendered valuable aid in getting together enough fit men for the two New England regiments.   His two sons, Lewis H. and Charles R. Douglass, who are still living in Washington and are honored citizens, were among the first to enlist. Their father's influence with the colored people of the country was so great that his services were almost indispensable.   He was distressed by the restrictions placed on these soldiers, but said : " While I, of course, was deeply pained and saddened by the estimate thus put upon my race, and grieved at the slowness of heart which marked the conduct of the loyal government, I was not discouraged, and urged every man who could enlist to get an eagle on his button, a musket on his shoulder, and the star and spangle over his head."   On March 2, 1863, he issued an appeal to his people which was in part as follows :

" Men of Color, To Arms.
" When first the rebel cannon shattered the walls of Sumter and drove away its starving garrison, I

predicted that the war then and there inaugurated would not be fought out entirely by white men. Every month's experience during these dreary years has confirmed that opinion. I have implored the imperiled nation to unchain against her foes her powerful black hand. Slowly and reluctantly that appeal is beginning to be heeded. Stop not now to .complain that it was not heeded sooner. That it should not, may or may not have been best. This is not the time to discuss that question. Leave it to the future. When the war is over, the country saved, peace established, and the black man's rights are secured, as they will be, history with an impartial hand will dispose of that and sundry other questions. Action! action! not criticism, is the plain duty of this hour. Words are now useful only as they stimulate to blows. The office of speech now is only to point out when, where and how to strike to the best advantage. From East to West, from North to South, the sky is written all over, 'Now or Never.' Liberty won only by white men will lose half its lustre. 'Who would be free, must themselves strike the blow.' 'Better, even to die free, than to live slaves.' This is the sentiment of every brave colored man amongst us. There are weak and cowardly men in all races. We have them amongst us. They tell you this is a 'white man's war'; that you will 'be no better off after the war, than you were before the war'; that the 'getting of you into the army is to sacrifice you on the first opportunity.' Believe them not. Cowards themselves, they do not wish to have their cowardice shamed by your example. Leave them to their timidity, or to whatever motive may hold them back. I have not thought lightly of the words I am now addressing to you. The counsel I give comes of close observation of the great struggle now in progress, and of the deep convic-

tion that this is your hour and mine.   In good earnest, then, and after the best deliberation, I now, for
the first time during this war, feel at liberty to call
and counsel you to arms.   By every consideration
which binds you to your enslaved fellow countrymen, and to the peace and welfare of your country;
by every aspiration which you cherish for the freedom and equality of yourselves and your children;
by all the ties of blood and identity which make us
one with the brave black men now fighting our
battles in Louisiana and in South Carolina, I urge
you to fly to arms, and smite with death the power
that would bury the government and your liberty
in the same hopeless grave.   I wish I could tell
you that the state of New York calls you to this
high honor.   For the moment her constituted authorities are silent on the subject.   They will speak
by and by, and doubtless on the right side, but we
are not compelled to wait for her.   We can get at
the throat of treason and slavery through the state
of Massachusetts.   She was first in the War of Independence ; first to break the chains of her slaves ;
first to make the black man equal before the law ;
first to admit colored children to her common
schools ; and she was first to answer with her blood
the alarm-cry of the nation, when its capital was
menaced by rebels.   You know her patriotic governor, and you know Charles Sumner.   I need not
add more.

" Massachusetts now welcomes you to arms as soldiers.   She has but a small colored population from
which to recruit.   She has full leave of the general
government to send one regiment to the war, and
she has undertaken to do it.   Go quickly and help fill
up the first colored regiment from the North.   I am
authorized to assure you that you will receive the
same wages, the same rations, the same equipments,
the same protection, the same treatment, and the

same bounty, secured to white soldiers.   You will
be led by able and skilful officers, men who will
take special pride in your efficiency and success.
They will be quick to accord to you all the honor
you shall merit by your valor, and to see that your
rights and feelings are respected by other soldiers.
I have assured myself on these points.   More than
twenty years of unswerving devotion to our common cause may give me some humble claim to be
trusted at this momentous crisis.   I will not argue.
To do so implies hesitation and doubt, and you do
not hesitate ; you do not doubt.   The day dawns.
The morning star is bright upon the horizon.   The
iron gate of our prison stands half open.   One
gallant rush from the North will fling it wide open,
while four millions of our brothers and sisters shall
march out into liberty.

" The chance is now given you to end in a day the
bondage of centuries and to rise in one bound from
social degradation to the place of common equality
with all other varieties of men.   Remember Den-
mark Vesey, of Charleston ; remember Shields
Green, and Copeland, who followed noble John
Brown, and fell as glorious martyrs for the cause of
the slave.   Remember that in a contest with oppression, the Almighty has no attribute which can take
sides with the oppressors.   The case is before you.
This is our golden opportunity.   Let us accept it
and forever wipe out the dark reproaches unspar-
ingly hurled against us by our enemies.   Let us win
for ourselves the gratitude of our country, and the
best blessings of our posterity through all time.
The nucleus of this first regiment is now in camp at
Readville, a short distance from Boston.   I will undertake to forward to Boston all persons adjudged
fit to be mustered into the regiment, who shall apply to me at once, or at any time within the next
two weeks."

The immediate effect of the enlistment of colored troops in the Union army was to call forth a feeling of resentment on the part of the white soldiers of the South. It is asking too much of human nature to have expected anything else. The prejudice instantly found official expression in the proclamation by the Confederate government that it would treat white officers of colored troops and colored soldiers when captured, as felons; Negro Union prisoners would be shot or sent back to slavery. This threat was literally carried out in several instances. For nearly a year the Confederate armies pursued this course toward black men who were caught wearing the uniform of a Union soldier.

During all this time the Federal government was silent: no word of protest and no threat of retaliation. Horace Greeley in the *Tribune* put the matter in strong terms when he stated that "every black soldier now goes to battle with a halter about his neck. . . . The simple question is, Shall we protect and insure to our Negro soldiers the ordinary treatment of a prisoner of war? Every Negro yet captured has suffered death or been sent back to the hell of slavery, from which he had escaped."

The colored people in the North were for a time thoroughly discouraged. The government, it seemed to them, put a low estimate upon them as soldiers. When Mr. Douglass was appealed to by Major George L. Stearns, an Abolitionist, and friend of John Brown, he expressed himself in part as follows:

"I am free to say, dear sir, that the case looks as if the confiding colored soldiers had been betrayed into bloody hands by the government in whose defense they had been so heroically fighting. . . . If the President is ever to demand justice and humanity for black soldiers, is not this the time for him to do it? How many Fifty-fourth men must be cut to pieces, its mutilated prisoners killed and the living sold into slavery or tortured to death by inches, before Mr. Lincoln shall say, 'Hold! Enough'?"

Appeals of this kind finally had the effect of moving the government to action. In order himself to be sure as to just what it intended to do, and before inducing any other colored men to go to the front, Mr. Douglass made up his mind to see the President personally. It was, at this time, an unheard-of thing for a colored man to go to the White House with a grievance, but he had many influential friends and admirers in Washington, who assured him that he would be well treated. Senators Sumner, Wilson, and Pomeroy; Secretary of the Treasury Salmon P. Chase, Assistant Secretary of War Dana, all guaranteed him a safe passage into Mr. Lincoln's presence. Senator Pomeroy introduced Mr. Douglass, and they soon found that they had much in common. The one had traveled a long hard journey from the slave-cabin of Maryland, and the other a thorny road from the scant and rugged life in Kentucky, to the high position of President. The one was too great to be a slave, and the other too noble to remain, in such a national crisis, a private citizen. Mr. Douglass's account of this historic

interview with the President, the first instance of
the kind, I believe, in the history of the country, is
worth reproducing :

"I was accompanied to the Executive Mansion
and introduced to President Lincoln by Senator
Pomeroy. Long lines of care were already deeply
written on Mr. Lincoln's brow, and his strong face
lighted up as soon as my name was mentioned. As
I approached and was introduced to him, he arose
and extended his hand and bade me welcome. I at
once felt that I was in the presence of an honest
man—one whom I could love, honor, and trust
without reserve or doubt. Proceeding to tell him
who I was and what I was doing, he promptly but
kindly stopped me, saying, 'I know who you are,
Mr. Douglass ; Mr. Seward has told me about you.
Sit down. I am glad to see you.' I then told him
the object of my visit ; that I was assisting to raise
colored troops ; that several months before I had
been very successful in getting men to enlist, but
that now it was not easy to induce the colored men
to enter the service because there was a feeling
among them that the government did not, in several
respects, deal fairly with them. Mr. Lincoln asked
me to state particulars. I replied that there were
three particulars which I wished to bring to his
attention. First, that colored soldiers ought to receive the same wages as those paid to white soldiers.
Second, that colored soldiers ought to receive the
same protection when taken prisoners, and be exchanged as readily and on the same terms as any
other prisoners, and that, if Jefferson Davis should
shoot or hang colored soldiers in cold blood, the
United States government should, without delay,
retaliate in kind and degree upon Confederate
soldiers in its hands as prisoners. Third, when colored soldiers, seeking 'the bubble reputation, at the

cannon's mouth' performed great and uncommon service on the battle-field, they should be rewarded by distinction and promotion precisely as white soldiers are rewarded for like services.

"Mr. Lincoln listened with patience and silence to all I had to say. He was serious and even troubled by what I had said and by what he himself had evidently before thought upon the same points. He, by his silent listening, not less than by his earnest reply to my words, impressed me with the solid gravity of his character.

"He began by saying that the employment of colored troops at all was a great gain to the colored people ; that the measure could not have been successfully adopted at the beginning of the war ; that the wisdom of making colored men soldiers was still doubted ; that their enlistment was a serious offense to popular prejudice ; that they had larger motives for being soldiers than white men ; that they ought to be willing to enter the service upon condition ; that the fact that they were not to receive the same pay as white soldiers seemed a necessary concession to smooth the way to their employment at all as soldiers, but that ultimately they would receive the same. On the second point, in respect to equal protection he said the case was more difficult. Retaliation was a terrible remedy, and one which it was very difficult to apply ; that, if once begun, there was no telling where it would end ; that if he could get hold of the Confederate soldiers who had been guilty of treating colored soldiers as felons he could easily retaliate, but the thought of hanging men for a crime perpetrated by others was revolting to his feelings. He thought that the rebels themselves would stop such barbarous warfare ; that less evil would be done if retaliation were not resorted to and that he had already received information that colored soldiers were being treated as prisoners of war.

In all this I saw the tender heart of the man rather than the stern warrior and commander-in-chief of the American army and navy, and while I could not agree with him, I could but respect his humane spirit.

" On the third point he seemed to have less difficulty, though he did not absolutely commit himself. He simply said that he would sign any commission to colored soldiers whom his Secretary of War should commend to him.   Though I was not entirely satisfied with his views, I was so well satisfied with the man and with the educating tendency of the conflict that I determined to go on with the recruiting."

From the White House, Mr. Douglass went directly to the War Department and had an interview with Stanton.   Contrary to his expectation, he found the Secretary most cordial, listening to the complaints with interest and patience.   Douglass says that Stanton made " the best defense that I had heard from any one of the treatment of colored soldiers by the government.   I was not satisfied, yet I left in the full belief that the true course to the black man's freedom and citizenship was over the battle-field and that my business was to get every black man I could into the Union army.

"Both the President and Secretary assured me that justice would ultimately be done to my race and," he adds, " I gave full credit and faith to these promises."   He was now better than ever prepared to say to his people that, if they would be free, they must not be afraid to suffer injustice and, if need be, cruelty.

In his interview with Mr. Stanton, the question

came up as to the advisability of commissioning
colored men as officers of colored regiments. The
Secretary expressed his willingness and readiness
to issue a commission to Mr. Douglass, if he would
accept. On being assured that he would, Stanton
promised to make him assistant adjutant to General
Thomas, who was recruiting and organizing
troops in Mississippi. He returned to his home in
Rochester, N. Y., confidently expecting that the
commission would be sent him, but for some reason,
not explained, it was never issued. Mr. Douglass's
only comment on this lapse of the Secretary of War
was: "The government, I fear, was still clinging
to the idea that positions of honor in the service
should be occupied by white men and that it would
not do to inaugurate the policy of perfect equality."

At length the outlook improved. Signs appeared
of better treatment of the colored soldiers by the
Confederate armies. On July 30, 1863, President
Lincoln issued an order "that for every soldier of
the United States killed in violation of the laws of
war, a rebel soldier shall be executed ; and for every
one enslaved by the enemy or sold into slavery, a
rebel soldier shall be placed at hard labor on the
public works." All the Union generals readily
coöperated with the President's efforts to have his
black troops receive equal consideration. General
Grant was especially interested in this matter and
gave instructions to the white men in his ranks to
treat the colored soldiers as comrades.

The Negro troops, by their soldierly qualities,
displayed at Fort Wagner, Vicksburg, Port Hudson,

Morris Island, and other places, had fully earned the right to honorable treatment, and such deserving had its good effects. When the government finally recognized the services of its black defenders, there was no trouble in getting the colored men to enlist. From each state and territory in and out of the Union, they offered themselves to the Federal government with as much eagerness as if they were already in possession of every right they hoped to receive.

The following table of figures will show how largely black men responded to President Lincoln's call to the defense of the Union:

Connecticut	1,764
Maine	104
Massachusetts	3,966
New Hampshire	125
Rhode Island	1,837
Vermont	120
New Jersey	1,185
New York	4,125
Pennsylvania	8,612
Colorado	95
Illinois	1,811
Indiana	1,537
Iowa	440
Kansas	2,080
Minnesota	104
Michigan	1,387
Ohio	5,092
Wisconsin	165
Delaware	954
District of Columbia	3,269
Kentucky	23,703
Maryland	8,718
Missouri	8,344
West Virginia	196
Alabama	4,969
Arkansas	5,526

Florida	1,044
Louisiana	3,480
Mississippi	17,869
North Carolina	5,035
South Carolina	5,462
Tennessee	20,123
Texas	47
At large	733
Not accounted for	5,083
Officers	7,122
Total	186,017 [1]

In addition to this impressive total it is estimated that there were about 92,576 colored men serving with regiments in other capacities. That the Negroes proved to be good soldiers, whenever or wherever their fibre was put to trial, is the unvarying testimony of every officer and commander who had any opportunity to know their conduct in the field. The exigencies of the war were such that the troops thus furnished were sorely needed. The whole fighting strength of the North was none too great to cope with the Southern armies, and the enlistment of black men was effected at a critical moment in the struggle.

From another point of view, this employment of colored troops with their good conduct on the field was an important event in the history of the Negro. It was the first opportunity given to him to demonstrate, on a large scale, that he was superior to the estimate put upon him at that time by the American people. The current of popular feeling against the race rapidly changed. The Southern soldiers also

[1] *History of the Negro Race in America*, George W. Williams, Vol. II, p. 299.

altered their attitude when they discovered in black
skin courage and character worthy of honor and
respect.

On both sides of the firing-line the colored men
proved themselves to be friends of the white race.
They shrank from no danger, however great; they
refused no task, however difficult; but worked, and
fought, and died without complaint. Negro men
and women, as non-combatants, secretly fed, hid,
and protected thousands of Union soldiers who were
in perilous positions and without a friend or hope
of favor in a hostile country. Many a man in blue
owed life and liberty to the nursing and protection
of some tender-hearted slave. It was to the care
and devotion of these same humble folk that the
Southern masters, when summoned to war, entrusted
the cultivation of their lands and the lives and
property of their families. The Negro was the
"good Samaritan" in those terrible days, when
white men were savagely bent upon destroying one
another.

The armies on both sides of the conflict were in-
debted to the black man as friend and as fighter.
In the South, he fought against himself; in the
North, he fought for himself. In helping to save
the Union by his service and by his death on battle-
fields, he put himself in a position to claim a share
in the fruits of reëstablished peace, and in the good-
will of a reunited country. In view of his recorded
part in this civil contest, it can never be said that
the Negro was a mere passive recipient of the freedom that came to all the members of his race.

After the government had fully committed itself to the policy of enlisting colored men in the Union army, the struggle began to assume the character of a war for liberty. It became so as a military necessity. President Lincoln's Proclamation of Emancipation, issued on the first day of January, 1863, sounded the death-knell of slavery, and was an expression of a changed attitude on the part of the government and of the people generally, foretelling the end of the war.

The President had been criticised by the Abolitionists, because he chose to fight battles for the preservation of the Union, rather than for the extirpation of slavery. If Douglass had ever faltered in his faith in Mr. Lincoln's desire for Abolition, he was reassured by an incident which occurred at this time. Shortly after the Proclamation was issued, the President summoned him to the White House. He reports that Mr. Lincoln was somewhat anxious because the slaves in the South were not coming into the Union lines as fast as he expected and wished. He said that he might be forced into arrangements for peace before his purposes could be realized, and if so, he wanted the greatest possible number of slaves within the territory of freedom. The President thought that Douglass could, in some way, bring his Proclamation to the knowledge of the Negroes, and organize raiding parties, which would aid them to escape from bondage and reach Union ground. Referring to this interview Mr. Douglass said :

" Mr. Lincoln saw the danger of premature peace,

and like a thoughtful and sagacious man, he wished
to provide means of rendering such consummation
as harmless as possible. I was most impressed by
this benevolent consideration because he had before said, in answer to the peace clamor, that his
object was to save the Union. . . . What he
said on this day showed a deeper moral conviction
against slavery than I had ever seen before in anything spoken or written by him. I listened with
the deepest interest and profoundest satisfaction and
at his suggestion agreed to undertake the organization of a band of scouts, . . . and urge the
slaves to come within our boundaries."

This plan, however, was soon rendered unneces-
sary by Union victories in the field and a better
military outlook.

Two incidents occurred at this meeting which
showed the President's strong and almost affectionate regard for Frederick Douglass. What these
were are best told by Douglass himself. He says:
"While in conversation with him, his secretary
twice announced Governor Buckingham of Connecticut, one of the noblest and most patriotic of
the loyal governors. Mr. Lincoln said : 'Tell
Governor Buckingham to wait, for I want to have a
long talk with my friend, Frederick Douglass.' I
interposed and begged him to see the governor at
once, as I could wait, but no, he persisted that he
wanted to talk with me and that Governor Buckingham could wait. . . . In his company I was
never in any way reminded of my humble origin, or
of my unpopular color."

The other pleasing incident of this visit is likewise best told in Douglass's own words : "At the door of my friend, John A. Gray, where I was stopping in Washington, I found one afternoon the carriage of Secretary Dole, and a messenger from President Lincoln with an invitation for me to take tea with him at the Soldiers' Home, where he then passed his nights, riding out after the business of the day was over at the Executive Mansion. Unfortunately, I had an engagement to speak that evening and having made it one of the rules of my conduct in life never to break an engagement if possible to keep it, I felt obliged to decline the honor. I have often regretted that I did not make this an exception to my general rule. Could I have known that no such opportunity could come to me again, I should have justified myself in disappointing a large audience for the sake of a visit with Abraham Lincoln."

The Emancipation Proclamation, as Mr. Douglass at the time said, was "the turning point in the conflict between freedom and slavery." He and his race lived through the first two years of the administration of the "party of liberty," in a kind of agony of hope and doubt. What the colored race, North and South, wanted in a hurry came with slowness. As the time approached for the word of deliverance, the country was in a state of feverish excitement. For those who had been connected with the movement for Abolition, everything else, for the moment, seemed to lose its interest, its importance, and its value in the presence of this impending event.   Indeed, the whole country vibrated with expectation.

In Tremont Temple, in Boston, on the day when Mr. Lincoln's Proclamation was looked for, there was gathered a memorable company.   Many of the most notable men in New England were present to join with the colored people in the song of jubilee. To quote Mr. Douglass :   " A line of messengers was established between the telegraph office and the platform, and the time was occupied with brief speeches from Hon. Thomas Russell, Anna Dickinson, J. Sella Martin, William Wells Brown, and myself. . . .   At last when patience was well-nigh exhausted and suspense was becoming agony, a man, I think Judge Russell, with hasty step advanced through the crowd and with a face fairly illumined with the news he bore, exclaimed, in tones that thrilled all hearts :   ' It is coming, it is on the wires.'   The effect of this announcement was startling beyond description, and the scene was wild and grand."

When the message finally came and was read, there was a scene of indescribable rejoicing.   The crowd was so crazy with excitement that midnight came upon them before they were aware of it and they adjourned to a colored Baptist church where the jubilation did not fully exhaust itself until morning. Mr. Douglass described it as " the most affecting and thrilling occasion I ever witnessed and a worthy celebration of the first step on the part of the nation in its departure from the thraldom of ages."

The Proclamation put new energy into all war

measures and as the four years of Mr. Lincoln's first administration approached the end, there was no one to oppose him for a renomination. His reëlection seemed to be an overwhelming vindication of his policy. Frederick Douglass was a prominent figure at the inauguration ceremonies and was looking gratefully and joyously up into the kindly face of the great President when he uttered these noble words : "Fondly do we hope, and fervently do we pray that this mighty scourge of war may speedily pass away. Yet if God wills that it continue until all the wealth piled by the bondsmen's two hundred and fifty years of unrequited toil shall be sunk, and until every drop of blood drawn with the lash shall be paid for by another drawn with the sword, as was said three thousand years ago, so still it must be said, that ' the judgments of the Lord are true and righteous altogether. ' "

Speaking of this event Mr. Douglass said :

" In the evening of the day of the inauguration, another new experience awaited me. The usual reception was given at the Executive Mansion, and though no colored person had ever ventured to present himself on such an occasion, it seemed, now that freedom had become the law of the republic, and colored men were on the battle-field mingling their blood with that of white men in one common effort to save the country, that it was not too great an assumption for a colored man to offer his congratulations to the President with those of other citizens. It is never an agreeable experience to go where there can be any doubt of welcome, and my colored friends had too often realized discomfiture

from this cause to be willing to subject themselves
to such unhappiness.   It was plain, then, that some
one must lead the way, and that if the colored man
would have his rights, he must take them ; and now,
though it was plainly quite the thing for me to attend President Lincoln's reception, they all with one
accord began to make excuses.   It was finally
agreed that Mrs. Dorsey should bear me company,
so together we joined in the grand procession of
citizens from all parts of the country and moved
slowly toward the Executive Mansion.   Upon
reaching the door, two policemen stationed there
took me rudely by the arm and ordered me to stand
back, for their directions were to admit no persons
of my color.   I told the officers I was quite sure
there was some mistake for no such order could have
emanated from President Lincoln ; and that if he
knew I was at the door, he would desire my admission.   They then, to put an end to the parley, as I
suppose, assumed an air of politeness, and offered
to conduct me in.   We followed their lead, and we
soon found ourselves walking some planks out of a
window, which had been arranged as a temporary
passage for the exit of visitors.   We halted as soon
as we saw the trick, and I said to the officers, ' You
have deceived me.   I shall not go out of this building till I see President Lincoln.'   At this moment a
gentleman who was passing in, recognized me, and
I said to him : ' Be so kind as to say to Mr. Lincoln
that Frederick Douglass is detained by officers at
the door.'   It was not long before Mrs. Dorsey and
I walked into the spacious East Room, amid a scene
of elegance such as in this country I had never before witnessed.   Like a mountain pine, high above
all others, Mr. Lincoln stood, in his grand sim-
plicity and home-like beauty.   Recognizing me,
even before I reached him, he exclaimed, so that all
around could hear him, ' Here comes my friend

Douglass.' Taking me by the hand, he said, 'I am glad to see you. I saw you in the crowd to-day listening to my inaugural address. How did you like it?' I said, 'Mr. Lincoln, I must not detain you with my poor opinion, when there are thousands waiting to shake hands with you.' 'No, no,' he said, 'you must stop a little, Douglass; there is no man in the country whose opinion I value more than yours. I want to know what you think of it.' I replied, 'Mr. Lincoln, that was a sacred effort.' 'I am glad you liked it,' he said; and I passed on, feeling that any man, however distinguished, might well regard himself honored by such expressions from such a man."

The events of the war moved rapidly toward the end and to peace. Mr. Douglass was in Boston when Richmond was captured. New England was more stirred over the fall of the Confederate capital than by any other single event of the war, except the Emancipation Proclamation. Faneuil Hall was again the scene of a great gathering. The victory was to be celebrated in song and speech. The governor of the state, Senator Wilson, and Robert C. Winthrop were among the speakers, and with them was Frederick· Douglass. A meeting of this kind anywhere in New England would at that time have been incomplete without him. His presence on the platform, sharing honors with the patrician Winthrop, served to illustrate the change of fortunes that are possible under a democratic form of government. Less than twenty-five years before, Douglass, a fugitive from Maryland, had stood behind Mr. Winthrop's chair at table as a waiter, at a dinner in

his honor in New Bedford.   He had won the position he now occupied by his services to a people
whose cause men in the North had come at length to
recognize as their own, because it was the cause of
humanity.

Mr. Douglass at this time had reason to feel not
only joy but gratitude.   It was clear that all he
had hoped and struggled for was soon to be realized.
The close of the war and the overthrow of the institution of slavery was for him a sort of personal victory.   But his rejoicing was soon turned to mourn-
ing.   At the time of the assassination of President
Lincoln he was in Rochester, and he spoke at a meeting held to give expression to the sorrow which that
event created.   The circumstances are thus related
by a friend :

"Rochester court-house never held a larger crowd
than was gathered to mourn over the martyred
President.   The meeting was opened by the most
eloquent men at the bar and in the pulpit, with carefully prepared and earnestly uttered addresses.   All
the time the people were not aroused.   Douglass,
who told me that he would not speak because he
was not invited, sat crowded in the rear.   At last
the feeling could be restrained no more ; and his
name burst upon the air from every side and filled
the house.   The dignified gentlemen who directed
had to surrender.   Then came the finest appeal in
behalf of the father of his people, who had died for
them especially, and would be mourned by them as
long as one remained in America who had been a
slave.   I have heard Webster and Clay in their best

moments ; Channing and Beecher in their highest inspirations. I never heard truer eloquence ; I never saw profounder impression. When he finished the meeting was done."

CHAPTER XIII

EARLY PROBLEMS OF FREEDOM

THE close of the Civil War left many of the agencies of emancipation without a cause. The anti-slavery publications, the state and national anti-slavery societies, "vigilance committees," and the vast Underground Railroad system, saw their purposes accomplished in the terms of peace. The American Anti-Slavery Society, which had been the longest in existence, and which, under the leadership of William Lloyd Garrison, had done more for freedom than any other single agency, was now ready to wind up its affairs. When a proposition was made for its dissolution, Frederick Douglass opposed it, giving his reasons in these words: "I felt that the work of the society was not done, that it had not fulfilled its mission, which was not merely to emancipate but to elevate the enslaved class . . . that the Negro still had a cause and that he needed my pen and voice to plead for it."

In taking this position, he showed that he had a clear and far-reaching comprehension of the many and serious problems and obligations that would in time result from the enforced emancipation of his people. He clearly foresaw that these problems were of a kind which had never before come within the range and scope of our national experience, and that if the country were to make the most of the good results of the war, and minimize its evils, the machinery of liberation and destruction must somehow be converted to the service of peace and construction. Two great questions had been settled, that the United States was to remain an indivisible nation, and that slavery was henceforth impossible in this nation.

The problems growing out of these achievements are still difficult. Before the Civil War, the people of the United States might have been classified as non-slave-holding and slave-holding white people; enslaved and free Negroes. Now, two of these classes, the slave-holders and the enslaved Negroes, disappeared and in the latter's stead, a new element was injected into the population, the freedmen, 4,000,000 souls, utterly destitute, without learning, without experience, and without traditions; dependent for their guidance, and almost for bare existence, upon the direction and good-will of the older elements. If, after the war, the South and the North could have united to repair the damages and solve the problems the conflict had left behind it, the history of the colored people in America, as well as their present condition, might have been different from what it is.

In facing the problems of reconstruction, the people of the North had no precedents and little knowledge of the Negro's character to guide them. The men who had the responsibility of providing for the present and future, of rehabilitating the South on the basis of freedom, were trained to treat

every question, social and political, from the standpoint of party politics.   But reconstruction needed
the services of the sociologist more than of the
party leader.   There were but few in public life
capable of treating these matters in a non-partisan,
a non-sectional, and a scientific spirit.   Men could
not so quickly overcome the animosities engendered
by the Civil War.   Abraham Lincoln, who alone
seemed to have a spirit large enough to be the President of all the people, even to the least of them, was
gone, and there was none in public service to take his
place.   While others acted in the spirit of war, he
acted in the spirit of peace.   In managing large
questions, he had a wonderful insight into the things
that would aggravate conditions and a fine courage
in avoiding them, until they had spent their force
with as little harm as possible.   His penetrative
powers, the contagion of his kindly spirit, his unswerving love for what was just, were needed quite
as much after as before and during the civil strife.
Had Mr. Lincoln lived, his clear vision, it is safe to
say, would have avoided many of the evils to which
the country has since fallen heir.   As it was, however much the white people in slavery's former
domain may have suffered, the Negro has borne the
brunt of every mistake of the period of Reconstruction.

The Southern people had lost (so it seemed at the
time at least) everything that was worth having and
fighting for,—their "cause," their property in
slaves, their prestige, and their political supremacy.
Their homes were devastated and their plantations

ravaged by the conquering Yankees. Their task was not to build up what had been destroyed, but to begin anew. It is asking too much to expect that they could have faced these conditions with a cheerful spirit. The slaves, as property, were now free, and this freedom was regarded as a punishment visited upon their former masters.

Free labor was new, and apart from this there was none of it to take the place of that of the liberated slaves. Furthermore, the white people had little or no faith in their possible usefulness. They feared that the Negro as a free man would not work, would not honor his contracts, and would use his liberty to commit all sorts of crimes against society. They could not, at once, rid themselves of the feeling that physical compulsion was the only way to keep the Negro within the bounds of law and labor. Carl Schurz, who, under the authority of the President, made a very thorough and statesman-like investigation of conditions, issued an official report of his findings, and it is clear from this paper that, if the Southern people could have overcome their fears of Negro freedom, the work of reconstruction would have been greatly simplified. They, however, were in no frame of mind to accept and honor any program for reconstruction emanating from the North. They insisted that they alone knew the Negro and what was best to be done for him and with him.

Between the North and the South, stood the ex-slave, free/ and that was all. His situation was anomalous. As Mr. Douglass aptly says, "He was free from individual masters, but the slave of society." Yet, because of his long service to the country, either as a slave or a freeman, he deserved more than he could possibly have been paid in terms of law, defining and defending his rights. He was without power and, as Mr. Douglass in describing him, said, "a man without force, is without the essential dignity of human nature."

In this almost totally helpless condition, the North expected too much of him and the ex-masters too little. It required more than the shock of four years of internecine war to change the solidarity of slavery into a society of organized self-helpfulness. A people who had been so long enslaved could not help being slavish in habits and instincts. They had little family life, no society, no institution except the church, a rudimentary conception of common interests, and very few traditions and ideals. No race ever came into the domain of freedom, independence, and democracy so little furnished with the elements of self-protection and self-determining purpose, as did the emancipated slaves forty years ago. Yet there were everywhere in the South important exceptions to this condition of race helplessness. Many free colored people, especially in the cities, were not hopelessly behind in the procession of progress. They fully understood the meaning of the war and its results. When the last gun was fired and they saw emancipation as a reality, their joy was unbounded. In many of the Southern cities, thousands of them gathered in the open streets and commons, where they shouted and prayed with full hearts, voicing in songs of jubilee and thanksgiving their gratitude for their great deliverance. There has been nothing like these demonstrations in the history of American liberty. No one who saw them could have any doubt whatever as to the Negro's appreciation of his freedom. It is a notable fact that in none of them was ever heard a word of hatred or revenge toward those who had been responsible for their long enslavement. Their gratitude was too great to leave room for resentment. God, Lincoln, and Freedom formed a mysterious trinity in the new awakening of these emancipated people.

All this was perfectly natural and hopeful, so far as it went, but it was not long before exultation gave way to the consciousness that this dearly bought liberty was a serious thing. The Negro capacity for happiness was large, but he could not live and sustain himself by this alone. Owning nothing, he had no place to live. Having nothing, he could get nothing. In addition to the ex-slaves, who were still fastened to the places where slavery left them and freedom found them, a great multitude, known as refugees, after emancipation made their way into the Union lines. When the war closed these were still with the Union army and dependent upon it for rations. It soon became apparent to those in authority, that something must be done in a large way by the Federal government itself to provide for this unorganized horde. To meet this serious condition, Congress, in the spring of 1865, passed an act establishing the "Freedmen's Bureau for the Relief of Freedmen and Refugees.'' Its main provisions were as follows :

The Bureau was to have supervision and management of abandoned lands.

It was to look after all subjects relating to refugees and freedmen.

It was to be under the control of a commission appointed by the President and to continue its labors for one year after the close of the war.

The Secretary of War was given authority to issue provisions, clothing, and fuel for the immediate and temporary needs of freedmen and their wives and children.

The War Department was to set apart for the use of loyal refugees and freedmen abandoned lands under the control of the United States Army and assign to such freedmen, not more than forty acres of land, and to protect such persons in the possession of such land for at least three years at an annual rent, not to exceed six per cent. upon the appraised value of the land. At the end of that time, the tenant was allowed to purchase it and receive therefor from the government a certificate of purchase.

In addition to these provisions, the Freedmen's Bureau was intended to be a ''friendly intermediary'' between the ex-masters and ex-slaves. Nothing could have been done more surely to smooth the way for a kindly relationship between the two parties in question, if such a relationship had been possible. General O. O. Howard was the first commissioner of that Bureau. He had made a record as a soldier in the Union Army, but, better still, he was a man of humane impulses, without sectional bias, and of exalted Christian character. The value of his services in the work of Reconstruction can be easily seen by a glance at some of his reports made to Congress in 1865–1870.

In these five years of work on the part of the Bureau to bring order out of chaos, there had been established over 4,000 schools, employing 9,000 teachers and giving instruction to about a quarter of a million pupils of all ages. In 1870 the school attendance in the old slave-states amounted to nearly eighty per cent. of the enrollment. The demand for learning on the part of the colored people, as shown by the Bureau's work, was amazing, and afforded a gratifying evidence of their sense of responsibility as freedmen. The Negroes themselves made a good showing of what they were able to do by their own efforts in creating the means for their instruction. They sustained over 1,300 schools and built over 500 school buildings, contributing more than $200,000 out of their earnings to further the cause of education.

The value of the Freedmen's Bureau in thus stimulating an interest in this important subject and in developing a serious sense of responsibility on the part of the freedmen cannot well be overestimated. Carl Schurz in his report says:

"The Freedmen's Bureau would have been an institution of the greatest value, under competent leadership, had not its organization, to some extent, been invaded by mentally and morally unfit persons. . . . Nothing was needed at this time so much as an acknowledged authority, standing guard between the master and the ex-slave, commanding and possessing the confidence and respect of both, to aid the emancipated black man to make the best possible use of his unaccustomed freedom, and to aid the white man to whom free Negro labor was a well-nigh incurable idea, in meeting the difficulties, partly real and partly conjured up by the white man's prejudiced imagination."

The lack of fit men, in sufficient numbers, to continue the good work inaugurated by the Freedmen's Bureau was the cause, in great part, of the failure of Reconstruction methods of helpfulness.   There were employed men of partisan spirit whose vision was clouded by political aspirations, and thus the future well-being of both races in the South was not kept paramount.   The cause of most of the evils that in a few years followed and overwhelmed the colored people in the South, was lack of men strong in character, patriotism, justice, and understanding for the work in hand.   This is true, in spite of the fact that there were those who were equal to the occasion, but who alone had not the power to perform the tasks set for them.   No greater injury has been done the colored people of this country than that which resulted from putting them in a position of political antagonism to their former masters.

But the purposes of this biography do not require a full statement of the causes that led to the over-throw of the temporary supremacy held by the freedmen and their Northern allies.   A careful reading of the history of the Southern states since the adoption of the Thirteenth Amendment to the Constitution of the United States in 1865, must convince the impartial reader that the Negroes were less the instigators than the victims of the mistakes of Reconstruction. Many of those who played the false rôle of friends and leaders left the freedmen to bear the brunt of the punishment which they have since suffered patiently, heroically, and alone. The Negroes of the South during the Reconstruction period were always amenable to wise direction. Those who were on hand to guide them, easily won their favor. There seems to be no reason to doubt that, had it been offered, the freedmen would have followed the leadership of the best elements in the South as willingly, if not more willingly, than that which they did accept.

The difficulty was that the Southern people could not in a day, or in a decade, change their inborn conviction that emancipation was forced upon them as a punishment. They accepted this punishment in a spirit in which injured pride, the sense of loss of property, loss of "cause," and revenge were elements. But with all these losses and defeats, the imperious temper of the Southern people suffered no impairment, and they were in no mood to take hold of the work of Reconstruction in the spirit of the victorious North.

The South hesitated to act, and the ex-slave had no power to do so. As a result, the responsibility for movements for the protection of the Negroes fell to the North. It sought to accomplish this object by giving freedmen all the rights of citizen-

ship.   Under the presuppositions upon which
our government was founded, this step was logical,
even though it may have been, and indeed seems to
have been, at that time unwise.

What has been said in the foregoing pages indicates what may be called the new field of labor for
Frederick Douglass after emancipation.   When the
great war came to an end and the object for which
he had so long labored was indeed an accomplished
fact, he confessed that his great joy was somewhat
tinged with a feeling of sadness.   He said, "I felt
that I had reached the end of the noblest part of
my life."   He was still in his prime, and all his
faculties were clear and ready for action.   He had
no occupation, no business, no profession.   His
training and associations, during the previous thirty
years, had unfitted him for manual labor, and he
had no fortune that would enable him to live without exertion of some kind.   But thoughts and feelings of this sort were soon swept aside by new
interests and anxieties of the most absorbing character.

In the first place, fresh evidences of his popularity
began to manifest themselves.   His struggle for
emancipation had been so conspicuous, his eloquence
so stirring, and his participation in all the great
questions of the day so earnest and compelling, that
his vogue continued as before.

In the great diversity of distinguished men and
women who figured in the history of the quarter of
a century immediately preceding the Civil War,
Frederick Douglass was in the fullest sense of the

word, a "self-made man." All kinds of persons were interested in him. His authority on every matter that concerned the Negro, North or South, was seldom questioned. His leadership, up to this time, was not often disputed. The American people manifested greater desire to hear him than ever before and invitations to lecture began to pour in upon him from colleges, lyceums, literary societies, and churches. It is scarcely too much to say that he was one of the most popular men on the lecture platform, and at a time when such illustrious personages as Henry Ward Beecher, Wendell Phillips, Theodore Tilton, Anna Dickinson, and Mary A. Livermore gave to the American lyceum its highest distinction. His themes were no longer anti-slavery in character. His new lectures bore such titles as, "Self-made Men," "The Races of Men," "William, the Silent," "John Brown," etc., all of which showed a wide reading, and a mastery of the art of eloquence. In addition to these lectures, he was called upon from every direction for informal talks on an almost endless variety of subjects.

But whatever might be the theme or the occasion, he could not get away from the Negro problem. As he said, "I never rise to speak before any American audience, without a feeling that my failure or success will bring harm or benefit to my whole race." When the all-important question of reconstruction came to be considered, Mr. Douglass was found to be fully conversant with the progress of events, prepared to say his word, and play his part. While other men were uncertain, confused, and

timid, Douglass's stand was bold, direct, and fearless. When it was time for him to speak and act,
his words attracted wide attention and many persons
in and out of Congress were willing to follow his
leading. He had always been frank, honorable,
and resourceful on the question of just treatment
for his race and he was so far in advance of most
of the men who had it in their power to make and
unmake the laws, that it would have been a decided
misfortune for the colored people to have been without his guidance. He had a wide acquaintance
among men in public life. No other Negro in this
country, at the time, knew political leaders in and
out of Congress so intimately. His qualities of
prudence and sagacity, as well as his great personal
charm, made him welcome in the councils of his
party. He was the soul of honor. Being thus
gifted, Douglass was able to be as much for his
people in a personal as in a public capacity. He
had a way of getting close to the men in power and
of reaching their hearts and enlisting their sympathies for the objects in whose service he was engaged. This was most fortunate. His race was without official connection with the government, without experience, and with no clearly defined status as
citizens. If ever the colored people needed a strong
man capable in every way to represent them, it was
now, when the war was over and the question, what
to do with the free Negro, must be answered in definite terms of law and governmental policy. Aside
from his commanding abilities, and his personal at-
tractiveness to men, Mr. Douglass had lived through

the very experiences that fitted him to know and feel what the Negro needed and ought to have. He had been a slave, a fugitive slave, and a freedman, at a time, too, when Negro freedom was most despaired of. No white man could appreciate, as he could and did, the sweetness of the terms, Freedom and Liberty. One of his earliest utterances on this subject indicates his feeling at this period. "I saw no chance," he said, "of bettering the condition of the freedman, until he should cease to be merely a freedman and should become a citizen, and that there was no safety for him or for anybody else in America, outside of the American government."

At the time when Mr. Douglass publicly took this position, he was far more radical than some of the most ardent of his anti-slavery associates. This declaration was then regarded as a challenge to the sense of justice of the American people. Many earnest friends of the Negro thought it was asking too much, even though the race deserved the franchise. Others argued that the Negro was unfit for the suffrage and that it would aggravate the already strained relations between the two races in the South. Opposition was expected by Mr. Douglass and he was ready to meet it. No one understood better than he that his people had had no training for citizenship, but he was accustomed to say, that "if the Negro knows enough to fight for his country, he knows enough to vote; if he knows enough to pay taxes to support the government, he knows enough to vote; if he knows as much when sober as an Irishman knows when he is drunk, he knows enough to vote." He anticipated the evils that would follow the enfranchisement of the ex-slaves, but insisted that such evils would be temporary and that the good would be permanent. He further insisted that it was worth all the suffering endured by his race to have that principle established; that the right of suffrage would be an incentive to arouse the latent energies of the Negro to become worthy of full citizenship, and that such impulse was imperatively needed. He always declared that political equality was a widely different thing from social equality. He vigorously protested that the right of suffrage did not mean Negro domination in the slave states, if the best white people would wisely assume the leadership of the blacks. He believed in the domination of the fittest, and insisted that the white people of the South, because of their superiority in intelligence and in all the forces that make for supremacy, were in no danger of being overwhelmed by the new voters. He believed in the rule of the competent and that in the long run intelligent supremacy would be tempered with justice and the true spirit of democracy. He believed that those who were strong enough, either to help the ex-slave to get upon his feet or to crush him in his efforts to rise, would choose the more generous course.

At any rate, he deemed the time ripe to claim for the freedmen full citizenship and equality before the law. When the question came forward for discussion, the people of the North were filled with enthusiasm over the results of the war and for the great objects they believed to have been achieved by it. It was the occasion to make a hero of every one who had taken part in the civil contest on the side of the Union. Even the Negro, for the first time, became the recipient of more than respectful consideration. The people of the North were as proud of his freedom as he was himself. If to give the Negro the franchise, and laws to protect him in the exercise of it as a citizen, would make more lasting the results of the war, the North was now in a mood to grant it to him, since it seemed to add to the significance of the great struggle which had just been so victoriously concluded. Douglass took advantage of this condition of things to advocate suffrage for his people. By speech and print and personal appeals to the leaders of public opinion, he urged this cause upon them in and out of season. There was no lack of evidence that it was gaining in every direction. The number of those who thought the suffrage ought to be granted, because it was right; those who thought it a good thing from a partisan standpoint, and those who thought the results of the war would be lost unless the Negro were given the privilege, increased rapidly.

What Douglass calls one of the first steps in the direction of popular favor for universal suffrage, was an interview that he had with President Johnson on the 7th of March, 1866. He headed a delegation of prominent colored men, including George T. Downing, Lewis H. Douglass, William E. Matthews, John Jones, John F. Cook, Joseph E. Otis, A. W. Ross, William Whipper, John M. Brown, and Alexander Dunlop. The visit of these black men to the President for the purpose of urging upon the government the policy of the franchise for the freedmen, attracted the attention of the entire nation. Nothing better could have been devised to bring the whole question before the people and obtain a hearing for it.

The delegation soon found that Mr. Johnson was not in sympathy with their plans for Negro enfranchisement. The President had evidently anticipated their purpose in calling upon him and he was fully prepared to answer their arguments. He spoke to them at great length and left no ground for them to doubt his position in the matter. He also gave them no opportunity to reply. On returning from the White House, his colleagues empowered Mr. Douglass to prepare an address to the public, to be printed simultaneously with Mr. Johnson's address to them. Mr. Douglass's paper was in the form of a reply to the President's arguments against the suffrage proposition, and was as follows :

" Mr. President : —In consideration of a delicate sense of propriety as well as of your own repeated intimations of indisposition to discuss or listen to a reply to the views and opinions you were pleased to express to us in your elaborate speech to-day, the undersigned would respectfully take this method of replying thereto.

" Believing as we do that the views and opinions you expressed in that address are entirely unsound and prejudicial to the highest interest of our race, as well as to our country at large, we cannot do other than expose the same and, as far as may be in our power, arrest their dangerous influence. It is not necessary at this time to call attention to more than two or three features of your remarkable address. The first point to which we feel especially bound to take exceptions, is your attempt to found a policy opposed to our enfranchisement, upon the alleged ground of an existing hostility on the part of the former slaves to the poor white people of the South. We admit the existence of this hostility, and hold that it is entirely reciprocal. But you obviously commit an error by drawing an argument from an incident of slavery, and making it a basis for a policy adapted to a state of freedom. The hostility between the whites and blacks of the South is easily explained. It has its root and sap in the relation of slavery, and was incited on both sides by the cunning of the slave-masters. These masters secured their ascendency over both the poor whites and blacks by putting enmity between them.

"They divided both to conquer each. There was no earthly reason why the blacks should not hate and dread the poor whites when in a state of slavery, for it was from this class that their masters received their slave-catchers and slave-drivers and overseers. They were the men called in upon all occasions by the masters whenever any fiendish outrage was to be committed upon the slaves. Now, sir, you cannot but perceive that, the cause of this hatred removed, the effect must be removed also. Slavery is abolished. The cause of this antagonism is removed, and you must see that it is altogether illogical to legislate from slave-holding and slave-driving premises for a people, whom you have repeatedly declared it your purpose to maintain in freedom.

"Besides, if it were true, as you allege, that the hostility of the blacks toward the whites must necessarily project itself into a state of freedom, and that this enmity between the two races is even more intense in a state of freedom than in a state of slavery, in the name of Heaven, we reverently ask, how can you, in view of your proffered desire to promote the welfare of the black man, deprive him of all means of defense, and clothe him, whom you regard as his enemy, in the panoply of political power? Can it be that you recommend a policy which would arm the strong and cast down the defenseless? Can you, by any possibility of reasoning, regard this as just, fair, or wise? Experience proves that those are most abused who can be abused with the greatest impunity. Men are whipped oftenest who are whipped easiest. Peace between races is not to be secured by degrading one race and exalting another, by giving power to one and withholding from another, but by maintaining a state of equal justice between all classes. First pure, then peaceable.

"On the colonization theory you were pleased to broach, very much could be said. It is impossible to suppose, in view of the usefulness of the black man in time of peace as a laborer in the South and in time of war as a soldier in the North, and a growing respect for his rights among the people and his increasing adaptation to a high state of civilization in his native land, that there can ever come a time when he can be removed from this country without a terrible shock to its prosperity and peace. Besides, the worst enemy of the nation could not cast upon its fair name a greater infamy than to admit that Negroes could be tolerated among them in a state of the most degrading slavery and oppression, and must be cast away, driven to exile, for no other cause than having been freed from their chains."

When the question reached Congress, the Negro was not lacking in friends who were willing to go the full length of the Frederick Douglass program of Reconstruction. The first step taken was a report made to the Senate by a committee having the subject in charge. This report in effect provided that the whole matter of franchise be left to the option of the several states concerned. Mr. Douglass believed he saw in this proposition the continued political enslavement of his people, and he was on his guard. The following communication written and sent to the Senate by the delegation which had visited President Johnson speaks for itself:

"To the Honorable, the Senate of the United States:—The undersigned, being a delegation representing the colored people of the several states, and now sojourning in Washington, charged with the duty to look after the best interests of the recently emancipated, would most respectfully, but earnestly, pray your honorable body to favor no amendment of the Constitution of the United States which will grant any one or all of the states of this Union to disfranchise any class of citizens on the ground of race or color, for any consideration whatever. They would further respectfully represent that the Constitution as adopted by the Fathers of this Republic in 1789 evidently contemplated the result which has now happened, to wit, the abolition of slavery. The men who framed it, and those who adopted it, framed and adopted it for the people, and the whole people, colored men being at the time legal voters in most of the states. In that instrument as it now stands, there is not a sentence or a syllable conveying any shadow of right or authority by which any State may make color or race a disqualification for the exercise of the right of suffrage, and the undersigned will regard as a real calamity

the introduction of any words expressly or by impli-
cation, giving any state or states such power ; and
we respectfully submit that if the amendment now
pending before your honorable body shall be
adopted, it will enable any state to deprive any class
of citizens of the elective franchise, notwithstanding it was obviously framed with a view to affect
the question of Negro suffrage only.

"For these and other reasons the undersigned respectfully pray that the amendment to the Constitution recently passed by the House and now before
your body, be not adopted. And as in duty
bound," etc.

In addition to this letter addressed to the United
States Senate, Mr. Douglass and his associates saw
and argued the matter with every member of that
body who would grant them an audience. The
"Option Measure" was defeated and to a considerable extent through Mr. Douglass's influence. By
this time the question of Negro suffrage had become
a leading issue. For the purpose of obtaining the
sense of the country on this subject, there was
arranged what was known at the time as the
"National Loyalists' Convention," to be held at
Philadelphia in September, 1866. It was made up
of delegates from all parts of the Union, including
many influential men in and out of public life.
Rochester elected Mr. Douglass as its sole representative, which was a great tribute to him, giving
new recognition to the Negro race. The entire
country was quick to take notice of the city's action,
in so important a gathering, and there was not only
objection but open opposition to Mr. Douglass's

taking a seat in the convention. Some of the leading delegates united in an effort to persuade him
not to go.

Speaking of the situation, Mr. Douglass says that
at Harrisburg, there was attached to his train cars
loaded with representatives from some of the western states.

"When my presence became known to these
gentlemen," he continues, "a consultation was
immediately held among them upon the question
of what was best to be done with me. It seems
strange, in view of all the progress which had been
made, that such a question should arise. But the
circumstances of the times made me the Jonah of
the Republican ship, and responsible for the contrary winds and misbehaving weather. I was duly
waited upon by a committee of my brother delegates
to represent to me the undesirableness of my attendance upon the National Loyalists' Convention. The
spokesman of these sub-delegates was a gentleman
from New Orleans. . . . He began by telling
me that he knew my history and my works and that
he entertained no very slight degree of respect for
me ; that both himself and the gentlemen who sent
him, as well as those who accompanied him, regarded me with admiration ; that there was not
among them the remotest objection to sitting in the
convention with me, but their personal wishes in
the matter they felt should be set aside for the sake
of our common cause ; that whether I should or
should not go in the convention was purely a matter
of expediency ; that I must know that there was a
very strong and bitter prejudice against my race in
the North as well as in the South and that the cry
of social and political equality would not fail to be
raised against the Republican party if I should

attend this loyal National convention.   .   .   .
I listened very attentively to the address, uttering
no word during its delivery; but when it was finished, I said to the speaker and the committee, with
all the emphasis I could throw into my voice and
manner, ' Gentlemen, with all respect, you might as
well ask me to put a loaded pistol to my head and
blow my brains out, as to ask me to keep out of this
convention to which I have been duly elected.
Then, gentlemen, what would you gain by the ex-
clusion? Would not the charge of cowardice, certain to be brought against you, prove more damag-
ing than that of amalgamation ; would you not be
branded all over the land as dastardly hypocrites,
professing principles which you have no wish or intention of carrying out? As a matter of policy or
expediency, you will be wise to let me in.   Everybody knows that I have been duly elected as a delegate by the city of Rochester.   This fact has been
broadly announced and commented upon all over
the country.   If I am not admitted, the public will
ask, "Where is Douglass? Why is he not seen in
the convention?" and you would find that inquiry
more difficult to answer than any charge brought
against you for favoring political or social equality ;
but ignoring the question of policy altogether and
looking at it as one of right and wrong, I am bound
to go into that convention ; not to do so would be to
contradict the principles and practice of my life.' ''

The delegates withdrew from the car in which
Mr. Douglass was riding without accomplishing
their purpose.   It was soon made evident to him
that his argument had not changed the prejudices
of his visitors.   When he reached Philadelphia and
learned of the plans of the convention, he easily detected a concerted scheme to ignore him altogether.

"I was," he says, "the ugly and deformed child of the family and to be kept out of sight as much as possible, while there was company in the house."

It had been arranged that the delegates should assemble at Independence Hall and from there march in a body through the streets to the building where the convention was to be held. Mr. Douglass was present at Independence Hall at the appointed time, but he at once realized the situation. Only a few of the delegates, like General B. F. Butler, had the courage even to greet him. He was not only snubbed generally, but it was hinted to him that if he attempted to walk in the procession through the streets of a city where but a few years ago Negroes had been assaulted and their houses and schools burned down, he would be jeered at, insulted, and perhaps mobbed. It required no little courage to act in the face of these conditions, but Douglass never wavered. He was strong enough not to falter even at the desertion of men whom he had a right to regard as his friends.

When the procession was formed, the delegates were to march two abreast. By this arrangement, the man who would have the hardihood to walk beside the only Negro in line would be an easy mark for scorn and contempt if not bodily attack. It was believed that no white man, under these conditions, would dare to march with Douglass. One delegate after another, those who had formerly taken counsel with him, passed him by. But to use his own words: "There was one man present who was broad enough to take in the whole situation and brave enough to meet the duty of the hour ; one who was neither afraid nor ashamed to own me as a man and a brother. One man of the purest Caucasian type, a poet, a scholar, brilliant as a writer, eloquent as a speaker, and holding a high influential position, the editor of a weekly journal having the largest circulation of any weekly paper in the state of New York, and that man was Theodore Tilton. He came to me in my isolation, seized me by the hand in a most brotherly way, and proposed to walk with me in the procession.''

The delegates marching through the streets of Philadelphia met with a great ovation, and Mr. Douglass was singled out for special marks of favor. Along the entire way he was loudly cheered, applauded, and congratulated by the multitude. Those who had misjudged the sentiments of the Philadelphians were ashamed of themselves when they saw that he was apparently the most popular man in the procession.

A very pleasing incident occurred on the line of march that day which served to call special attention to him. As his eyes caught a glimpse of a beautiful young woman among the spectators, he was seen suddenly to leave his place and fervently greet her. She was a member of the Auld family, and Mr. Douglass, recognizing her at once, paid her homage publicly. It appears that she had come to Philadelphia from her home in Baltimore when she heard that the ex-slave was to be there and walk in the procession as one of the great men of the occasion, and had been following the line for over an hour with the hope of catching a view of the man who, but for his desire for freedom, might still have been a servant in her family. The newspapers made much of the incident, and described it as one of the most dramatic features of the day.

By the time the marchers had reached the hall, the fear of Mr. Douglass's presence, as a delegate, had given way to a feeling of respect, pride, and comradeship. He threw off all restraint, and went in to win from this body a resolution in favor of the franchise for his people. He delivered one of those powerful and convincing addresses that he was well able to make when aroused. As a result, he quite captured and controlled the sentiment of the convention in favor of his resolution, and when it adjourned Mr. Douglass was congratulated for having achieved a personal triumph that was remarkable for its completeness.

After the adoption of the Thirteenth, Fourteenth, and Fifteenth Amendments, there was some curious speculation as to what place Frederick Douglass would take in this larger world of citizenship that he had helped to create. A number of his friends and admirers thought that he had led his people so successfully out of the wilderness of slavery that he should now put himself into a position where he could guide them further in the proper use of their rights and privileges as citizens of the republic. Many urged that the South was the right place for one of his power and standing. No colored man in this country had such training for large responsibilities as Mr. Douglass had had, during the previous thirty years of service. It was also feared that, without such leadership as he could bring to the South, small men, of mere political training and of partisan methods and ambitions, would assume the direction of the newly-made citizens, and, by their selfishness and greed, bring down upon these poor people more miseries than could be cured in many generations. Everything seemed to invite Frederick Douglass to these new duties and new responsibilities. It was pointed out to him how easily he could become a pioneer by being elected to the House of Representatives, or even to the Senate, from some of the reconstructed states of the South.

He thought long and seriously over the project, but finally concluded not to change his habitation for the sake of gaining political power. He expressed his conclusions on the matter as follows :

"That I did not yield to this temptation was not entirely due to my age, but the idea did not entirely square well with my better judgment and sense of propriety. The thought of going to live among a people in order to gain their votes and acquire official honors was repugnant to my sense of self-respect, and I had not lived long enough in the political atmosphere of Washington to have this feeling blunted so as to make me indifferent to its suggestions. . . . I had small faith in my aptitude as a politician, and could not hope to cope with rival aspirants. My life and labors in the North had in a measure unfitted me for such work, and I could not have readily adapted myself to that peculiar oratory found to be most effective with the newly enfranchised class. Upon the whole,

I have never regretted that I did not enter the arena
of Congressional honors to which I was invited.
Outside of mere personal considerations, I saw, or
thought I saw, that, in the nature of the case, the
sceptre of power had passed from the old slave-
states to the free and loyal states, and that hereafter, at least for some time to come, the loyal North,
with its advanced civilization, must dictate the policy and control the destiny of the republic. I had
an audience ready made in the free-states, one
which the labors of thirty years had prepared for
me, and before this audience the freedmen needed
an advocate as much as they needed a member in
Congress. I think that in this I was right, for thus
far our colored members in Congress have not largely
made themselves felt in the legislation of this country, and I have little reason to think that I could
have done better than they."

CHAPTER XIV

SHARING THE RESPONSIBILITIES AND HONORS OF FREEDOM

THE course of events in the succeeding thirty years proved that Frederick Douglass was wholly right in his determination not to take up his residence in one of the Southern states for political purposes. Had he followed the advice of some of his friends, his career would have been considerably marred by the exigencies of party and sectional politics, and his character as a natural leader of his people would, in all probability, have shrunken to that of a state politician. He did the wise thing, however, in changing his residence from Rochester to Washington. This brought him in closer touch with his people, as well as near to the law-making forces of the nation.

After he became settled in his new home, he soon found his heart and hands full of occupations that tried his soul. He was fairly overwhelmed with all kinds of schemes and propositions that were carried to him, urging him to do this or that for the protection and elevation of the race. It required a mind of more than ordinary shrewdness to discriminate between the practical and impractical. Many of the Negroes seemed to think him capable of performing miracles in the way of undoing the effects of slavery. It required a stout spirit to listen un-

moved to the wail that came from the hearts of his
sadly distracted people. Those of us who are living forty years after the close of the war, can little
appreciate to what an extent the glory of emancipation was shadowed by the miseries of a whole race
suddenly set free with no preparation for freedom.
When one studies the history of the years that followed emancipation, and learns of the many sins
and errors of the time, and the retribution that
they brought upon the bewildered people in whose
name they were committed, it must seem strange
that the Negro race could survive and make the
progress it has made. Through all the confusion
and clamor of wants, sorrows, sufferings and disap-
pointments, Mr. Douglass kept his head, and was
at all times philosophical, certain that the good accomplished was more important than the seeming
failures; that the hindrances to progress were transitory, the forces of progress permanent. After
he had settled in Washington, two things at once
engaged his attention: the publication of another
paper, *The New National Era*, and the Freedmen's
Bank.

There was apparently a pressing need for a
national organ to advance the cause of the Negro,
and it was believed that the name of Frederick
Douglass at its head would surely bring it a wide
circulation, as well as a commanding influence. He
took hold of the project with characteristic vigor
and invested a large amount of his savings in the
venture. With the assistance of his two sons, both
practical printers, the paper proved to be one of the

greatest helps of the hour. Some of Mr. Douglass's best utterances are to be found in the *New Era*. Its columns were open to the leading colored men and women of that time and it exerted a wide and salutary influence. However, it failed of support. The enterprise cost Mr. Douglass between nine and ten thousand dollars. He seems to have anticipated its financial misfortunes, but said of it afterward : "The journal was valuable, while it lasted, and the experiment was to me full of instruction which has to some extent been heeded, for I have kept well out of newspaper undertakings since, so I have no tears to shed."

When Mr. Douglass went to Washington, he found established there the Freedmen's Bank. It was chartered by Congress and was run and managed in connection with the Freedmen's Bureau. "It was," as Mr. Douglass says, "more than a bank. There was something missionary in its composition." Its managers were men of character and religion, and were interested in everything that could point the way of true living to the ex-slave. To teach the important lesson of thrift was its main object.

For a time this bank flourished very well. Branches were established in various parts of the South. The poor freedmen in the bottom lands of Mississippi and other isolated places quickly learned the use and meaning of the institution ; and eagerly and gratefully committed to its keeping their small earnings. Thousands of these depositors first came to know and realize their relationship to the government at Washington through it. The owners of United States bonds did not feel more secure than did these trusting new citizens of the republic.

The bank and its purposes appealed to Mr. Douglass. He felt it his duty to do anything in his power to help the benevolent enterprise. It was not long before he was elected one of its trustees. He accepted the post and, as an earnest of his interest and confidence in it, placed several thousand dollars in its keeping. He says : "It seemed fitting to cast in my lot with my brother freedmen and help build up an institution which represented the thrift and economy of my people to so striking an advantage, for the more millions accumulated there, I thought, the more consideration and respect would be shown to the colored people by the whole country."

At first he was not active in his new office. He seldom attended the board meetings. The men in charge were of so high a character and had brought the bank up to such rank that his faith in it was well-nigh absolute. He was surprised when soon notified that he had been elected president. Before assuming this post, in 1871, he asked for a statement of the bank's affairs, not because he was suspicious, but that he might the more intelligently take hold of his new duties. He received assurances from the officers that everything was in excellent condition but he at once began a wholesale policy of retrenchment in the expenses of management. From the showing made by those in a position to know and to be believed, Mr. Douglass felt

so confident that everything was as it appeared to
be that he loaned the bank $10,000 of his own
money, until it could realize on a part of its secu-
rities. Soon afterward several things connected
with the bank's management excited his distrust.
The money loaned by him was not repaid so
promptly as it should have been; some of the
trustees had removed their own deposits and opened
accounts with other banks ; and the new president
discovered that through dishonest agents, heavy
losses were sustained in the South ; that there was a
discrepancy in the accounts amounting to about
$40,000 ; that the "reserve" which the bank by its
charter was obliged to maintain was entirely exhausted. All this Mr. Douglass learned after he
had been president for only three months. Being
convinced that things were rapidly going from
bad to worse, he immediately reported the condition of the bank to the Finance Committee of
the United States Senate. The trustees upon whose
figures and reports Mr. Douglass relied for his
action, now tried to retract their statements and did
their utmost to stay the hand of the government,
but the Senate committee accepted his representa-
tions and immediately proceeded to bring the bank
to the end of its remarkable career.

Mr. Douglass did not take advantage of his private
knowledge of its insolvency to remove his $2,000
on deposit, as some trustees had done. In this,
as in other things, he acted with perfect openness
and absolute honesty. Nevertheless the bank's
troubles brought to him no end of bitter criticism.

The number of open accounts at the time of failure was over 60,000 and the total amount deposited during the period of its existence was about $57,000,000.

Bad management may truthfully be written on the face of this greatest single setback to the Negro's progress. Viewed in the light of the condition of these people, striving by might and main to promote their own interests, the failure of the Freedmen's Bank was little less than a crime. The mischief had all been done before Mr. Douglass took charge of the institution. As he says: "Not a dollar of its millions was loaned by me or with my approval. The fact is, and all investigation will show, that I was married to a corpse. When I became connected with the bank I had a tolerably fair name for honest dealing. I had expended in the publication of my paper in Rochester thousands of dollars annually and had often to depend upon my credit to bridge over immediate wants. But no man here or elsewhere can say that I ever wronged him out of one cent."

This miserable failure distressed Mr. Douglass more than any other man in the country, because he saw how wide-spread would be the loss of confidence in him and in his people. The mere fact that his own conscience was clear and that his prompt action prevented further losses did not soften his disappointment. On the contrary, the subject continued to be a source of public bitterness and suspicion for many years, but he was large enough to grow out of and beyond any evil effects

arising from it, so far as his own standing and reputation were concerned.

Important as was the Freedmen's Bank, both as
a success and as a failure, it was but a small part
of the many evidences that the black race was
everywhere awake to the fact that it was living in
a new era. The transformation of the Negro's status
from that of a quasi-denizen to that of a full-fledged
citizen of America was a revolution of far-reaching
import, but it was accompanied by little demonstration. The only proof that a great change had been
brought about was the eagerness with which the
colored people attempted to realize all the benefits
belonging to full citizenship. Up to this time, of
course, they had never had any part in politics, but
it did not take them long to learn the game. Educated Negroes and those who had but little education, very quickly mastered its tricks and made the
most of their opportunities. In every Southern
state colored men were easily elected to the state
legislatures and to other high offices.

In Louisiana, Oscar J. Dunn, P. B. S. Pinchback,
and C. C. Antoine; in South Carolina, Alonzo J.
Ransier and Robert H. Gleaves; and in Mississippi,
Alexander Davis, were elected Lieutenant-Gov-
ernors. Colored men were also chosen for important county and town offices;—there were Negro
sheriffs, county clerks, justices of the peace. To
this period also belongs the election of the only two
colored men ever given seats in the United States
Senate, Hiram R. Revels and Blanche K. Bruce, of
Mississippi. In the lower house of Congress, nearly

every state in the South was represented by Negroes. In addition to these elective offices of honor and distinction, a large number of the leaders of the race held appointive Federal offices, as postmasters, and as collectors of customs and internal reve-nue, and for the first time in the history of the United States, colored men were appointed to dip-lomatic positions.

In recent years, students and writers of the Re-construction period, have indulged in a good deal of unmerited abuse of the colored men who, for a brief season, and without previous training, under the leadership of white politicians, held political posts. It is a deplorable fact that too many inferior persons were elected to fill important state and county offices in the reconstructed states. It is quite true that the colored citizen voted for unfit men of his own race because there was no one else to vote for. This same freedman would more willingly have used his franchise for a white man of character and ability, if he had had the opportunity. The fact is that democracy does not stand still for want of fit men, whether in the Bowery district in New York or in the Black Belt of South Carolina. The Negroes who were elected to Congress, however, were, with but few exceptions, men of character and superior intelligence. B. K. Bruce of Missis-sippi, John R. Lynch, Robert Brown Elliot, A. J. Ransier, and Robert Smalls were highly creditable representatives of a race that had just emerged from the night of slavery. In fact, it is surprising that there were any colored men in the South who had

enough spirit and intelligence even to aspire to the
things that but yesterday were beyond their reach.
It is also worthy of note that among the Negroes
holding positions of dignity and trust, there were
only a few cases in which that trust was know-
ingly betrayed.

The eagerness with which colored men, of any
ability at all, sought public posts was largely due
to the fact that there were few places open to honorable ambitions, outside of public office, to which
they could aspire. Not many at that time had
any training for school-teaching or the professions.
Politics was the one door that opened most widely
to Negroes of ability. The people at large seemed
to enjoy the novelty of seeing these new citizens of
the country so quickly take their places in the
civil service of the government, and wear whatever
honors they could win. The same sentiment that
forced the Fourteenth and Fifteenth Amendments
into the Constitution of the United States, was
gratified when educated and eloquent ex-slaves took
their seats in both branches of Congress.

While it lasted, this was all very pleasing, hopeful, and interesting, but a reaction was bound to
come. The constituency behind these representative leaders lacked the necessary intelligence, knowledge, and business experience. By such an elect-
orate men may be chosen to power, but they cannot
long be held in power.

It was an unfortunate thing, too, that the freedmen
learned their first lessons in politics when public
morals were at so low an ebb. Many sins were

committed and tolerated in the interest of party success. Many desperate men in a spirit at once predatory and partisan, invaded the South and attempted to instruct the colored people in ways that were dark, but ways that led to party victory. These men were bad models for a learning race to follow. Although it was unreasonable to expect these newly-emancipated people to be superior to their white leaders, yet, by recent writers, they have been held accountable for whatever sins were committed in this office-holding era.

Mr. Douglass, in the midst of the political prosperity of his race, was not misled as to the outcome. No one saw more clearly than he the uncertainty of the position to which it had been elevated by recent events. While it is true he was at no time a political power in the South, the colored men who came into office looked to him for counsel and advice. He rejoiced in the many evidences of personal worth and talent displayed by Negroes who, for the first time in American history, were having some real part in the government of the country. Yet experience made him feel and declare that, after all, "the true basis of rights is the capacity of the individual." He urgently pleaded that the government should give the freedman education that he might have knowledge to use his suffrage in such a manner as to preserve his own liberty, and contribute to the public welfare.

Mr. Douglass enjoyed a full share of the honors and responsibilities of office-holding. In each succeeding administration after the war, posts and

places came to him almost as a matter of course, because of his prominence as a representative of the enfranchised race. During the administration of President Grant, he was appointed one of the council-
men of the District of Columbia, and afterward was
elected a member of the legislature of the District.
He soon resigned the last position to accept the
secretaryship of the commission appointed by
Grant to visit San Domingo for the purpose of
negotiating a treaty for the annexation of that
island to the United States. The commission
was composed of Senator B. F. Wade, Dr. S. G.
Howe, and Andrew D. White, President of Cornell
University. The country was somewhat startled by
the innovation of placing a colored man in a position to represent the government on so important a
mission. Its purpose failed. Opposition on the part
of Senator Sumner and other influential Republicans
was of the most bitter and uncompromising sort.

The political feud that arose from General Grant's
San Domingan policy carried many men out of the
Republican party. Mr. Douglass was placed in an
awkward position in accepting the appointment,
because his great friend, Senator Sumner, was the
leader of the opposition to the President's plan of
annexation. He admired and was personally attached to both because of their heroic services in the
cause of freedom and citizenship for his people.
Explaining his attitude, he said : "I am free to say
that, had I been guided only by the promptings of
my heart, I should, in this controversy, have followed Charles Sumner. He was not only the most

clear-sighted, brave, and uncompromising friend of my race who had ever stood upon the floor of the Senate, but he was to me a loved, honored, and precious personal friend.''

After Senator Sumner had arraigned President Grant in a notable speech in the Senate, Mr. Douglass happened to be a caller at the White House and was asked by the President what he now thought of his friend from Massachusetts. True to his feelings, Douglass frankly replied that, in his opinion, the Senator was sincere in his position, believing that in opposing annexation he defended the cause of the colored race, as he had always done. "I saw that my reply was not satisfactory," Douglass observes, "and I said, 'What do you think, Mr. President, of Senator Sumner?' He replied with some feeling, 'I think he is mad.'"

By his perfect frankness, Mr. Douglass was able to retain the respect and confidence of both men. He agreed with President Grant in his annexation policy and had, at the same time, a special fondness for the Massachusetts Senator. He frequently dined with the latter and they were often seen walking arm in arm in the corridors of the Capitol, while Douglass embraced every opportunity to sound the praises of his friend. In an address delivered at New Orleans before a convention of colored men, during this Grant-Sumner feud, he said : "There is now at Washington a man who represents the future and is a majority in himself,—a man at whose feet Grant learns wisdom. That man is Charles Sumner. I know them both ; they are great men, but Sumner is as steady as the north star ; he is no flickering light. For twenty-five years he has worked for the Republican party and I hope I may cease forever, if I cease to give all honor to Charles Sumner." And later he said: "As a man of integrity and truth, Charles Sumner was high above suspicion, and not all the Grants in Christendom will rob him of his well-earned character."

Notwithstanding his repeatedly declared loyalty to the Senator, Mr. Douglass was found in the ranks doing valiant service for the reëlection of General Grant for a second term. His coöperation was needed in some quarters, because the colored voters were not a little confused when such stalwart friends as Sumner, Senator Trumbull, of Illinois ; Carl Schurz, of Missouri ; and Horace Greeley, of New York, were found in the "camp of the enemy," fighting the Republican party. The National Convention of Colored Men, held in New Orleans in April, 1872, affords an interesting example of how puzzling was the split in the Republican organization to the average Negro voter. This was a very large and representative body. The members were in a state of grave apprehension, on account of the division in the ranks of the black man's party. Many of the leading delegates in attendance were uncertain to whom their allegiance should be given. It was difficult for a colored man in those days not to be with Sumner, right or wrong.

It was here that Mr. Douglass demonstrated his power as a political leader. His speech as president of the convention was a notable effort. It was telegraphed in full to the New York *Herald*, and throughout the country it was widely circulated and read, as a campaign document. It did more than any other one thing to hold the colored people in party lines. In addition to this, Douglass took an active part in the ensuing struggle, and no orator in the Grant-Greeley contest was more popular than he. To the black voter, who wanted to follow the Liberal Republicans led by Senator Sumner, he urged that there was "no path out of the Republican party that did not lead directly into the camp of the Democratic party—away from our friends, directly to our enemies." It was in this campaign, too, that he made use of the well-known party aphorism, "The Republican party is the ship, and all else is the sea."

What was more important and interesting than any other thing in this contest, so far as Mr. Douglass was concerned, was the singular recognition shown him by the Republicans of New York, who placed his name on the ticket as one of the electors of that state. No other colored man in the history of the country had ever been so honored. When the electoral college met in Albany, he was commissioned to carry the New York vote to the capital of the nation.

Though he had done valiant service for the re-election of General Grant, Mr. Douglass neither asked nor received any reward in the form of an office. At that time there were but few honors in the gift of the President that could be considered within the reach of a colored man. The one diplomatic post which he could have obtained for the asking—as minister to Hayti—he made no effort to get, but generously supported his friend E. D. Bassett, of Philadelphia, for it.   Mr. Bassett was a man of fine attainments and exceptionally well qualified for the office.   This act of deference to the claims of others was characteristic of Mr. Douglass in all of his relationships to the prominent Negroes of his generation.

In 1877, and after the election and inauguration of President Hayes, the whole country was more or less startled by the announcement that Frederick Douglass had been appointed Marshal of the District of Columbia.   This office was one of much political and social responsibility, and the appointment of an ex-slave produced a sensation in Washington.   As Mr. Douglass says, "It came upon the people of the District as a great surprise and almost a punishment, and provoked something like a scream, I will not say a yell, of popular displeasure."   This was not an exaggerated statement of the public feeling directed against the appointment.   Plans were set on foot to secure the defeat of his nomination in the United States Senate.   It seemed impossible for the people at the capital to view the President's action in any other way than as the degradation of an exalted office.   They were sure that Mr. Douglass would use his place to "Africanize the District courts"; and the great social functions of the White House, with a Negro as "Lord High Chamberlain," would become the laughing-stock of the enlightened world.

If Mr. Douglass had been a man of less tact and intelligence, and had not occupied so high a place in popular esteem, he could not have withstood the strength and bitterness of the opposition. His good standing, in spite of his color, saved him and the Hayes administration from a humiliating surrender to popular prejudice. When his name reached the Senate, it was confirmed without serious discussion. Senator Conkling had charge of the matter, and swept away all opposition in a perfect storm of eloquent ridicule of the reasons presented for rejection. Unfortunately, the Senate's action did not wholly end the agitation. Every word and act of Mr. Douglass's was scrutinized for some proof of his unfitness. Shortly after the confirmation of his appointment, he delivered an address in the city of Baltimore, taking as his theme "Our National Capital." It was an interesting mixture of praise and criticism, though in no way the result of recent occurrences, for he had delivered the same speech in Washington some months before and it provoked no discussion. He was, therefore, greatly surprised to find, when he returned to the capital, that the old animosity which had spent itself in attempting to defeat his appointment, was again aroused. The objectionable portions of his Baltimore lecture were quoted and commented upon in terms of unqualified bitterness. An effort was made to induce the sureties on his bond to withdraw, and in this way disqualify him to act in his official capacity. Strong pressure was brought to bear on the President to relieve the capital of the nation of the insufferable offense of an official who had so little sense of the proprieties as to hold up Washington and its citizens to public ridicule. All this, however, proved to be of no effect. His bondsmen, one of whom was a wealthy and prominent Democrat of the District, could not be persuaded to embarrass the Negro marshal by withdrawing their names. Hayes was likewise firm in resisting all efforts to remove Mr. Douglass, who refers gratefully to the President as follows: "When all Washington was in an uproar, and a wild clamor rent the air for my removal from the office of marshal, on account of the lecture delivered by me in Baltimore, and when petitions were flowing in upon him demanding my degradation, he nobly rebuked the mad spirit of persecution by openly declaring his purpose to retain me in my place."

Douglass's successful fight in retaining his position of honor was interesting, not so much because of his personal standing, as because it was typical of the whole struggle of his race, since emancipation, to win their way into the confidences of the American people by proving themselves capable of using their liberty and their citizenship in a proper manner.

If Mr. Douglass had been sacrificed to the demands of popular prejudice, it would have served as a disqualifying precedent in the matter of future opportunities of colored men with honorable ambitions. In a short while, all opposition was quieted, and the new marshal pursued the routine of his duties without hindrance or serious embarrassment.

The judges and attorneys of the District soon learned to treat the Negro official with respect and courtesy. None of the awful things predicted came to pass, and the powers that stood behind him and were responsible for him were wholly vindicated.

During the trying ordeal from which he had so successfully emerged, Mr. Douglass complained somewhat petulantly that "no colored man in the city uttered one public word in defense or extenuation of me or my Baltimore speech, except Dr. Charles B. Purvis." He was always sensitive to the least evidence of opposition or slight on the part of his own people. For a man who had done so much for his race at a time when it was unable to do anything for itself, it was, perhaps, quite natural for him to feel as he did, now that so many voices were lifted against him. Whatever hostility or indifference the colored people in the District exhibited toward Mr. Douglass, was probably due to jealousy of his leadership and a professed chagrin on account of the alleged willingness on his part to accept the office with the abridgment of the social privileges enjoyed by previous marshals.

His answer to these complaints was such as to satisfy any reasonable person that it meant no surrender of principle. All the functions that legally belonged to his office he performed. The ornamental duties that had grown up by custom and usage, he willingly left to others. He had enjoyed more social opportunities than any colored man in the country and he possessed infinite tact and a fine sense of discrimination as to rights and privileges.

Frequently while he was marshal, he was called upon to introduce distinguished strangers to the President.   He said :   "I was ever a welcome visitor at the Executive Mansion on state occasions and on all others while Rutherford B. Hayes was President of the United States."

As time passed, his own people, as well as other men in Washington, came to admire Douglass's good sense as well as his fine bearing on all occasions.   The proudest event in his official life was associated with the inauguration of General James A. Garfield as President of the United States.   The Marshal of the District of Columbia was called upon to act an important part in the greatest of all national ceremonies.   He was brought into touch with the retiring as well as the incoming President. He had the honor of escorting them both from the chamber of the United States Senate to the east front of the Capitol where the oath of office was to be taken by President Garfield and where he delivered his inaugural address to a vast concourse of people.

In speaking of that experience, Douglass says with pardonable pride :

"I felt myself standing on new ground, on a height never before trodden by any of my people, one heretofore occupied only by members of the Caucasian race.   .   .   .   I deemed the event highly important as a new circumstance in my career, as a new recognition of my class, and as a new step in the progress of the nation.   Personally, it was a striking contrast to my early condition.   Yonder I was an unlettered slave, toiling under the ' Negro

breaker'; here I was the United States Marshal of
the capital of the nation, having under my care and
guidance the sacred persons of an ex-President and
the President-elect of a nation of sixty millions of
people, and was armed with a nation's power to
arrest any arm raised against them. While I was
not insensible or indifferent to the fact that I was
treading the high places of the land, I was not conscious of any unsteadiness of head or heart. I was
a United States Marshal by accident. I was no less
Frederick Douglass, identified with a proscribed
class, whose perfect and practical equality with
other American citizens, was yet far down the steps
of time. Yet I was not sorry to have this brief
authority for I rejoiced in the fact that a colored
man could occupy this height and that the precedent
was valuable."

Thus it was that Mr. Douglass esteemed every
honor or favor earned and received by him, to
mean some fresh recognition of the worth of
the Negro race. He sustained a very close and
cordial relationship to Mr. Garfield. He had done
effective service in the campaign that resulted in
the election of the new President, whose fine abilities and robust Americanism he greatly admired.
Shortly after the inauguration, Mr. Douglass was
summoned to the White House. Garfield wished
to discuss with this acknowledged leader of the
Negro race his policy in reference to appointments
of colored men to office. He assured Mr. Douglass
of his intention to place capable colored men in a
higher grade of positions in the diplomatic service,

and he asked if, in Douglass's opinion, nations composed of white people would object to receiving colored men as representatives of the American government. He also assured Douglass that Senator Conkling's wish for his (Douglass's) reappointment as Marshal of the District of Columbia would be granted with pleasure. The Negro leader found the position thoroughly congenial to him, and it was a matter of satisfaction to realize that he had so successfully lived down past objections that no one now raised a voice against him.   But for reasons that were never divulged to him, he was displaced, and another was appointed to the post.

Though he was keenly disappointed and chagrined, Douglass believed in Mr. Garfield and was not inclined to censure him because of his broken promise. He had strong faith that the President was about to carry out a policy of recognition of the colored race which would be more liberal than that of any of his predecessors.   He felt that the colored people at this time needed a firm friend.   He clearly saw that his race in respect to its rights of citizenship was slipping back from the high position occupied by it ten years prior to this time.   He feared that the reaction which began to set in after the withdrawal of Federal troops from the South in 1876 would carry his people to something like political serfdom unless some strong hand would come to their aid.

The assurances now given to him by President Garfield that the Negro and his cause would receive fair and honest treatment relieved his anxiety despite his own displacement, and he confidently expected that the administration of General Garfield would mean much to Negro progress in all directions.

Alas for human hopes! Before the big-hearted man could put his good intentions into effect, the assassin had done his evil work. Mr. Douglass, like every one else close to the President, was overwhelmed with grief. He said: "Few men in this country felt more keenly than I the shock created by the assassination of President Garfield and few men had better reason for this feeling."

When Vice-President Arthur succeeded to the presidency, Mr. Douglass was appointed Recorder of Deeds of the District of Columbia. This was a lucrative office and a good deal of patronage was attached to it. Being the first colored man to be appointed to the post, he had to face the opposition that usually attaches to an innovation ; but the objections were not of a serious nature and soon subsided.

He continued in this place for five years. When Mr. Cleveland came to the presidency he rather expected to be removed summarily ; but the Democratic chief magistrate proved to be less of a party man than either the Recorder or the average Republican expected. The new President was too high-minded to be a mere partisan, and to Mr. Douglass's surprise, he was treated with much respect and kindness. He and his wife were invited to all public functions given at the White House and Mr. Cleveland in every way showed that he shared the public esteem in which the great Negro was so universally held.   He was allowed to occupy the position for quite a year under the Democratic administration.   Then instead of removing or asking for his resignation in the usually abrupt way, the President graciously wrote to know when it would be convenient for him to give up the post.

Mr. Cleveland further indicated his kindly regard for the colored people of the country by promising them that his election would not mean a curtailment of their liberties, as some of them feared. For this assurance Mr. Douglass made public acknowledgment.   The statements of the President were timely and quieting, because for the first time in twenty years, the more ignorant of the Negroes were somewhat panic-stricken.   Speaking of their fears, Douglass testified "to the painful apprehension and distress felt by my people in the South from the return to power of the old Democratic and slavery party.   To many of them, it seemed that they were left naked to their enemies, in fact, lost; that Mr. Cleveland's election meant the revival of the slave-power and that they would now again be reduced to slavery and the lash.   The misery brought to the South by this wide-spread alarm can hardly be described or measured.   The wail of despair for a time from the late bondmen was deep, bitter and heart-rending.   . . .   It was well for the poor people in this condition that Mr. Cleveland himself sent word South to allay their fear and remove their agony."

Mr. Douglass always cherished a very sincere admiration for President Cleveland, for this and other reasons, and regarded it as highly fortunate that a man so just and non-partisan should be elected as the first Democratic President after emancipation. As a result of his fair treatment, the American Negroes first learned that the term Democratic did not necessarily mean for them loss of rights and citizenship. In fact, his liberal policy caused a great many of the more intelligent colored men very seriously to consider the advisability of a division of the Negro vote between the two great parties. Men of the high standing of Archibald H. Grimké, of Boston, Mass., and W. M. E. Matthews, of New York, argued with great plausibility that one way to convince the American people of his qualifications for citizenship, would be for the Negro to learn to vote for principles rather than for party leaders. They insisted that to take the pitn out of the Democratic opposition to his appearance in politics, a goodly portion of the voters should join themselves to that party. It was unfortunate that this tendency to political independence on the part of the enlightened colored men could not have been encouraged. However natural and human it may be for the Negro people to be allied wholly to one of two political parties, it is nevertheless a serious hindrance to the colored man's political freedom that he must continue to regard the Republican party as composed wholly of his friends and the Democratic party as composed wholly of his enemies. Mr. Douglass openly confessed his inability to take this new stand in politics, notwithstanding his admiration for Mr. Cleveland and his respect for the motives of the few colored men in the country who were independent enough to break away from party control. Though he personally could not join the movement he regarded it as a sign of progress for colored men of character and intellect to say that they cared more for their race than for party, and more for their country than for their race.

The last public office held by Mr. Douglass under the United States government was that of Minister Resident and Consul General to the Republic of Hayti. This seemed a fitting climax to the long list of honors that came to him, not so much as a reward of party service as for his own high deserving. The appointment was made by President Harrison and was wholly unsought. Douglass had, of course, and as usual, taken an active part in the campaign of 1888. The tariff was the main subject of contention and it was more than hinted to him that he was expected to make the most of this issue. He nevertheless had his own way, and everywhere he insisted that the paramount issue was the rights of men.

On the stump he was as popular as ever ; on all sides he found the people deeply interested in his fervent pleas for justice to his race. Speaking of his efforts in the last political campaign in which he took a prominent part, he said : "I held that the soul of the nation was in this question and that the gain of all the gold in the world would not compensate for the loss of the national soul. National honor is the soul of the nation and when this is lost all is lost. . . . As with an individual, so with a nation. There is a time when it may be properly asked, What does it profit a nation to gain the whole world and lose its own soul?"

In accepting the honor of representing this country in Hayti Frederick Douglass was about to realize a long cherished wish,—an opportunity to see and study the only republic established and carried on by black men in the Western world. In some respects his appointment at another time would have been more agreeable. Very much to his surprise and chagrin, and for causes of which he was wholly innocent, it was bitterly opposed. Antagonism to him came almost wholly from the East and was confined to interests that were bent upon obtaining valuable concessions from Hayti. Certain New York newspapers tried to make it appear that he was unfitted for the place, and insisted that the people wanted a white man to represent the United States, although every representative from this government to Hayti since 1869 had been a colored man. It was also urged that Douglass would not be well received, because at one time he favored the annexation of San Domingo.

Even after his appointment was confirmed by the United States Senate, the opposition still pursued him. For example, it was said that the captain of the ship designated by the government to convey the new minister to Port-au-Prince, refused to take him on board because of his complexion; that after he arrived at the capital of Hayti he was snubbed by the officials for the same reason; and that it was found he had not been duly accredited.

In these statements there was scarcely a grain of truth. There was no insult to Mr. Douglass by the captain of the boat; there was no lack of cordiality and respect on the part of the Haytians on account of his color; and there was no embarrassment of any kind to warrant the peculiar and insistent opposition that followed him from the moment his appointment was announced. There were two issues of commanding interest at this time which made the position of our Minister to Port-au-Prince a trying one. First in importance was a desire on the part of the United States to secure by treaty, Môle St. Nicolas as a naval station; and, second, a desperate determination by the Clyde Steamship Company to obtain from the Haytian government a subsidy of a half-million dollars to ply a line of steamers between New York and Hayti.

As an evidence of the mean spirit of Mr. Douglass's enemies, he was grossly misrepresented as being the cause of the failure of the United States to obtain the Môle. The great perversion of the real facts surrounding the diplomatic efforts on the part of the government to procure from Hayti the use of this port, led Mr. Douglass to publish in the *North American Review* for September and October, 1891, a full history of his connection with the affair. In this interesting account of the negotiations carried on during his official residence in Hayti, it will be seen that he was in no way responsible for the re-

sult. In the first place, he was not vested with
authority to arrange with Hayti for a United
States naval station. He had been there as a representative of this government over one year before
the matter was taken up. When the United States
got ready to negotiate a treaty, the subject was entrusted wholly to a special agent in the person of
Rear-Admiral Gherardi. Mr. Douglass's only instructions were to coöperate with and assist the
Admiral in every possible way. The news of the
appointment of a special commissioner by the
United States government was viewed by Mr.
Douglass as "sudden and far from flattering." It
placed him in an unenviable light, both before the
community of Port-au-Prince and the government of Hayti, and made his position very humble,
secondary, and subordinate. He said : "The situation suggested the resignation of my office as due to
my honor, but reflection soon convinced me that
such a course would subject me to misconstruction
more hurtful than any which, in the circumstances,
could justly arise from remaining at my post."

He cordially and energetically assisted Admiral
Gherardi. He secured audiences with the President
and the Minister of Foreign Affairs of Hayti, and did
not allow anything like offended dignity to diminish his zeal and alacrity in carrying out his instructions.

In the conference, Mr. Douglass supplemented the
arguments of the commissioner in an earnest appeal
in behalf of the United States. He urged that the
concession asked for by his government, "was in

line with good neighborhood, and advanced civilization, and in every way consistent with Haytian
autonomy ; that such a concession would be a source
of strength to Hayti ; that national isolation was a
worn-out policy, and that the true policy of Hayti
ought to be to touch the world at all points that
make for civilization and commerce.''

All arguments, however, failed to overcome the
deep-seated suspicion of the Haytian people of any
proposition to yield even one inch of their national
dominion. While in Mr. Douglass's opinion, the
negotiations were ill-timed, being prejudiced by the
previous demands of the agents of the Clyde Company, and by the apparent threat in the presence of
a part of the United States Navy in the Haytian
harbor, he yet gave it as his deliberate opinion that
no earthly power outside of absolute force could
have obtained for the American government a naval
station at Môle St. Nicolas.

He also found that Hayti was somewhat suspicious of the United States on account of the
national prejudice against the color of its citizens.
While loyal to his own government, Mr. Douglass
scarcely blamed them for this feeling. He believed
in the future of the little republic, and said :
'' Whatever may happen of peace or war, Hayti will
remain in the firmament of nations and like the
north star will shine on, and shine forever.''

CHAPTER XV

FURTHER EVIDENCES OF POPULAR ESTEEM, WITH GLIMPSES INTO THE PAST

THE foregoing chapters contain the important incidents and events in the life of Frederick Douglass. He lived in a great transitional period, and, in his struggle to gain his own freedom, he personified the historic events which took place during that time. His life was so wholly under the public eye, and what he did and stood for during more than fifty years, were so much an integral portion of these years, that it is impossible to obtain an estimate of the man apart from the history of slavery. Frederick Douglass and Anti-slavery, are almost interchangeable terms. In himself he was both the argument and demonstration of the things that gave interest and meaning to his life and times. Yet he had another side not exhibited in the history of which he was a part and which he helped to make. Much of a personal nature that would add interest to his life and partly explain the sources of his strength as a leader of men, can be added to the portrait.

The limitations of this volume will permit only a brief outline of some of the things that Frederick Douglass said and did during the last thirty years of his life, which chronologically belonged to pre-

vious chapters, but which for the sake of their
peculiar significance are reserved for this.

As may be inferred from what has appeared in the
course of this narrative, Frederick Douglass was a
more than ordinarily interesting personality. He
was a figure to attract attention anywhere, and especially so during the last twenty-five years of his
life.   He was over six feet in height, broad-shoul-
dered, well-proportioned, and his movements had
all the directness and grace of a man who had been
bred a prince rather than a slave. His features
were broad, strong, and impressive. His complexion was that of a mulatto. His head was strikingly
large, and crowned with an abundant crop of white
hair of almost silken fineness. His eyes were
brown and mildly animated. His voice was strong,
but of mellow tone. When he was aroused, however, it would fairly thunder with the passionate
earnestness of the man. In conversation he was delightful. His manner was graceful and wholly free
from personal mannerisms. His mental and moral
faculties were well balanced. He was a man without technical education, yet he had more than ordinary learning. All that he knew was acquired outside of schoolrooms and without school teachers.
His great library bore witness to his love of books.
In the history of governments and of races, and in
mental philosophy and poetry, he found special delight. No trained elocutionist could recite verse with
better effect. He was especially fond of Byron,
Burns, Coleridge, and Pierpont.

He was always quick to recognize ability in one

of his race, and so had a peculiar fondness and interest in Paul Laurence Dunbar, who, at his death, was just beginning to be known as a poet, and who received his first real encouragement from Frederick Douglass.

He had an unfailing memory, and consequently a good command of everything he ever saw, heard, or read. He was liked and honored by men and women, not only because he was interesting, but also because he was singularly free from crotchets, idiosyncrasies, and ill-temper. He was of a lovable disposition, and especially so in the latter days of his life. The all too common character blemishes of selfishness, envy, and jealousy were never charged against him. His whole nature was keyed to high, generous impulses. He loved the right, and hated wrong in any form.

No man of his prominence was freer from vices : he was of temperate habits, clean speech, and personal rectitude. His sense of honor was not partial, but a controlling force in all of his relationships to men and things.

He was also fortunately free from family troubles, except the loss by death of a beloved little daughter, whose few gentle and beautiful years had been his delight, a sorrow which deeply shadowed the earlier period of his public career. His wife, who had helped him to gain his freedom, devoted her life to his comfort and to the happiness of his home. His three stalwart sons, Lewis, Charles, and Frederick, Jr., honored him by lives of usefulness, and there was always the closest intimacy between him and them. His oldest girl, named Rosa, was very dear to him. She grew up by his side as a faithful helper in his work as well as a devoted daughter. She is widely known and loved for her culture and unselfish disposition. In short, Frederick Douglass's family was worthy of him. If by his deeds he brought to them honor and opportunity, he lived long enough to see his example and precepts honored again in them.

His home in Cedar Hill, overlooking the Capitol, was a delightful spot. Everything about it bespoke the character of the man. The broad grounds, shaded with trees, the well-cultivated garden, all told of his love of nature. Within the ample house there was a quiet, restful refinement, revealing the taste and habits of the scholar. Books, busts, and pictures all bore witness to that instinctive thirst for culture which no one who knew him well could fail to recognize. He had an extraordinary passion for the violin, and, although he did not place a very high estimate upon his own ability, yet he, as well as his nearest friends, received much enjoyment from his knowledge of the use of this instrument.

In later years he found a special delight in the fact that his grandson, Joseph Douglass, exhibited a decided taste and a real genius for the violin. A more affecting picture of the power of music could scarcely be imagined than that of the old man sitting and listening with rapt and tearful attention when this boy played for him some of his favorite tunes.

But perhaps these glimpses of the personality of

Frederick Douglass are sufficient to suggest that, behind the great orator, the active politician, the anxious leader in a critical period, there was a real man, whose domestic tastes and disciplined heart give an added value to his public life. It is not at all surprising that one thus gifted should have had many intimates among the best people of his generation. The leading statesmen, educators, and literary men were counted as his close and personal friends. Behind the respect that was felt for his natural talents and his unusual achievements was a sincere admiration and even fondness for the large and warm-hearted nature which could laugh and cry and be touched by the social delights of home and fireside. He was a man of opinions, of ideals, of imagination, and had the gift of adequate expression for every thought and emotion.

After the death of his first wife, Mr. Douglass married again, in 1884, and for this step he was severely criticised. The fact that his second wife, Miss Helen Pitts, was a white woman caused something like a revulsion of feeling throughout the entire country. His own race especially condemned him, and the notion seemed to be quite general that he had made the most serious mistake of his life. Just how deep-seated was the sentiment of white and black people alike against amalgamation has never been so clearly demonstrated as in this case. Douglass was sorely hurt by the many unkind things said about his marriage by members of his own race.'

The woman whom he married he had known and

admired for many years. She had helped him in
various ways in his literary work. She belonged to
one of the best families in western New York, and
in following the natural impulse of his attachment,
he failed to take into consideration the offense his
act might give to public feeling. The resentment
felt by the people because of his disregard of its unwritten law never entirely died out in his lifetime,
but he himself got over the personal discomfiture of
it. In addressing a large audience of white and
colored people in Springfield, Mo., in the fall of
1893, he referred to this incident in the following
words : " I am strongly of the opinion that you
will want me to say something concerning my
second marriage. I will tell you : My first wife,
you see, was the color of my mother, and my second
wife the color of my father ; you see I wanted to be
perfectly fair to both races." This clever bit of
raillery on a very delicate subject put him on good
terms with his audience and if any were inclined to
think the less of him because of his marriage the
fact did not then appear.

In the period from 1865 to the Columbian Exposition at Chicago, in 1893, Mr. Douglass was interested in many things. He made various addresses
outside of the range of politics, and was busy to the
limit of his waning strength. What he wrote found
ready acceptance in important publications, and his
absence from any great national gathering was a
matter of regret.

Among the many tokens of respect that continued
to come to him from all parts of the country, he

cherished none so much as the tribute paid to him by the city of Rochester, his home during the twenty-five formative years of his career. In the name of the city, some of its leading citizens caused to be placed in Sibley's Hall, at Rochester University, a noble bust of Frederick Douglass. It was a gracious recognition of the esteem in which he was held by the people who had had the best opportunity of knowing him. The Rochester *Democrat and Chronicle* expressed the sentiment of the city in the following eulogy written at the time :

"Frederick Douglass can hardly be said to have risen to greatness on account of the opportunities which the republic offers to self-made men, and concerning which we are apt to talk with an abundance of self-gratulation. It sought to fetter his mind equally with his body. For him it builded no schoolhouse, and for him it erected no church. So far as he was concerned, freedom was mockery, and law was the instrument of tyranny. In spite of law and gospel, despite of statutes which enthralled him and opportunities which jeered at him, he made himself, by trampling on the laws and breaking through the thick darkness that encompassed him. There is no sadder commentary upon human slavery than the life of Frederick Douglass. He put it under his feet and stood erect in the majesty of his intellect ; but how many intellects, brilliant and powerful as his, it stamped upon and crushed, no mortal can tell until the secret of its terrible despotism is fully revealed. Thanks to the conquering might of American freedom, such sad beginnings of such illustrious lives as that of Frederick Douglass are no longer possible ; and that they are no longer possible, is largely due to him, who when his lips were unlocked, became a deliverer of his people. Not alone did his voice proclaim emancipation. Eloquent as was that voice, his life in its pathos and in its grandeur, was more deeply eloquent still ; and where shall be found, in the annals of humanity, a sweeter rendering of poetic justice than that he, who has passed through such vicissitudes of degradation and exaltation, has been permitted to behold the redemption of his race ?

" Rochester is proud to remember that Frederick Douglass was, for many years, one of her citizens. He who pointed out the house where Douglass lived, hardly exaggerated when he called it the residence of the greatest of our citizens, for Douglass must rank as among the greatest men, not only of this city, but of the nation as well—great in gifts, greater in utilizing them, great in the persuasion of his speech, greater in the purpose that informed it.

" Rochester could do nothing more graceful than to perpetuate in marble the features of this citizen in her hall of learning ; and it is pleasant for her to know that he so well appreciates the esteem in which he is held here. It was a thoughtful thing for Rochester to do, and the response is as heartfelt as the tribute is appropriate."

Among his notable addresses during the period under review was one delivered on Decoration Day in 1871 at Arlington. His theme was " The Unknown Loyal Dead." President Grant, the members of the Cabinet, and a large number of the most prominent people of Washington were present, and the occasion was unusually impressive. He rose grandly to the need of the hour. The oration was in his best vein and is in part as follows :—

"Friends and Fellow Citizens :—Tarry here for a moment. My words shall be few and simple. The solemn rites of this hour and place call for no lengthened speech. There is, in the very air of this resting-ground of the unknown dead, a silent, subtle and all-pervading eloquence, far more touching, impressive, and thrilling, than living lips have ever uttered. Into the measureless depths of every loyal soul it is now whispering lessons of all that is precious, priceless, holiest and most enduring to the nation in human existence.

"Dark and sad will be the hour to this nation when it forgets to pay grateful homage to its greatest benefactors. The offering we bring to-day is due alike to the patriot soldiers, dead, and their noble comrades who still live ; for, whether living or dead, whether in time or in eternity, the loyal soldiers who imperiled all for country and freedom are one and inseparable.

"These unknown heroes whose whitened bones have been piously gathered here, and whose green graves we now strew with sweet and beautiful flowers, choice emblems alike of pure hearts and brave spirits, reached in their glorious career that last highest point of nobleness beyond which human power cannot go. They died for their country.

"No loftier tribute can be paid to the most illustrious of all the benefactors of mankind than we pay to these unrecognized soldiers when we write above their graves this shining epitaph.

"When the dark and vengeful spirit of slavery, always ambitious, preferring 'to rule in Hell than to serve in Heaven' fired the southern heart and stirred all the malign elements of discord ; when our great republic, the hope of freedom and self-government throughout the world, had reached the point of supreme peril ; when the union of the states was torn and rent asunder at the centre, and the armies of a gigantic rebellion came forth with broad blades and bloody hands to destroy the very foundation of American society, the unknown braves who flung themselves into the yawning chasm, where cannon roared and bullets whistled, fought and fell.   They died for their country.

" We are sometimes asked, in the name of patriotism, to forget the merits of this fearful struggle, and to remember with equal admiration those who struck at the nation's life and those who struck to save it; those who fought for slavery and those who fought for liberty and justice.

" I am no minister of malice.   I would not strike the fallen.   I would not repel the repentant; but may my right hand forget her cunning and my tongue cleave to the roof of my mouth, if I forget the difference between the parties to that terrible, protracted and bloody conflict.

" If we ought to forget a war which has filled our land with widows and orphans; which has made stumps of men of the very flower of our youth; which has sent them on the journey of life armless, legless, maimed and mutilated; which has piled up a debt heavier than a mountain of gold, swept uncounted thousands of men into bloody graves and planted agony at a million hearthstones—I say, if this war is to be forgotten, I ask in the name of things sacred, what shall men remember? "

Five years later Mr. Douglass was again honored with an invitation to deliver the address in memory of Abraham Lincoln, at Lincoln Park, in Washington.   The occasion and the man were happily blended.   No orator ever had a more inspiring theme.   The rulers of the nation in the persons of President Grant and his Cabinet advisers, members of the United States Senate, Justices of the Supreme

Court, and a great many high officials were present to evidence the importance of the day ; and in such a company of distinguished people Douglass delivered what many call his supreme effort as an orator. The speech later was printed as a pamphlet, and extensively read throughout the country.

His closing words addressed to his own people, prescient, as they seemed to be of days and dangers as yet but vaguely understood, made an ineffaceable impression upon men of his color who heard him :

"We have done a great work for our race to-day. In doing honor to the memory of our friend and liberator, we have been doing highest honor to ourselves and those who are to come after us. We have been attaching to ourselves a name and fame imperishable and immortal. We have also been defending ourselves from a blighting scandal, when now it shall be said that the colored man is soulless, that he has no appreciation of benefits or benefactors ; when the foul reproach of ingratitude is hurled at us, and it is attempted to scourge us beyond the range of human brotherhood, we may calmly point to this monument we have this day erected to the memory of Abraham Lincoln."

In his address before the Tennessee Colored Agricultural and Mechanical Association at Nashville, September 18, 1873, he furnished the country new evidence of his ability to give instruction, to inspire hope and ambition, and to encourage thrift. Though not an agriculturist by occupation, his speech can still be used as a manual for the young farmer.

It, like his other addresses, is full of practical and useful maxims. His quotation from Theodore Parker, "All the space between man's mind and God's mind is crowded with truths which wait to be discovered and organized into law for the practice of men," indicates the tone of high hopefulness that ran through all his appeals to the people. "If we look abroad over our country and observe the condition of the colored people," he said, "we shall find their greatest want to be regular and lucrative employment for their energies. They have secured their freedom, it is true, but not the friendship and favor of the people around them. . . . On account of bad treatment, great numbers are driven from the country to the larger cities where they quickly learn to imitate the vices and follies of the least exemplary whites. Under these circumstances, I hail agriculture as a refuge for the oppressed."

Insisting that the condition of the Negro in this country is exceptional, he reminded his hearers that "the farm is our last resort, and if we fail here, I do not see how we can succeed elsewhere. We are not like the Irish, an organized political power ; we are not shrewd like the Hebrews, capable of making fortunes by buying and selling old clothes."

The address is rich with maxims that are good to remember and to use as rules of conduct ; such as :

"Emancipation has liberated the land as well as the people."

"It is not fertility, but liberty that cultivates a country."

"The state of Tennessee is now to be cultivated by liberty, by knowledge which comes of liberty, by the respectability of labor."

"Neither the slave nor his master can abandon all at once the deeply entrenched errors and habits of centuries."

"There is no work that men are required to do, which they cannot better and more economically do with education than without it."

"Muscle is mighty but mind is mightier, and there is no field for the exercise of mind other than is found in the cultivation of the soul."

"As a race we have suffered from two very opposite causes, disparagement on the one hand and undue praise on the other."

"An important question to be answered by evidences of our progress is : Whether the black man will prove a better master to himself than the white master was to him."

"Accumulate property. This may sound to you like a new gospel. No people can ever make any social and mental improvement whose exertions are limited. Poverty is our greatest calamity. . . . On the other hand, property, money, if you please, will produce for us the only condition upon which any people can rise to the dignity of genuine manhood."

"Without property there can be no leisure. Without leisure there can be no invention, without invention there can be no progress."

"We can work, and by this means we can retrieve all our losses."

"Knowledge, wisdom, culture, refinement, manners, are all founded on work and the wealth which work brings."

"In nine cases out of ten a man's condition is

worse by changing his location.   You would better
endeavor to remove the evil from your door than to
move and leave it there."

"If you have a few acres, stick to them."

"Life is too short, time is too valuable, to waste
in the experiment of seeking new homes.   People
are about as good in your neighborhood as anywhere else in the world, and may need you to make
them better."

The foregoing extracts sufficiently indicate the
character and importance of this Nashville address.
It was quite unlike speeches that had been made by
most of the colored leaders to their people.   While
emphasizing the importance of hard work, of
duties, and patience, he indulged in no false
hopes and made no extravagant claims.   The
every-day facts, needs, and responsibilities of the
people on the soil were, he held, the paramount
things for men who were beginning their social development.   In short, it was a strong and stirring
call to the Negroes to look about them, and not
afar, for the instruments and forces that must be
utilized for their salvation.

Belonging to this latter period of his life, another
address, in character quite different from the one
just referred to, illustrates how the colored people
have been carried from one extreme of hopefulness
to the other of despair and uncertainty by the
changes in public sentiment concerning them.

In 1883 the Supreme Court of the United States
rendered a decision declaring unconstitutional what
was known as the "Civil Rights Bill."   This was

one of the Reconstruction measures, championed by
Senator Sumner, and, when brought forward it was
regarded by the colored people and their friends
as a sort of charter of liberty. It undertook to
prevent discriminations against Negroes in hotels,
restaurants, and other places of public accommo-
dation. At the time of its enactment it was
considered a necessary appendage to the Fourteenth and Fifteenth Amendments, and the colored
people everywhere felt a strong sense of protection
in its provisions.

When the Supreme Court's opinion declaring the
law, outside of the District of Columbia and other
national territory, to be null and void, was made
known, it produced a sensation of alarm and almost
despair among Negroes everywhere. They saw
in this decision a complete reversal of the public
sentiment that a few years before was so strongly
favorable to them. They began to lose faith in the
potency of the letter of the law, either to define or
protect their rights. It was a sort of rude reminder
that, if they would be secure in their rights, they
must rely upon something else than mere statutes.
Here was an apt illustration of the maxim that
what the law gives, the law can take away. In relying upon only this for his salvation, the Negro
had been suspended between hope and despair, until
it seemed to him that there was no such thing as sta-
bility of sentiment toward him. The first impulse
was to protest, in the name of all the colored people,
not only against the letter of the decision, but also
against haunting implications that they had no

rights which the law of the land was bound to respect.

The spirit of resentment found adequate expression in a great mass-meeting arranged for and held
in the city of Washington in 1883. Frederick
Douglass was selected, as a matter of course, as the
one colored man in the country who could best voice
the feelings of the people affected by the decision.
The other speaker was the eloquent Robert G.
Ingersoll. The meeting was a notable one in every
respect. The most distinguished leaders of the race
were there, and the audience was large and earnest.
There were present, too, a great number of prominent white people who sympathized with the colored
race. The address of Mr. Douglass was one of the
most interesting ever made by him. In it he showed
his ability to put into the most telling form the arguments with which it seemed possible at that time
to counteract, to some extent, the moral effect of
the decision upon the colored and the white communities. His speech showed a wide acquaintance
with the principles of the law and more than usually profound knowledge of the philosophy of democracy. The following extracts will indicate its
character, and reflect, no doubt, the opinions and
sentiments of the meeting and the time :

"It makes us feel as if some one was stamping on
the graves of our mothers, or desecrating our sacred
temples."

"We have been, as a class, grievously wounded
in the house of our friends."

"This decision has swept over the land like a cyclone, leaving moral desolation in its track."

"Inasmuch as the law in question is in favor of liberty and justice, it ought to have had the benefit of any doubt which could arise as to its strict constitutionality."

"If any man has come in here with his breast heaving with passion and expecting to hear violent denunciation of the Supreme Court on account of this decision, he has mistaken the object of this meeting. Its judges live, and ought to live, an eagle's flight beyond the reach of fear or favor, praise or blame, profit or loss."

"In humiliating the colored people of this country, this decision has humbled this nation."

"No man can put a chain about the ankle of his fellow-men without at least finding the other end of it about his own neck."

"Prejudice is a spirit infernal, against which enlightened men should wage perpetual war."

"We want no black Ireland in America. We want no aggrieved class in America. Strong as we are without the Negro, we are stronger with him than without him."

"Our legislators, our President, and the judges should have a care lest by forcing these people outside the law, they destroy that love of country, which in the day of trouble is needful to the nation's defense."

"Oh, for a Supreme Court of the United States which shall be as true to the claims of humanity as the Supreme Court formerly was to the demand of slavery."

"What is a state in the absence of the people who compose it?"

"Land, air, and water do not discriminate.

What does it matter to the colored citizen that a state may not insult him if the citizen of the state may? The decision is a concession to race pride, selfishness, and meanness, and will be received with joy by every upholder of caste in the land, and for this I deplore and denounce the decision."

The few addresses just referred to are, in point of the subject-matter and the occasions that called them forth, the most important and able made by Frederick Douglass after emancipation. On each occasion there was a call for the supreme man of the Negro race and there were few, except a small group of colored people, to question his right to be so regarded.

Frederick Douglass, however, was something more than a "race leader"; he was always an eminent citizen of the republic, and as such his interests were not wholly rimmed about by the sorrows and aspirations of his own people. He was a careful student of his times and had an intelligent concern in all the great questions that arose and called for an opinion. It was quite in keeping with his cosmopolitan spirit that he should be opposed to the policy of our government in excluding the Chinese from American shores because, as he said, "I know of no rights of race superior to the rights of humanity." His views on the question, which twenty-five years ago was an urgent one, are more fully expressed in the following extract from one of his addresses on the subject of the "Composite Nation" :—

"Our republic itself is a strong argument in favor

of cosmopolitan nationality. . . . Let the China-
man come ; he will help to augment the national
wealth. He will help to develop our boundless re-
sources ; he will help to pay off our national debt.
He will help to lighten the burden of our national
taxation. He will give us the benefit of his skill as
a manufacturer, and as a tiller of the soil in which
he is unsurpassed. Even the matter of religious
liberty, which has cost the world more tears, more
blood, and more agony than any other interest, will
be helped by his presence. I know of no church more
tolerant, of no priesthood, however enlightened,
which could safely be trusted with the tremendous
power which universal conformity would confer.
We should welcome all men of every shade of religious opinion, as among the best means of check-
ing the arrogance and intolerance which are the
almost inevitable concomitants of general conformity. Liberty always flourishes best amid the
clash and competition of rival religious creeds.''

Reference has already been made to Douglass's
services to the cause of female suffrage. His
presence at nearly all of the anniversaries and
other important gatherings of those who advocated
the enfranchisement of women was expected and his
utterances were warmly received.

In the matter of religion, Mr. Douglass was not
strictly orthodox in his beliefs, although it will be
remembered that during his enslavement he found
much consolation in the Bible, and was for a time a
Methodist exhorter. His religious views, as he
grew older, underwent a radical change. He had

no patience with hypocrites. He had seen and
heard so much that was cruel, unjust, and almost
fiendish under the name of religion, that his faith
in sectarianism was badly shaken. In his early
anti-slavery addresses, he indulged in many absurd
parodies of the pious frauds whom he had known.
However, he was not an atheist. He had a deep religious sense, but was more fully under the influence of the theological opinions of Theodore
Parker than of any other school of religious thought.
His best friends and associates were among the
Unitarians, the Quakers, and others of liberal faith.
His views on religion are finely expressed in a bit of
correspondence published by Mr. Holland in his
biography. In response to a cordial invitation to
speak before the "Free Religious Association" in
Boston, in 1874, he wrote :

"I cannot be present at your Free Religious
Convention in Boston. This is, of course, of
smaller consequence to others than to myself, for I
should come more to hear than to be heard. Freedom is a word of charming sound, not only to the
tasked and tortured slaves, who toil for an earthly
master, but for those who would break the galling
chains of darkness and superstition. Regarding the
Free Religious movement as one for light, love, and
liberty, limited only by reason and human welfare,
and opposed to those who convert life and death
into enemies of human happiness, who people the
invisible world with ghastly taskmasters, I give it
hearty welcome. Only the truth can make men
free, and I trust that your convention will be guided
in all its utterances by its light and feel its power.

I know many of its good men and women, who are likely to assemble with you, and I would gladly share with them the burden of reproach which their attacks upon popular error will be sure to bring upon them.''

Extracts from letters to friends indicate still more clearly the deeper currents of his thought.

"I once had a large stock of hope on hand, but like the sand in the glass, it has about run out. My present solace is in the cultivation of religious submission to the inevitable, in teaching myself that I am but a breath of the infinite, perhaps not so much. I was very sorry not to be able to attend the Free Religious Convention. I shall, hereafter, try to know more of these people. . . . I sometimes, at long intervals, try my old violin; but after all the music of the past and of imagination is sweeter than any my unpracticed and unskilled bow can produce. So I lay my dear old fiddle aside, and listen to the soft, silent, distant music of other days which, in the hush of my spirit, I still find lingering somewhere in the mysterious depths of my soul.''

"I do not know that I am an evolutionist, but to this extent, I am one. I certainly have more patience with those who trace mankind upward from a low condition, even from the lower animals, than with those who start him at a point of perfection and conduct him to a level with the brutes. I have no sympathy with a theory that starts man in Heaven, and stops him in Hell. . . . An irrepressible conflict, grander than that described by the late William H. Seward, is perpetually going on. Two hostile and irreconcilable tendencies, broad as the world of man, are in the open field ; good and evil, truth and error, enlightenment and superstition.''

One of the stirring incidents of this post-slavery period was the "exodus movement." In the summer of 1879, great numbers of Negroes, as if by concerted action, began to emigrate from the South and the southwestern states toward the North and West. This movement was the first manifestation of discontent ever made by the colored people on a large scale. It was in no way due to politics, but was rather an effort to free themselves from the conditions under which they were compelled to work and live. Their economic state was bad, and there seemed to be little hope of improvement. The exodus grew to such an extent that it produced something like national alarm and there were grave apprehensions that much suffering would attend the efforts of the Negroes to escape from poverty and dependence. Mr. Douglass has given the following reasons for the dissatisfaction:

"Work as hard, faithfully, and constantly as they may, live as plainly and as sparingly as they may, they are no better off at the end of the year than at the beginning. They say that they are the dupes and victims of cunning and fraud in signing contracts which they cannot read and cannot fully understand; that they are compelled to trade at stores owned in whole or in part, by their employers; and that they are paid with orders and not with money. They say that they have to pay double the value of nearly everything they buy; that they are compelled to pay a rental of ten dollars a year for an acre of ground that will not bring thirty dollars under the hammer; that land-owners are in league to prevent land owning by Negroes ; that when they work the land on shares, they barely make a living ; that outside the towns and cities no provision is made for education, and, ground down as they are, they cannot themselves employ teachers to instruct their children."

As a general rule, the colored people in the North looked upon the exodus hopefully. To them it was a sign of courage on the part of their Southern brethren, and a protest against bad treatment. Frederick Douglass, however, who was always expected to have an opinion and express it, deplored the "unintelligent and somewhat aimless running away from the ills they have to others they know not of." He could see no salvation for the Negro in the Northern states. "For him, as a Southern laborer," he said, "there is no competition or substitute," and he insisted that the freedman is always to be "the arbiter" of Southern "destiny." He held that the best place for the Negro to work out his salvation was at home. His arguments are condensed in the following extracts from his published views :

"It may well enough be said that the Negro question is not so desperate as the advocates of this exodus would have the public believe ; that there is still hope that the Negro will ultimately have his rights as a man, and be fully protected in the South ; that in several of the old slave states his citizenship and his right to vote are already respected and protected ; that the same, in time, will be secured by the Negro in other states. . . . The Fourteenth Amendment makes him a citizen, and the Fifteenth Amendment makes him a voter. With power behind him, at work for him, and which cannot be taken from him, the Negro, at the South may wisely bide his time.

"As an assertion of power hitherto held in bitter contempt; as an emphatic and stinging protest against high-handed, greedy, and shameless injustice to the weak and defenseless; as a means of opening the blind eyes of oppressors to their folly and peril, the exodus has done valuable service. Whether it has accomplished all of which it is capable in this particular direction for the present, is a question which may well be considered. With a moderate degree of intelligent leadership among the laboring classes at the South, properly handling the justice of their cause, and wisely using the exodus example, they can easily exact better terms for their labor than ever before. Exodus is medicine, not food; it is for disease, not health; it is not to be taken from choice, but necessity. In anything like a normal condition of things, the South is the best place for the Negro. Nowhere else is there for him a promise of a happier future.

"Let him stay there if he can, and save both the South and himself to civilization. The American people are bound, if they are or can be bound to anything, to keep the north gate of the South open to black and white and to all people. The time to assert a right, Webster says, is when it is called into question. If it is attempted by force or fraud, to compel the colored people to stay, then they should by all means go; go quickly and die if need be in the attempt. Thus far and to this extent any man may be an 'emigrationist.' In no case must the Negro be bottled up or caged up. He must be left free like any other American citizen, to choose his own habitation, and to go where he shall like. Though it may not be for his interest to leave the

South, his right and power to leave it may be his best means of making it possible for him to stay there in peace. Woe to the oppressed and destitute of all countries and races, if the rich and powerful are to decide when and where they shall go or stay."

These sentiments of Mr. Douglass are interesting, not only as having a bearing on a question still vital to the South, but also as showing the orator's secret affection for the land of his birth and early struggles. In spite of his fifty years of life and triumphs in the North, he was still a Southerner in spirit and in his primary attachments. His imagination and memory still traveled back to the associations that contained more of bitterness than joy, —yet some joy. There seemed to be in the depths of his soul a living sympathy for those who were enslaved with himself, and who were still wearing the scars of servitude. The land that was worked by the toil and sweat of generation after generation of his people, and the land in which they were still laboring and hoping on, he loved in spite of himself. He believed in the race in spite of its apparent helplessness, and he believed in the South in spite of all that he had suffered. It pained him to see his people flee from the land of their birth, of their sorrows, but also the land of their better destiny. He would not have them abandon what would some day be theirs if they could but endure, and work, and wait.

With this sort of attachment to the South, it is not strange that, even after fifty years of complete separation, he still cherished the hope and eagerly welcomed an opportunity when it was offered him, to return to Talbot County, Md., his birthplace.

The time of his visit to the land upon which he had formerly been held as a slave, was happily chosen so as to heighten the contrast between the past and present, for he was now United States Marshal of the District of Columbia. It required a vivid imagination to see anything in common between the barefooted, half-naked, half-starved, and penniless slave boy of fifty years ago and the stately-mannered gentleman and high government official of this day.

The man whose misfortune it was at that time to have been Douglass's master, lay on a bed of sickness with little hope of recovery. Thomas Auld had passed the allotted three score years and ten. When he learned that Marshal Douglass was actually on his ground as a visitor, he at once sent for him. The name of Thomas Auld was made noted all over the land wherever Douglass had spoken concerning slavery and slave-holders, and because of this he had for several years harbored a strong resentment against his one-time runaway slave. Now all was wonderfully changed, and each was in a mood to make amends for the wrongs he was impelled to commit against the other. Mr. Douglass feelingly says:

"Had I been asked, in the days of slavery to visit this man . . . it would have been an invitation to the auction block; now he was to me no longer a slave-holder, either in fact or spirit, and I regarded him as I did myself, as a victim of circumstances of birth and education, law and custom. Our courses had been determined for us and not by us. We had both been flung by powers that did not ask our consent, upon a mighty current of life which we could neither resist nor control. . . . Now as our lives were verging toward a point where differences disappear, even the constancy of hate breaks down and the clouds of pride, passion and selfishness vanish before the brightness of infinite light."

The meeting between the ex-master and ex-slave was impressive and beautiful. They were both so overcome with emotion for some moments that neither could speak. Tears dimmed their eyes and the silence was more eloquent than words. As soon as he regained his power of speech, Mr. Douglass, with that instinctive politeness which was characteristic of him, made apology to his former master for the many harsh accusations uttered in the days of slavery, when passion was in the ascendency. The old master was equally frank and said : "I always thought, though, that you were too smart to be a slave, and had I been in your place, I should have done as you did."

"Captain Auld," replied Douglass, "I did not run away from you, but from slavery. It was not that I loved Cæsar less, but Rome more."

With this exchange of apologies and expressions of mutual good-will, the visit came to an end. If Mr. Douglass had any lingering bitterness in his soul, on account of the past, this face-to-face meeting, after so many years and so many changes, had now forever removed it. The laws and customs that so often made it impossible for good men, standing in the intimate relation of master and slave, to understand and respect each other, no longer existed.

Shortly after this interview Mr. Auld passed away, and the fact that the Marshal of the District of Columbia had once been the property of the dead man became a matter of wide comment.

Two years later, Mr. Douglass was again a visitor to Talbot County. He now went on the private yacht of John L. Thomas, United States Collector of Customs at the port of Baltimore. This time he returned to the scenes of his early life on the Lloyd plantation. It will be remembered that it was here the boy was separated from his grandmother, and left the only home he ever had before he became free. His master, Captain Anthony, lived on the Lloyd estate. It was at this place, too, that he was cuffed and half-starved by the hated Aunt Katy, and saw his own loving mother for the last time. Standing amid the scenes of his childhood miseries, looking in vain for faces that he once saw or knew in the long ago, he embodied in himself, perhaps, more changes than have been experienced in the life of any other American.

Colonel Lloyd was away at the time, but every one on the estate was made aware of the visit of Marshal Douglass. The place was rich in traditions concerning this strange visitor, who had come out of a strange past, an era known to but few now living, and he was treated with marked deference by all.

He also visited Easton, which will be remembered as the county-seat of Talbot County, where young Douglass, with his companions, was locked up in jail on the charge of conspiracy to escape from slavery. The old sheriff, who had placed him behind prison-bars, was still living, and said that he was proud to shake hands across the chasm of nearly fifty years. White and black crowded into the little court-house and listened with profound interest to the address he was asked to deliver. The young people, who belonged to the new era of freedom, wondered at his eloquence, and the older ones heard with confused and bewildering emotions.

There seemed to be more of romance than reality, more of apparition than of real substance, in this man, for whom, at one time, the jail, and not the court-house, would have been regarded as a more fitting place.

In the same year Frederick Douglass had another opportunity to revive the memories of the days preceding the war. He was asked to deliver an address on John Brown at Harper's Ferry. He gladly accepted the invitation, and spoke to an immense concourse of Virginians, white and black, on the very spot where, less than twenty years before, he would, very possibly, have been tried and hanged on the charge of high treason, had he not escaped those who made efforts to arrest him. On the platform close beside him sat the man who was the attorney for the commonwealth of Virginia in the prosecution of Brown. Douglass spoke with boldness in his eulogy of the old raider, and what he said was heartily cheered.

In 1859 Douglass had fled to England as a fugitive from justice because of his presumed complicity in what was then called John Brown's "crime." In less than twenty years he was honored by many of the same people who had then hated his name and thirsted for his blood. He could rightly claim to be a part both of the cause and the effect of this remarkable revolution of public opinion. The possibilities of American life were, perhaps, never better illustrated than in his person.

In the fall of 1886, Mr. Douglass, accompanied by his wife, made an extensive tour of Europe and Egypt. He revisited some of the cities in Italy, and crossed the Mediterranean to the land of the Pharaohs. He has written most delightfully of his travels in his *Life and Times*. Everything of historical value in Europe meant a great deal to him, because he was so earnest a student of men and events. Of Victor Hugo, he said, on seeing a memorial to him, that "he was a man whose heart was broad enough to take in the whole world and to rank among the greatest of the human race."

Upon returning to this country, he had many pleasing evidences that he was greatly missed in his absence, and that his opinions were as eagerly sought as ever on any question that came within the range of his interest.

One of the first public addresses made by him after his return from abroad was in behalf of woman's suffrage, in Washington, at a meeting of the International Council of Women. He spoke ardently of the progress of the human mind as evidenced by the unveiling of a statue to Galileo, which he had witnessed in Rome. He said :

" Whatever revolutions may have in store for us, one thing is certain : the new revolution in human thought will never go backward. When a great truth once gets abroad in the world, no power on earth can imprison or proscribe its limits, or suppress it. It is bound to go on until it becomes the thought of the world. Such a truth is woman's right to equal liberty with man. She was born with it, it was hers before she comprehended it. It is inscribed upon all powers and faculties of her soul, and no custom, law, or usage can ever destroy it. Now that it has got fairly fixed in the minds of the few, it is bound to become fixed in the minds of the many, and be supported at last by a great cloud of witnesses which no man can number and no power can withstand."

In the same year, addressing a suffrage association in Boston, he said : " If the whole is greater than a part ; if the sense and sum of human goodness in man and woman combined are greater than that of either alone and separate, then this government that excludes women from all participation in its creation, administration, and perpetuation demeans itself."

In the matter of the education of his people, Mr. Douglass had a deep and abiding interest. It will be remembered that he believed in the broadest and

best possible schooling of the masses.   He regarded
it as important to consider the Negro's opportunity
in planning for his education.   Hence it was that,
in addressing the students of Tuskegee in 1892 on
the subject of "Self-Made Men," he laid special
stress on the necessity of the learning of trades in
connection with other training.   Hence his saying
that "the earth has no prejudice against color;
crops yield as readily to the touch of the black
man's hand as to that of his white brother."

"Go on," he continued; "I shall not be with
you long ; you have heights to ascend and breadths
to fill such as I never could and never can.   Go on.
When you are working with your hands they grow
larger ; the same is true of your heads.   .   .   .
Seek to acquire knowledge as well as property, and
in time you may have the honor of going to Congress.   Congress ought to be able to stand a Negro,
if the Negro can stand Congress."

In these addresses before students in college or
trade-schools, he took pains to urge that the man
with a trade, as well as the man with a profession
should be respected and honored, according to the
amount of character and intelligence he puts into
his work.   He insisted that there was no such thing
as servility or degradation for one who made his
way through the world with an honest heart and
skilled hands.

His earnestness in this conviction is further evidenced by one of his last acts in behalf of his people, when he helped to found the Industrial School
at Manassas, Va.

CHAPTER XVI

FINAL HONORS TO THE LIVING AND TRIBUTES TO THE DEAD

THE last public office held by Frederick Douglass was that of Commissioner for the Haytian Republic at the World's Columbian Exposition in Chicago, in the summer of 1893. The government of Hayti erected an artistic pavilion on the Fair grounds, and here from May 1st to November 1st, he was stationed, dispensing the hospitalities demanded by his position and the occasion.

Interesting as was the Haytian display, it did not attract as much public attention as did the Commissioner. No person or exhibit at the Exposition so illustrated and exemplified human progress as did Frederick Douglass. In him it was personified. Everywhere his presence excited interest and admiration. In his movements through the grounds he was ever a striking figure. His form, towering far above the average man, and his snow-white hair, hanging in waves about his massive head, commanded instant attention. People, young and old, crowded about him, wherever he went. But not all were curiosity seekers. Thousands knew Mr. Douglass personally, had heard him speak, or were familiar with his history. Parents brought their children, that they might shake hands with him.

He was sometimes quite embarrassed by these manifestations of admiration and interest.

The Exposition officials appreciated the importance of the man, as well as his position as the Haytian Commissioner.   No honors were unshared by him on account of his race.   Whenever the representative men of the civilized governments met in administrative councils, Frederick Douglass was an honored guest and participant.   His old-time eloquence was aroused on many interesting occasions, and especially when the cause of the Negro needed a champion.   An official of the Exposition was reported as saying that Frederick Douglass, more than any other orator there, voiced the sentiment of the brotherhood of man.   While various representatives would extol the people of this or that government or nationality, this self-made and self-educated man of a belated race, was always insisting that the man himself, as God made him, was greater than any geographical or national label could possibly render him.

He was constantly sought for addresses on all kinds of occasions, and he generously responded, whether the call came from some obscure religious organization, literary society, or one of the great international parliaments, convened in connection with the Exposition.

There were two very notable addresses by him in the summer of 1893, that almost excel the best of his many great speeches.   One of these was made on what was known as "Negro Day" at the Exposition in the month of August.   The vast auditorium

in Music Hall was filled by an audience that was
more thoroughly international in the variety of
races represented, than any other gathering assembled during the progress of the Fair.   In voice,
gesture, and spirit, he seemed like some great
prophet, bearing a message to the civilized world.
No one who listened to this masterful plea for justice for the Negro race, can ever forget the inspiration of that hour.

The other speech was delivered before one of the
parliaments on the subject of "good government."
There were present students of civil government,
sociologists, judges of courts, representatives of the
woman's suffrage movement, like Susan B. Anthony,
and others.   Some striking addresses followed Douglass's, but he had left the audience completely
under his spell.

With the closing of the Exposition in the autumn
of 1893, ended the last chapter in his life as a
public official.   As office-holding, however, was by
no means the most important part of his career, it
did not require an office to keep him in view of the
people.   His prominence outlasted that of many of
his contemporaries who were more favored than he
in the matter of public service.   He remained, up
to the very last hour of his life, one of the few men
of the nation of whom it never tired.   This was so,
largely because he was more a part of the present
than of the past.   Though he compassed in his life
over a half-century of national history, he never got
out of touch with current events, retaining to the
end his influence on public opinion in all those mat-

ters in which he was peculiarly interested, and in regard to which his views had special authority.

When he closed his official business with the World's Fair, he yielded to a strong pressure from the people of the West for a limited course of lectures. The one thing which induced him to undertake this arduous task, after the months of exhausting duties at the Exposition, was the opportunity it would offer him to speak his word of protest and condemnation of the crime of lynching. Nothing in his long life of anxiety and struggle for his race so depressed him as did this new manifestation of contempt for his people. His first itinerary included Des Moines, Omaha, and other cities. He was cordially received everywhere and his denunciation of mob law made a deep impression. These addresses were in the nature of his last message and warning to the American people against the unchecked lawlessness that spent itself on those who were not strong enough to protect themselves.

He returned to his restful and delightful home in Washington with some apparent fatigue, but no permanent harm in consequence of his long journey.

The last two years of his life seem to have been more free from care and active duties than any previous period. He merited a rest and he had everything about him to contribute to his ease and enjoyment. Among the trees and flowers of his ample grounds on Cedar Hill, and surrounded by his books and the comforts of his classic home, life went on serenely and happily.

One of the interesting sights here was the procession of people of all kinds making pilgrimages every day to the home of " the Sage of Anacostia," [1] as he was fondly called by his friends and neighbors. Thousands of colored persons visited him to pay their respects to the man whose life had been consecrated to the cause of their emancipation and citizenship. To all he was kindly and considerate. His mind was as alert and keen as ever, and thoroughly alive to passing events. He had a special fondness for the young men of his race, and particularly those who were educated and progressive. It was always an inspiration to him to see the numbers of young colored men, who were fitting themselves by study and application to pass civil service examinations, and gain for themselves positions of importance in all departments of the government. He frequently invited them to his home to dine with him, and would discuss with them the possibilities for their advancement in all lines of endeavor. He was always hopeful regarding the progress of these young men in business and in the professions.

He was generous, almost to a fault, with his time, money, and services in behalf of any cause that meant a step forward for his people. His health was uniformly good. Every day he was either riding or walking about the streets of Washington, or in conference with those who needed his advice and assistance in all kinds of helpful enterprises. He had a part in every civic event of any impor-

[1] Anacostia is a suburb of Washington, and was Frederick Douglass's home so long as he lived in the District of Columbia.

tance in the District of Columbia. No one colored
man before or since his death has wielded so much
influence in all directions. He had not only won
the esteem of the people of Washington, but he
knew how to deserve and retain it. In the District
government, in the public schools, and at Howard
University, his influence was felt and respected.

What he himself was, he had gained by hard
work, consecration, temperate habits, and God-fear-
ing conduct toward all his fellows. His life and
achievements spoke eloquently to the young men
about him and pointed the way to progress. Mr.
Douglass had richly earned everything that he had,
and those who took him as a model were made to
realize that success comes not as a gift, but must be
deserved and won as a reward for right thinking
and high living. Poor as were his people in all
things, Frederick Douglass found enough to be
proud of in them and urged continuously upon the
younger generation the necessity of cultivating a
spirit of race pride,—of setting before themselves
and the race of which they were members clear and
definite ideals.

In nothing else was the life of Mr. Douglass so
important as in the uplifting influence he exerted,
directly and indirectly, upon the young men of his
time. There were many good leaders worthy
of emulation, but none who exercised the authority
that he did over the opinions of the other members
of his race. His life was an open book. Naturally
there were those of his color who envied him; who
sought to discredit his worth and work; who felt

that so long as he lived and spoke, none other could be known or heard. The young men of force and intelligence, however, who had it in them to do something large and important looked up to and were inspired by the "old man eloquent" of the Negro race.

It is easily possible to extend observations of this kind concerning the personality and influence of this great man during those restful years when he was happily free from care and public responsibilities. How little he thought of death! Sound of body and sane of mind, and always thinking and planning for what should come after, he lived as if there was no claim upon his future existence which he could not adjust. When death did come on the second day of February, 1895, it found him with no preparation, in the ordinary sense, for its message. And yet it had always been his expressed wish that he should go as he did—"to fall as the leaf in the autumn of life."

On that day he had been attending the Council of Women which was meeting in Metzerott's Hall in the city of Washington, and was much interested in the proceedings. He was an honorary member of that body. They were in quest of larger liberties for themselves, as he so long had been for himself and his people. When Frederick Douglass appeared at the convention in the morning, he was greeted with applause and escorted to the platform by a committee. He remained there nearly the entire day. When he returned to his home on Cedar Hill for dinner, he was in the best of spirits, and with a great deal of animation and pleasure, discussed with Mrs. Douglass the incidents of the meeting.

After the meal he prepared himself to deliver an address in a colored Baptist church near by. His carriage was at the door. While passing through the hall from the dining-room, he seemed to drop slowly upon his knees, but in such a way that the movement did not excite any alarm in his wife. His face wore a look of surprise as he exclaimed, "Why, what does this mean?" Then, straightening his body upon the floor, he was gone. The men who responded to Mrs. Douglass's agonized cries for help, came hurriedly with physicians, but it was too late. Douglass was dead—without pain, without warning, without fear, and at a time when life was sweet, full, and complete. His last moment of enthusiasm, like his first hours of aspiration when a slave-child, was for liberty; if not for himself, then for some one else.

The announcement that Frederick Douglass was dead came like a shock to every one, especially to those who had seen him about the city during the day, full of animation and apparent physical vigor. The sad news spread rapidly and produced a profound sense of bereavement among all classes of people.

The scene at the Women's Council, where he had been during the day an honored guest, was an affecting one. The president, Mrs. May Wright Sewall, in attempting to voice the sentiment of the members, said:

"A report, as unwelcome as sad and solemn, has come to us of the sudden and most unexpected death of Frederick Douglass. The news cannot be received in silence by the Council. That historic figure which individually and intellectually was the symbol of the wonderful transition through which this generation has lived has been with us in our Council during both of our sessions to-day. When he arrived, an escort was directed to conduct him to the platform. We felt that this platform was honored by his presence. I am sure there was no divided sentiment on this subject, although we have here women whose families are related to all political parties of our country, and connected by ancestry with both sides of the great question. It is surely to be regarded as a historic coincidence that this man, who embodied a century of struggle between freedom and oppression, spent his last hours a witness of the united efforts of those who have come from so many different places and along such various avenues to formulate some plan for a new expression of freedom in the relation of woman to the world, society, and the state."

The mortuary arrangements at Washington were on the scale and of the dignity of a state funeral. Throngs of people lined the streets through which the *cortége* passed to the Metropolitan Church where the ceremonies were held. Delegations of prominent colored men and women, from almost every part of the Union, came to pay their last respects to the dead statesman.

Within the spacious church, the scene was such as perhaps had never before been witnessed in this country. All colors and nationalities were present, moved by a common sorrow. Men like Senators

Hoar and Sherman; members of the Supreme Court like Justice Harlan; members of the House of Representatives, officials of the District of Columbia, members of the National Council of Women, the faculty of Howard University, several Bishops of the African Methodist Episcopal Church, and other distinguished men and women were present and gave to the sad occasion the character of a national bereavement.

Floral tributes in profusion were sent by organizations of all kinds as well as by individuals. There were two that had special significance; the one sent by the Haytian government, and the other by Colonel B. F. Auld of Baltimore, the son of Frederick Douglass's former owner. Fervent words of appreciation were spoken by Dr. J. T. Jenifer, pastor of the Metropolitan Church, Rev. F. J. Grimké, Susan B. Anthony, Mrs. May Wright Sewall, John S. Durham, Bishop W. B. Derrick, and M. J. N. Nichols, representing Hayti. The city of Washington, where Mr. Douglass lived so long and was so much esteemed, paid every possible tribute of respect to his memory in these impressive ceremonies.

While the fallen Douglass was thus being honored at the national capital, the city of Rochester was sorrow-stricken at the loss of its "foremost citizen" and at once set about making "suitable arrangements to give his remains according to the desire he so often expressed,—a resting-place in beautiful Mount Hope, the city of the dead." Rochester always claimed Frederick Douglass as her son by right of adoption, and that at a time when many other Northern cities would not have tolerated his presence. By order of the mayor, a special meeting of the city council was convened "for the purpose of taking such action as might be necessary and appropriate in connection with the funeral of Hon. Frederick Douglass, for many years a respected and beloved citizen of this city."

At the meeting thus called, a memorial, couched in terms at once touching and flattering, was read and spread upon the records. The council also passed a resolution that the members attend the funeral in a body, and it was arranged that the remains should lie in state in the city hall, and that on the day of the funeral the public schools be closed, so as to give the pupils an opportunity to view the face of a man whose life and character were worthy of their remembrance and emulation.

Thus all the proceedings partook of a civic nature and were impressive beyond anything ever witnessed in honor of a Negro citizen. The services in Rochester were held in the Central Presbyterian Church. The Douglass League acted as a guard of honor in conducting the remains to the city hall and to the church. Rev. W. C. Gannett, of the Unitarian Church, delivered the funeral oration. No other in the United States was better qualified by natural disposition and breadth of mind to give adequate estimate of Douglass as a man. The portion of the address here quoted will afford some notion of the character of the eulogies uttered in all parts of this country and in England in recognition

of the worth of Frederick Douglass and his work.
Mr. Gannett said in part :

"This is an impressive moment in our city history. There was a man who lived in one of its
humbler homes, whose name barred him from the
doors of the wealthiest mansions of our city. This
man has come home to a little circle of his best beloved ones. He has come, as it were, alone, and
our city has gone forth to meet him at its gates.
He has been welcomed for once in the most impressive way. His remains have laid in our city hall.
Our school children have looked upon his face, that
they may in the future tell their children that they
have looked on the face of Frederick Douglass.
What a difference! What a contrast! What does
it all mean? It means two things. It is a personal
tribute and it is an impersonal tribute. It is a personal tribute to the man who has exemplified before
the eyes of all America the inspiring example of a
man who made himself. America is the land of
opportunities. But not all men in this land can use
their opportunities. Here was a man who used to
the uttermost all the opportunities that America
held forth to him, and when opportunities were not
at hand he made them. Nature gave him birth,
nature deprived him of father and almost mother.
He was born seventy-eight years ago, forty years
before anti-slavery was heard of as a watchword.

"He is not simply a self-made man, although he
was one of the greatest. A man self-made but
large-hearted. Who ever had better opportunity to
be a greater-hearted man than Frederick Douglass?
Think of the results for which he labored almost to
the end of his life. Notwithstanding that the lash
had been lifted from his back, still he encountered
shrugs of the shoulders, lifting of the eyebrows, and

an edging away of his fellow-men when he approached them, always under that opportunity of insult.

"But that was not all. It is not a simple tribute to the man. The personal tribute rises and loses itself in a grander and nobler thought. It becomes transfigured into an impersonal thought. We are in an era of change on a great subject. White people are here honoring a black people. An exception? Yes. Great men are always exceptions. An exception? Yes, but an instance as well, an example of how the world's feeling is changing. I like to think over our 140,000 people of Rochester and pick out the two or three who will be called our first citizens twenty or thirty years hence. Very few in Rochester are famous through the North, very few are famous throughout the world. Yet the papers of two continents had editorials about the man whose remains lie before us. We have but one bronze monument in our streets. Will the next be that of Frederick Douglass, the black man, the ex-slave, the renowned orator, the distinguished American citizen? I think it will be. In and around our soldiers' monument we group the history of the war. It is not only the monument of Lincoln, although Lincoln's figure is represented there. It is the monument of the war.

"The nation to-day, thank God, is not only celebrating the emancipation of slavery, but also its emancipation from the slavery of prejudice and from the slavery of caste and color.

"Let me end with one word. There are but six words in the sentence, and it is one of the great sentences worthy to be painted on the church walls and worthy to be included in such a book as the Bible. It is his word. It is: 'One with God is a majority.'"

The vast audience that listened to these words of praise sadly followed Douglass's remains to their resting-place in Mount Hope Cemetery, beside the graves of his little daughter Anna, and his beloved wife, the mother of his children. Few great citizens of the state of New York were ever more signally honored than was he in these last funeral rites by the citizens of Rochester. And this was not all. The suggestion of a monument by Mr. Gannett in his funeral address found quick and hearty response from the people of the city in an effort led by John W. Thompson without regard to race or color. Not only in that place, but throughout the country, the idea of erecting a bronze statue of Douglass, at his home, was taken up and acted upon. Generous contributions began to pour in from every direction. The great state of New York, that had honored him in so many ways during his lifetime, appropriated out of the public treasury, the sum of $3,000 for this purpose.

The whole amount was soon raised. The ceremonies attending the unveiling of the monument partook of the character of a state event. Special excursions brought multitudes of people from all parts of New York. The Governor, Theodore Roosevelt, and many other state officials, were in attendance. His address, so impressively delivered, was the climax of the splendid ceremonies. His tribute to the great Negro was inspired by a sympathetic appreciation of the man and a profound sense of the significance of his life. He reminded the vast concourse of people that the lesson taught by the colored statesman was "the lesson of truth, of honesty, of fearless courage, of striving for the right; the lesson of distinguished and fearless performance of civic duty." The bronze figure of the great Negro stands in a con- spicuous site in the heart of Rochester, and is as much a monument to the generous spirit of its citizens, as to the worth and achievements of him whose career it commemorates.

Douglass lived long enough to see the triumph of the cause for which he had dreamed, hoped, and labored. But he had lived long enough, also, to realize that what slavery had been two hundred years and more in doing could not be wholly undone in thirty or forty years; could, in fact, hardly be wholly undone since the Future is always built out of the materials of the Past.

In his later years he came to understand that the problem, on the work of solving which he and others had entered with such high hopes in the Recon- struction period, was larger and more complicated than it at that time seemed. If the realization of this fact was a disappointment to him, it did not cause him to lose courage. His faith in the future remained unshaken. He was sane and sanguine to the end. Least of all did he allow himself to feel aggrieved or become embittered by any personal inconvenience that he encountered because of the color of his skin. At the conclusion of his Auto- biography he says:

"It may possibly be inferred from what I have said of the prevalence of prejudice, and the practice of proscription, that I have had a very miserable sort of life, or that I must be remarkably insensible to public aversion. Neither inference is true. I have neither been miserable because of the ill-feeling of those about me, nor indifferent to popular approval ; and I think, upon the whole, I have passed a tolerably cheerful and even joyful life. I have never felt myself isolated since I entered the field to plead the cause of the slave, and demand equal rights for all. In every town and city where it has been my lot to speak, there have been raised up for me friends of both colors to cheer and strengthen me in my work. I have always felt, too, that I had on my side all the invisible forces of the moral government of the universe.''

Frederick Douglass's life fell in the period of war, of controversy, and of fierce party strife. The task which was assigned to him was, on the whole, one of destruction and liberation, rather than construction and reconciliation. Circumstances and his own temperament made him the aggressive champion of his people, and of all others to whom custom or law denied the privileges which he had learned to regard as the inalienable possessions of men. He was for liberty, at all times, and in all shapes. Seeking the ballot for the Negro, he was ardently in favor of granting the same privilege to woman. Holding, as he did, that there were certain rights and dignities that belong to man as man, he was opposed to discrimination in our immigration laws in favor of the white races of Europe and against the yellow races of Asia. In religion, also,

he was disposed to unite himself with the extreme
liberal movement. In all this he was at once an
American, and a man of his time.

But Mr. Douglass was not merely an American,
sharing the convictions and aspirations of the most
progressive men of his day. He was also a Negro,
and the lesson of his life is addressed in the most
particular way to the members of his own race :
"To those who have suffered in slavery, I can say,
I, too, have suffered. To those who have taken
some risks and encountered hardships in the flight
from bondage, I can say, I, too, have endured and
risked. To those who have battled for liberty,
brotherhood, and citizenship, I can say, I, too, have
battled. And to those who have lived to enjoy the
fruits of liberty I can say, I, too, live and rejoice.
If I have pushed my example too far, I beg them to
remember that I have written in part for the encouragement of a class whose aspirations need the
stimulus of success."

And then he ends : "I have aimed to assure
them that knowledge may be obtained under difficulties ; that poverty may give place to competency ;
that obscurity is not an absolute bar to distinction ;
and that a way is open to welfare and happiness to
all who will resolutely and wisely pursue that way ;
that neither slavery, stripes, imprisonment, nor proscription need extinguish self-respect, crush manly
ambition, or paralyze effort ; that no power outside
of himself can prevent a man from sustaining an
honorable character and a useful relation to his day
and generation ; that neither institutions nor friends

can make a race to stand unless it has strength in
its own legs ; that there is no power in the world
which can be relied on to help the weak against the
strong, or the simple against the wise; that races,
like individuals, must stand or fall by their own
merits."

As has been already indicated in the course of
this narrative, Frederick Douglass never formulated
any definite religious creed.   But no one who reads
the story of his life and work can doubt that he was
guided and inspired through his whole career by the
highest moral and religious motives.   The evidence
of this is not merely his steadfast optimism and faith
in the future, but in the sense in which he regarded
his personal mission.   From his own point of view,
the work he did for his race was not merely a duty,
it was a high privilege :

"Forty years of my life have been given to the
cause of my people, and if I had forty years more
they should all be sacredly given to the same great
cause.   If I have done something for that cause, I
am, after all, more a debtor to it than it is a debtor
to me."

BIBLIOGRAPHY

DOUGLASS, FREDERICK. Narrative of Frederick Douglass, 1845.

——— My Bondage and My Freedom, 1855.

——— My Escape from Slavery. *Century Magazine*, November, 1881.

——— Life and Times of Frederick Douglass, 1882.

HOLLAND, FREDERICK MAY. Frederick Douglass, the Colored Orator, 1891.

GARRISON, WILLIAM LLOYD. Frederick Douglass as Orator and Reformer, *Our Day*, August, 1894.

MAY, SAMUEL J. Recollections of the Anti-Slavery Conflict, 1869.

JOHNSON, OLIVER. William Lloyd Garrison and His Times, 1881.

AUSTIN, GEORGE LOWELL. The Life and Times of Wendell Phillips, 1899.

LIFE AND TIMES OF WILLIAM LLOYD GARRISON. By his children, 1889.

SIEBERT, WILLIAM H. The Underground Railroad, 1898.

REPORTS of the Anti-Slavery Society.

GOODELL, W. Slavery and Anti-Slavery, A History of the Struggle in Both Hemispheres; with a View of the Slavery Question in the United States, third edition, 1855.

STILL, WILLIAM. The Underground Railroad, 1872.

——— Underground Railway Records, New and revised edition with life of author, 1883.

GREELEY, HORACE. The American Conflict: Its Causes, Incidents, and Results, 1864-6.

WILSON, JOSEPH T. The Black Phalanx; a History of the Negro Soldiers of the United States in the Wars of 1775, 1812, and 1861-1865 ; 1888.

NICOLAY, JOHN G. AND HAY, JOHN. Abraham Lincoln ; a History, 1890.

RHODES, JAMES FORD. History of the United States from the Compromise of 1850, 1893.

WILLIAMS, G. W. Negro Troops in the Rebellion, 1888

INDEX

Covey, Edward, the "negro-breaker," 38.

Cox, A. L., delegate National Anti-Slavery Society, 96.

Crafts, William, fugitive slave, 163.

Crandall, Prudence, Abolitionist, imprisoned for teaching colored children, 88, 141.

Crandall, Doctor Reuben, Abolitionist, imprisoned for circulating Anti-slavery literature, 88.

Crofts, Mrs. Julia Griffith, takes business management of *North Star*, 125.

Dallas, George M., Minister to England, refuses Douglass passport, 194.

Dana, Charles A., Assistant Secretary of War, encourages Douglass to visit President Lincoln, 228.

Davis, Alexander, Lieutenant-Governor of Mississippi, 279.

Davis, Richard A., aids in rescue of Anthony Burns, fugitive slave, 169.

Day, J. Howard, colored anti-slavery orator, 155.

Delaney, Martin R., colored anti-slavery orator, 155.

Derrick, Bishop W. B., address at Douglass's funeral, 343.

Dickinson, Anna, at Boston celebration of Emancipation Proclamation, 239.

Discrimination against Negroes at public lectures done away with, 66.

Disraeli, Benjamin, Douglass meets, 101.

Dix, General John A., procla-

mation to Southern people, 218.

Dorr, Thomas W., leader of pro-slavery forces in Rhode Island contest over new constitution, 76.

Dorsey, Thomas L., agent for the Underground Railway, 161.

Douglass, Charles R., son of Frederick, enlists in army, 223.

Douglass, Frederick, born at Tuckahoe, 15; transferred to the Lloyd plantation, 19; starved by "Aunt Katy," 20; sees his mother for the last time, 20; sees a slave killed by an overseer, 23; goes to Baltimore to live, 24; is taught to read, 24; gains possession of a speller, 26; buys a copy of the *Columbian Orator*, 26; learns to write, 27; thoughts turned to religion, 28; sent back to the plantation, 31; justifies pilfering by slaves, 34; Sunday-school broken up, 36; sent to a negro-breaker, 37; starts a second Sunday-school, 42; plans to escape, 44; plot discovered, 48; sent back to Baltimore, 50; apprenticed as a ship-calker, 51; buys his own time, 56; makes his escape from Baltimore, 58; marries in New York, 62; seeks refuge in New Bedford, Mass., 63; changes his name, 63; denied opportunity to work at his trade, 65; attends anti-slavery convention at Nantucket, 70; invited to become a